The Contemporary Japanese Economy

THE CONTEMPORARY JAPANESE ECONOMY
AN OVERVIEW

Ryuichiro Tachi

translated by Richard Walker

UNIVERSITY OF TOKYO PRESS

HC
462.95
T2813
1993

This volume is a translation of *Nihon no Keizai* (1991, University of Tokyo Press). The publication was partially supported by a grant from the Federation of Bankers Associations (Zenginkyo).

ISBN 4-13-047059-0

ISBN 0-86008-499-X

Printed in Japan

CONTENTS

PREFACE

In today's world, the in-depth knowledge and mutual understanding that are bases for cooperation among nations have seldom been of greater importance. Economically, as in many other respects, the world has become increasingly interdependent; and yet, national and ethnic strife are apparent wherever we look.

First, self-knowledge, and then knowledge of other systems' culture, politics, and economics, are essential first steps towards achieving the understanding that leads to tolerance and international cooperation.

In the hope of contributing to the knowledge and understanding of Japan's economic system among readers in other countries, I have decided to undertake publication of my overview of the Japanese economy in English. Originally it had been written for Japanese students and readers who wanted to learn more systematically about their own country's economy. With this edition, I would be gratified to add to the store of knowledge about the workings of the world economic system and about one country's niche in it.

My second purpose is to illustrate Japan's path to economic development, in the language of general economics, for the benefit of people of other nations who are now traveling along the same path of growth and modernization.

In preparing this book, I have received assistance from a number of persons and organizations. The Federation of Bankers Associations in Japan contributed financially to the translation and publication of this volume. The translator, Richard Walker, took a difficult text and made it readable in English. My wife's friend, Anna Nakada, read the manuscript in draft and made a number of helpful comments and suggestions. Susan Schmidt of the University of Tokyo Press edited and shepherded the book through production. I am sincerely grateful to each of them for their advice and encouragement.

July 1993   RYUICHIRO TACHI

INTRODUCTION

The collapse of the Cold War framework, the subsequent war in the Persian Gulf, and the social and economic upheavals in the Soviet Union and Eastern Europe have set the world in search of a new order. Japan has not been immune to these global trends; the economy shows signs of a significant shift away from the development-orientation that has characterized it since the Meiji Restoration of 1868. To discuss the Japanese economy, therefore, we must look at its past, survey its present, and attempt to predict its future. That is what this book will attempt to do. Its goal is to elucidate some of the issues facing the Japanese economy today.

TIME FRAME

The first problem encountered in a study like this is the need to understand the Japanese economic past in order to grasp its present and future. But how far back need one go?

There are many different ways this could be approached. One could, for example, start in 1971, when the United States halted conversions between dollars and gold, destroying the IMF-led framework that had been at the root of the postwar international monetary system and forcing many of the world's countries to switch from fixed to floating exchange rates.

Another choice would be to go back to the point at which Japan, defeated in World War II, began to rebuild itself as a member of the Western alliance, anchored firmly on the U.S. side of the Cold War with the Soviet Union. Or maybe it would be enough to go back to around 1960, when the supply of surplus labor from Japan's rural communities finally dried up.

A third option would be to go back to the end of World War I. Japan had been steadily modernizing since the Meiji Restoration, and during the interwar period it reached the stage of advanced capitalism, with its economy focused on heavy chemical and industrial production and its population beginning to urbanize.

We could even go all the way back to 1868, the first year of the Meiji Period, when Japan decided to take the West as its model for modernization, or to 1854, the year in which the Japan–U.S. Treaty of Peace and Amity was signed and the country began to open up after centuries of seclusion. Then again, if we are going to emphasize the Japanese economy of today, we might start our discussion in 1985, when the Group of Five economic powers reached the agreement that came to be known as the "Plaza Accord."

There is much to be said for and against all of these choices. For the purposes of this book, I have decided to begin the discussion with the end of World War II. We will, however, look briefly at the reforms of the Meiji Restoration since they serve as a background to the formation of the development-oriented economic system that has continued in Japan until very recently.

CORRELATION WITH WORLD POLITICAL AND ECONOMIC TRENDS

The next problem one faces in organizing this type of study is how much to say about correlations between what happens in Japan and political and economic trends in the rest of the world. After the "Black Ships" of Commodore Perry awakened Japan from its long and tranquil slumber, the country quickly became integrated into the world economy. Today, it is so integrated that it is impossible to even discuss the Japanese economy without touching on relations with political and economic events elsewhere in the world. The death of President Kennedy in 1963 had an immediate effect on the Japanese share market; when war in the Middle East caused oil prices to soar a decade later, it hit the Japanese economy hard, causing prices to rise and production to stagnate. Likewise, comments and statements about the official discount rate from the governor of the Bank of Japan or the Finance Minister have a noticeable impact on both foreign exchange markets and foreign securities prices. Japanese economic trends have significant effects on the country's neighbors in Asia and the Pacific as well.

There is thus an interdependence at work here: not only are world economic trends something that Japan cannot afford to ignore, but Japanese economic trends and policies also have more and more impact on the economies of other countries, and these come back to affect Japan once again. One example can be seen in the skyrocketing crude-oil prices of the early seventies. Economic expansion in non-oil-producing industrialized countries like Japan led to the formation of a cartel among oil producers and a hike in prices. This in turn caused the prices of goods to rise in Japan and other countries. Similarly, trade friction with the United States has forced Japan to shift more of its export capacity inward in the direction of domestic demand. As a result, Japan imports fewer goods from its neighbors. But while recognizing this interdependence, in this book we will limit ourselves to an analysis of the Japanese response to such changed conditions as higher crude-oil prices and declining finished goods imports.

ECONOMIC POLICY AND IDEOLOGY

The same questions that we raised regarding correlations with world political and economic trends could also be raised regarding domestic political and social trends. But even more importantly, there is the question of the impact of philosophical and ideological changes and how much weight to assign them.

Obviously, economic policies are not discussed and enacted in a vacuum; they are related to the philosophy, ideology, and politics of the time. After World War II, for instance, the idea of the welfare state, as embodied in the British Labour Party slogan "From the cradle to the grave," carried vast sway in the policies of many countries and led to the creation of social security systems. By contrast, in the eighties the neoconservatism of U.S. President Ronald Reagan and British Prime Minister Margaret Thatcher influenced policy makers to begin focusing on "smaller government" and "privatization."

One thing that sets social phenomena apart from natural phenomena is that forecasts about the future are able to influence, trigger, and prevent them. And if forecasts have such an impact on the future, there is the temptation to manipulate them so as to push events in the direction one desires. One of the consequences is that there may emerge as many forecasts as there are interested parties. In the case of social development, there are always at least two: those who are pushing for further social progress, and the more conservative who are against social change. Because they play this role in social phenomena, it is easy for forecasts (policy positions) to become subject to ideology, which blurs the distinction in social phenomena between ideology and objective, scientific laws.

As we have seen in the examples above, a shift in the dominant ideology will result in large swings in actual economic policies. If, as political scientists maintain, the overriding concern of politicians in today's democracies is winning and maintaining their seats, then real problems are likely to matter less than ideology-fraught policy choices. For example, less attention will be given to objective arguments about how much rice would actually be imported should the restriction be lifted, and more to the choice between food self-sufficiency ("food security") and free trade.

The economic commentator is faced with the thorny question of how much weight to give such considerations. My basic stance is to avoid problems of ideology wherever possible and concentrate instead on objective descriptions. But the nature of the issues being discussed makes it difficult to avoid all subjective judgments, and readers should be aware of this from the beginning.

ECONOMICS AND HISTORICISM

From the standpoint of modern economic studies, research on the Japanese economy is one branch of applied economics. Modern analytical tools are used to describe the present state of the Japanese economy, elucidate problem areas therein, and, where possible, point to solutions. We will be using both macroeconomic and microeconomic tools. In addition to such standard aggregate concepts as savings, investment, and GNP, we will analyze the behavior of markets and such economic actors as households and corporations. However, I have tried to hold mathematical formulas and technical complexities to a minimum.

This brings us to the often-encountered problem of the relationship between modern economics and historical analysis. Regardless of whether or not it has actually achieved its ideals, modern economics is built on "refutable hypotheses" about events, which can theoretically be refuted by empirical data, if enough data are available and if test results do not match the predictions of the hypothesis.[1] For instance, the proposition "Individuals will behave so as to obtain maximum satisfaction from consumption" is not a refutable hypothesis since there is no objective way to measure satisfaction. If, however, we derive from this the proposition "A rise in prices will result in a decline in the demand for common goods," we have a hypothesis that is refutable. And as long as this proposition is not refuted, then the hypothesis "Households will behave so as to maximize the satisfaction obtained through consumption" is also deemed corroborated.

By contrast, trends induced from actual events—for example, the proposition that public expenditures grow as the economy develops— are experiential in nature and therefore not considered "laws" in the strict sense of the word employed in modern science and therefore in modern economics. Thus, there are questions about whether "growth theory," a tool often used to discuss the Japanese economy, is really a proper economic tool. One doubts that it can stand up to the rigorous tests demanded.

There is a long-standing debate among the historical school, the classical school, and the neo-Kantian school about the differences between historical science and natural science. Karl Popper proposed that "refutability" (or "falsifiability") be the criterion by which the scientific and non-scientific be divided. In this context, Popper vigorously attacked historicism, the view that general laws of social development determine the course of events, as holistic and therefore not worthy of the name "modern science."[2] Modern science must fulfill the condition of refutability, and Popper exposed the fraud of historicism in all its different manifestations because it appropriated the name of science ("the one and only scientific socialism") without meeting that condition. At the time, at least part of Popper's reason for criticizing historicism was a desire to attack totalitarianism, and this must be considered when reading his work. But even after discounting the critiques of totalitarianism, one must still recognize the

---

[1] We use the term "refutable" in almost the same sense as "falsifiable." The point is to distinguish refutability (or falsifiability) from verifiability. For example, the sentence "Unicorns exist" can be verified but not refuted, even if it is false, because failure to find a unicorn does not establish that none exists.

[2] After looking at the arguments between the classical and the historical schools, Popper coined the word "historicism" to describe the product that would emerge from a stronger version of traditional historicism. Karl Popper, *The Poverty of Historicism* (London: Routledge & Kegan Paul, 1957).

limits inherent in trying to derive "general laws of development" out of historical events which, by nature, are one-time-only phenomena.

Thus "growth theory" should be seen as a supplementary explanation designed to further one's understanding of the stylized facts and trends observed in history, but having no possibility of going beyond that. In this respect, there is much in modern economics that resembles the natural sciences, particularly biology and evolutionary theory. While some researchers carry on with the traditional methods of the natural sciences, analyzing individual cells and DNA chains, others use non-traditional methods to approach subjects like the growth and evolution of organisms. In our case, the techniques of modern economics are useful for analyzing the behavior of individual economic units, while growth theory, cultural anthropology, and the analytical techniques of the social sciences may prove more useful in analyzing economic history and development.

My aim in this book is to use economic techniques wherever possible to analyze economic conditions and problems, and in principle to avoid resorting to cultural anthropology for explanations, since the latter approach tends to devolve into theories of Japanese uniqueness. To quote Popper: "We can conceive of very few events which could not plausibly be explained by an appeal to certain propensities of 'human nature.' But a method that can explain everything that might happen explains nothing."[3] In the case of Japan, there are few things that cannot be "explained" by the characteristics described by the cultural anthropologist: the "culture of shame," "the emphasis on hierarchy," the "electric culture," "groupism," or what have you. But that is because these characteristics really explain nothing at all.

That having been said, we should emphasize that our range of tools for economic analysis will not be as limited as what Popper and his disciples would advocate. And by the same token, the reader should bear in mind that social phenomena are one-time-only in nature and therefore are governed to a large extent by chance.

THEORIES OF JAPANESE UNIQUENESS

I have already expressed my intention to avoid theories of Japanese uniqueness in the cultural anthropological sense. But there are some

[3] Karl Popper, *The Poverty of Historicism* (London: Routledge & Kegan Paul, 1957), p. 154.

things about Japan that truly are unique. Japan began the process of modernization much later than other industrialized countries, so while Europe and North America were the models for its economy, it is undeniably different from them on some very basic points.

The biggest difference is that, until the arrival of Commodore Perry's "Black Ships," Japan was in isolation; having been forced to open its doors, its major concern during the latter half of the nineteenth century was how to avoid being colonized like India or Indonesia or having its territory invaded and divided like China. That is what inspired its programs to modernize itself and enhance its power as a nation. Its rallying cries were "enrich and strengthen the country" and "promote industries"; its methods were protection of industry, promotion of education, and compulsory military service. The only way it could accomplish these goals with the urgency required was to set up a government-dominated, bureaucratically led, development-oriented state, even if that meant turning away from Western-style democracy and suppressing those who clamored for free competition rather than discretionary regulation.

Perhaps, too, the general public found this kind of system easier to accept because the Meiji Restoration was not a civil revolution to begin with and because since the advent of feudalism the Japanese had been accustomed to a system led by bureaucrats (originally, warriors). But however it came to be, the system has survived to this day with no basic changes—in spite of attempts to transplant an American-style emphasis on rules when the *zaibatsu* were dismantled and anti-monopoly laws introduced at the end of World War II. The need to rebuild and regain international competitiveness after the war allowed a national consensus to be reached, and the intensification of the Cold War brought on a shift in policy away from the goals of the initial Occupation period (this shift will be discussed in more detail later) that made possible the continuity and strengthening of the development-oriented system. The only exception to this pattern in modern Japanese history was the brief "Taisho Democracy" period of the twenties, when a relative liberalism in the political sphere was matched by a loosening of controls in the social and economic areas as well.[4]

[4]During the reign of the Taisho emperor (1912–1926), especially the latter part, the political institutions that had been established under the 1890 Meiji Constitution became vested with real authority, political parties contended for power, and elections were held for seats in parliament. In the arts, philosophy, and the economic sphere as

Inasmuch as it is different from Western market-oriented—
and particularly American rule-oriented—economies, the Japanese
development-oriented economy is indeed unique. But given the conditions Japan found itself in, this was the path to which trial and
error inevitably led. There is no reason to ascribe it to some unique
facet of Japanese culture like "groupism." That is exactly why today,
as Japan continues to modernize and internationalize, signs of radical
change can be observed everywhere.

We can see this by looking at the *keiretsu* system, one of the
favorite targets of foreign critics. *Keiretsu*, or corporate groups,
can be divided into vertical and horizontal types. For the moment,
we will concern ourselves with just the vertical *keiretsu* found
between parent companies and subsidiaries. The traditional critics of
keiretsu have been Marxist economists or those with similar lean-
ings. But as early as 1937 Ronald Coase and later Oliver E. Wil-
liamson discovered that when imperfect markets result in transaction costs or when there are uncertainties about the future, the
size of the transaction costs or the uncertainties will determine
whether, for example, automakers buy parts on the open market
or produce them within their own organizations. The choice will in
principle be for the route that is best able to minimize transaction
costs. But where large American companies tend to make their parts
in-house, Japanese companies tend to order them from *keiretsu* companies. Japanese companies thus purchase more parts from affiliates
than their American counterparts do, but both are involved in a vertical *keiretsu* nonetheless. The only questions are which arrangement
results in lower costs and which one minimizes risks, not about
Japanese uniqueness. Likewise, there is nothing terribly unique about
Japan's "share cross-holdings." Japanese anti-monopoly laws banned
holding companies because the purpose of the laws was to dismantle
the *zaibatsu*. That is why cross-holdings were adopted instead. In
short, theories of Japanese uniqueness tend to borrow heavily and
uncritically from the analyses of Japan's Marxist economists.

That is not to say that analysis by neoclassicists is not without its
faults. Much recent analysis, particularly that involving "information

---

well, it was a brief period of flowering. By 1925, however, the storm clouds of reac-
tion were beginning to gather: that year saw not only the institution of universal male
suffrage but also passage of the infamous Peace Preservation Law, which was to be a
tool of the military as the nation became aggressive abroad and repressive at home.

economics" and "transaction costs," leads to the generally dubious conclusion that "all that exists is rational." As with facile theories of Japanese uniqueness, this tendency needs to be rethought more carefully.

It is common in modern economics to analyze a "system" as "given conditions." The development of information economics and transaction cost theory, however, has caused a sharp increase in research where the "system" is analyzed as an internal variable. There is a pressing need for more research on the Japanese economy from this direction.

1

THE GROWTH AND DEVELOPMENT OF JAPAN'S ECONOMY

1. THE JAPANESE ECONOMY: A BRIEF INTRODUCTION

THE FACTORS OF WEALTH AND PRODUCTION. Adam Smith, the father of economics, begins his masterpiece *An Inquiry into the Nature and Causes of the Wealth of Nations* (1776) by defining a country's wealth as the product of the year-in, year-out labors of its people:

> The annual labour of every nation is the fund which originally supplies it with all the necessaries and conveniences of life which it annually consumes, and which consists always either in the immediate produce of that labour, or in what is purchased with that produce from other nations.
>
> According therefore as this produce, or what is purchased with it, bears a greater or smaller proportion to the number of those who are to consume it, the nation will be better or worse supplied with all the necessaries and conveniences for which it has occasion.
> —*The Wealth of Nations* (1986 Penguin Classics edition, p. 104)

Thus, rather than define the wealth of a nation as its holdings of treasure, Smith defines it as the aggregate of the "necessaries and conveniences of life" that are produced by the annual labor of the people. The per-capita size of these "necessaries and conveniences" is therefore an index of how wealthy the nation is. Smith goes on to say that annual production is a function of the quantity and quality of productive labor: how many workers are employed in manufac-

11

turing, their skills, abilities, and judgment, and the amount of capital stock employed.

Granted, there are some problems with trying to define the wealth of a nation as its per-capita "necessaries and conveniences." Some, for instance, would argue that "spiritual wealth" takes precedence over "material wealth"; others, that it is just as important how wealth is distributed as how much there is. Confucius was one such advocate of fair distribution. In *The Analects* he says, "Do not mourn scarcity, mourn inequality." Nonetheless, there can be little argument that per-capita "necessaries and conveniences" are one important yardstick of wealth; today's "national accounting" and "national income" are outgrowths of Smith's observations in this regard.

As Smith said, this annual "produce" is the product of labor and capital. Figure 1-1 below shows the schema involved. For our purposes, labor and capital (including land) will be considered the "factors of production."

As can be seen from Figure 1-1, part of what is produced goes to consumption, part to "investment." On the investment side, part goes to replenishing consumed fixed capital at the beginning of the period, and part to net investments (additional capital). How much output is generated is a function of three factors: the amount and quality of labor, the amount and quality of capital stock, and the level of manufacturing technology. We will use "manufacturing technology" in its broadest sense, encompassing the knowledge and ability to organize all of the other factors of production in addition to the more limited industrial meaning. In *Wealth of Nations*, Smith uses the example of a pin factory. Rather than having individual workers produce each pin from start to finish, the manufacturing process is

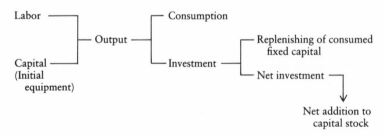

FIGURE 1-1   Relationship Between Production Factors and Output

broken down into simple steps, allowing each worker to specialize in his or her particular part of the process. This improves "training, ability, and judgment" and therefore increases production. The division of labor, Smith maintained, boosts productivity, but it is dependent on the size of the "market" in which the products of labor are exchanged. In this way the *quality* of labor has just as marked an impact on production as capital itself. Division of labor facilitates specialization in areas in which a person or group or country has a "comparative advantage," but in order to make this work, someone must be able to break down the production process and reorganize and manage it. This kind of knowledge and ability also has a significant impact on final output. The commonly used phrase "managerial resources" refers to the aggregate of this sort of expertise and skill.

The obvious question that arises is how to measure all the many different commodities that are produced. One idea, which was advocated by Smith, is to consider everything produced to be the product of labor and to measure the value of goods and services by the amount of labor required to produce them—the "labor input." Not surprisingly, this is known as the "embodied labor theory of value." It was later taken up and developed by Ricardo and Marx, to become what is commonly referred to as the "labor theory of value."[1] Another way to measure goods produced is in terms of their market value. This method is the base for the "national accounting" that we use today.

Later in this chapter, we will touch briefly on national accounting, but first let us enumerate the factors of production at work in Japan.

Labor: During the early Meiji Period (the 1870s), Japan had a population of only 35 million people. Since then its growth has been remarkable. In 1946, there were 75 million people in Japan, and in 1968 the population passed the 100-million mark. As can be seen from Table 1-1, the Japanese population stood at just over 121 million in 1985 and nearly 123 million in 1988. Recent statistics, however, show the growth rate to have slowed from 0.4% per annum to something closer to 0.3%. Likewise, the birth rate is less than 1.0% per annum, lower than that of Britain, the United States,

---

[1] Another variation on the labor theory of value, known as the "commanding labor theory of value," measures value as the amount of labor one is able to purchase or command through various commodities. This idea was also advanced by Smith in *The Wealth of Nations.*

TABLE 1-1   Japan's Population and Labor Force   (Units: 1,000 people; %)

	1975	1980	1985	1988	1990
Total population	111,940	117,060	121,050	122,780	123,610
Pop. of working age					
(over 15)	84,430	89,320	94,650	98,490	100,890
Labor force	53,230	55,360	58,070	61,110	62,490
Workers	52,230	55,360	58,070	60,110	62,490
Completely un-					
employed (%)	1,000 (1.9)	1,140 (2.0)	1,560 (2.6)	1,550 (2.5)	1,340 (2.1)
Non-working					
population	30,950	32,490	34,500	36,350	36,570

Note: The labor force consists of those between the ages of 15 and 65.
Source: Bank of Japan, Economic Statistics Annual.

or France, and the death rate has declined to 0.6–0.7%, the lowest in the world. Current forecasts are that the Japanese population will reach 129 million in 2010, after which it will begin to decline. Obviously, this decline in population will have a significant impact on the economy. Today's low population growth rates are accelerating the upward trend in the age structure (the "graying society"), with the result being an expected peaking of the labor supply around the year 2000 (though this will depend somewhat on that labor force participation rate, as will be discussed below). Its current population of 120 million ranks Japan as the seventh most populous nation in the world behind China, India, the Soviet Union, the United States, Indonesia, and Brazil.

From Table 1-1 it can be seen that the "working-age population" over 15 years old was 96,650,000 in 1985. Of this number, 59,630,000 actually wanted jobs: this is what is called the "labor force." The labor force participation rate is calculated by dividing the number in the labor force (those who want jobs) by the total working-age population. In 1985, this rate stood at 63.0%; in 1988, 62.6%; and in 1990, 63.3%. These figures represent a noticeable decline from the rates of 70% that were recorded in the late fifties. Behind the lower participation rate was a decline in the percentage of the very young and the very old in the labor force. Three factors were involved: 1) more young people have been matriculating to high school and college, rather than entering the work force; 2) agriculture has been contracting as a sector of the economy, resulting in fewer jobs for the elderly; and 3) fewer women are employed to-

TABLE 1-2   Number of Workers in Each Industrial Sector
(Units: 1,000 people; %)

	1975	1980	1985	1988	1990
Primary industry	6,610 (12.7)	5,770 (10.4)	5,090 (8.8)	4,470 (7.9)	4,510 (7.2)
Secondary industry	18,410 (35.2)	19,260 (34.8)	19,920 (34.2)	20,210 (33.6)	20,990 (33.6)
Tertiary industry	27,210 (52.1)	20,220 (54.8)	33,060 (56.9)	35,160 (58.5)	36,990 (59.2)
Total	52,230 (100)	55,360 (100)	58,070 (100)	60,110 (100)	62,490 (100)

Source: Bank of Japan, Economic Statistics Annual.

day on family farms. Another factor that could be pointed to is that the elderly have less need to work now that living standards have improved and the social security system has expanded.

This trend toward lower participation rates may be changing, however. In recent years, for one thing, more and more women have been entering the work force.

We will look at the reasons for unemployment later. Let it suffice to point out here that the rate of complete unemployment in Japan is only around 2.2–2.7%, far lower than in other industrialized countries.

Today, it is supply and demand in the labor market that determine what kinds of jobs are available to the people who want work. This was not always the case. As we shall see later on, until late in the nineteenth century, the population was divided into four castes (warriors, farmers, artisans, and merchants), and freedom of employment and freedom of movement were severely restricted.

In Table 1-2, I have followed Colin Clark's division of industry (in *The Conditions of Economic Progress*, 1940) into three broad groups and looked at the number of workers in each. As can be seen, less than 10% of the labor force is now employed in the primary sector (agriculture, forestry, and fishing). This is roughly equivalent to the situation in France. Likewise, 59% of the Japanese labor force is employed in tertiary industries (wholesale/retail, services, transportation/telecommunications, finance/insurance, and the like), which is again similar to France. By contrast, tertiary industries account for 69.7% of the U.S. labor force (1983) and 66.3% of the British (1984). Employment in secondary industries such as manufacturing

TABLE 1-3   Japan's National Assets and Liabilities   (Unit: ¥1 trillion)

	1975	1980	1985	1986	1987	1988
Tangible assets	736	1,338	1,817	2,087	2,550	2,766
Inventories	45	65	68	64	65	66
Net fixed assets (housing, buildings, machinery, tools etc.)	287	527	688	712	758	808
Non-reproducible tangible assets	404	746	1,060	1,309	1,725	1,891
Financial assets	700	1,297	2,120	2,446	2,799	3,226
Total assets	1,436	2,635	3,937	4,533	5,350	5,993
Liabilities	682	1,275	2,060	2,367	2,712	3,129
Shares	15	20	27	44	51	59
Net worth	739	1,340	1,850	2,120	2,586	2,803

Source: Economic Planning Agency, National Accounts of Japan, 1990.

and construction has tended to remain flat in the 33–35% range, with perhaps a slight trend downward.

Capital stock: "Annual product" is produced by labor together with "capital stock," so let us turn to this area next. Table 1-3 shows Japan's term-end capital stock for the years 1975–1988.

"Inventory," as is customary, comprises unshipped goods, goods in-process, materials, and goods in distribution.

"Net fixed assets" includes houses, factories, transportation equipment, machinery and tools, and "other structures," of which the largest portion (approximately one third) are roads and bridges. "Non-reproducible tangible assets" are mostly land holdings, as Japan has few mineral or other underground resources.

The "assets" category also includes "financial assets" (savings accounts, stocks, bonds, and the like), though most of these are offset by liabilities (since for everyone who owns a financial asset there is someone else with a corresponding liability). "Net worth" is therefore roughly equivalent to "tangible assets" plus "foreign assets." Table 1-3 gives Japan's net worth as of the end of 1985 at ¥1,850 trillion, of which ¥1,817 trillion was tangible assets.

This capital is used for production, and the value of the goods and services produced with it is generally expressed as either the GNP or the GDP, the two chief indexes of a country's economic performance. The total amount, at market prices, that a country produces (usually the goods and services exchanged on the market) during a given

Stage	Market price	Raw materials cost		Value added
Wheat	40 —	0	=	40
Flour	80 —	40	=	40
Bread	150 —	80	=	70
Total	270 —	120	=	150
	Gross output —	Intermediate input	= Net output	= Net added value

FIGURE 1-2   Gross Output, Net Output, and Value Added

period of time (for example, one year or one three-month quarter) is its "gross output." This figure, however, includes intermediate goods, whose value ("intermediate input") needs to be subtracted in order to arrive at final production.

For example, to make bread you need flour; and to make flour you need wheat. The price of bread, therefore, will include the price of flour, and the price of flour will of course include the price of wheat. But if you were to calculate the market prices of all the bread, flour, and wheat produced during a given time period, you would end up counting the flour twice and the wheat three times. This redundancy must be eliminated, which is why the intermediate input is subtracted to arrive at "net output," which is equivalent to the value, at market prices, of the final goods domestically produced by a country during a certain period of time. In our example above, the economy produces wheat, flour, and bread, but the wheat is the raw material for flour and the flour is the raw material for bread; bread alone is the final product. As Figure 1-2 shows,

Net output = Market price of final goods = Total value added.

This, in turn, is the equivalent of "gross domestic product" (GDP), a central index in the new System of National Accounts (SNA). "Product" in this case includes services as well as goods.

The difference between "domestic product" and "national product" (NP) is that domestic product includes all goods and services produced within the area of the country—a geographic measure; national product includes all goods and services produced by citizens of a country—a people-based measure. Thus, for Japan, GNP equals the GDP plus all income earned by Japanese nationals working overseas and sent back to Japan minus all income earned by foreign nationals working in Japan and sent overseas. (The latter is called "net factor income from overseas.") We can summarize this in mathematical form by saying:

$$\text{Gross output} - \text{Intermediate input} = \text{Net output} = \text{GDP} \quad (1a)$$

$$\text{GDP} + \text{Net factor income from overseas} = \text{GNP}. \quad (1b)$$

But some of the domestically produced goods and services are used to replenish capital that has been used and consumed. We therefore need to subtract that amount from GDP and GNP:

$$\text{GDP} - \text{Capital consumption allowance}$$
$$= \text{Net Domestic Product (NDP)} \quad (2a)$$

$$\text{GNP} - \text{Capital consumption allowance}$$
$$= \text{Net National Product (NNP)}. \quad (2b)$$

In recent years, the factor income from overseas on the Japanese national accounts has been small, and on a net base it has been negligible, so there is very little difference, in practice, between GNP and GDP or GDE (gross domestic expenditures). This is not the case in some countries, however, where the factor income from overseas is too large to be ignored. The situation could be changing in Japan, too, as the upsurge in foreign investments causes a corresponding increase in interest and dividend income from overseas.

Let us assume, for simplicity's sake, that all production is accounted for by "corporations," and that "households" obtain their income either by working for corporations or by lending them land or capital. Part of this income they use to purchase goods or services provided by corporations; the rest becomes savings. Figure 1-3 illustrates this relationship, and from the figure we can derive the following:

$$\text{Gross product} \equiv \text{Factor income (consumption + savings)}$$
$$\equiv \text{Expenditure (consumption + investment)}.$$

While the national accounts are not as simple as the case we are looking at, this basic relationship does not change:

$$\text{Gross product} = \text{Income (value added)} = \text{Expenditures}. \quad (3)$$

This is often referred to as the "triple equivalency" by Japanese economists.

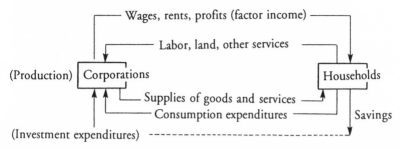

FIGURE 1-3   Relationship Between Corporations and Households in Production

We have already seen that, when measured at market prices, net income is equal to value added, and concluded that GDP (or GNP) is equal to income. However, market prices also include indirect taxes and subsidies (negative indirect taxes).

If a certain product is subject to a 10% commodities tax (or consumption tax), for example, 10% of the price goes to pay this tax and must be subtracted in order to arrive at the "net value-added" of the product—the amount that is imputed to households. Likewise, if the product is subsidized, we must correct for the decline in price this causes. We can therefore say:

Net domestic product − (Indirect taxes − Subsidies)
= Domestic factor income (aggregate value-added).   (4a)

Similarly,

Net national product − (Indirect taxes − Subsidies)
= National income.   (4b)

The difference between national income and domestic factor income is the same as the difference between GDP and GNP.[2] GNP is larger than GDP because it contains net factor income from overseas; likewise, national income includes net factor income earned by Japanese overseas.

National income comprises three broad categories of income: 1) worker income; 2) asset income (interest, dividends, rents); and 3) corporate income.

[2] We could also say that because factor prices equal market prices minus indirect taxes plus subsidies, NNP, as expressed by factor prices, is equal to national income (NI).

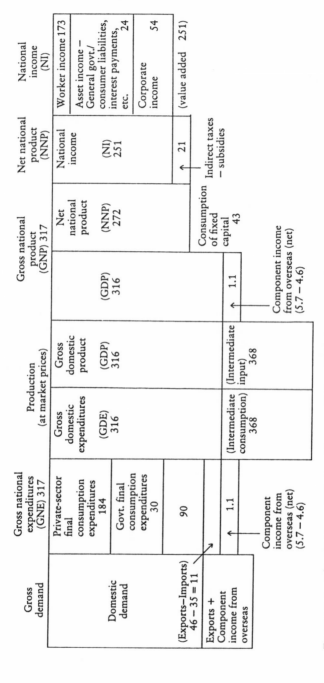

FIGURE 1-4 The Concept of National Income (Using 1985 as an Example)
Note: This diagram uses Japanese figures for 1985. The unit is trillions of yen and all values are according to market prices. There are therefore slight discrepancies between this diagram and Table 1-4.

TABLE 1-4 Special Categories of Domestic Gross Production and Factor Income (Nominal; 1985)   (Unit: ¥1 trillion)

Category of economic activity	Production value (1)	Intermediate input (2)	Gross domestic production (3) = (1) − (2)	Depletion of fixed capital (4)	Net domestic production (5) = (3) − (4)	Indirect taxes (less subsidies) (6)	Domestic factor income (7) = (5) − (6)	Worker income (8)	Operating surplus (9) = (7) − (8)
Industry (total)	634	339	296	41	255	20	235	143	92
Primary industries	18	8	10	2	8	—	7	2	5
Secondary industries	358	239	119	17	102	11	91	65	26
Mining	2	1	1	1	—	—	1	—	—
Manufacturing	296	202	94	13	81	10	71	48	22
(1) Light industry	91	59	33	4	29	5	24	17	7
Raw materials	17	11	6	1	5	—	4	3	1
Processing	74	47	27	3	24	4	20	15	5
(2) Heavy industry	205	144	62	10	52	6	46	31	15
Raw materials I	41	31	10	2	8	6	6	3	3
Raw materials II	50	36	14	2	11	1	11	6	4
Processing	114	77	38	6	32	1	30	21	8
Construction	59	35	23	3	20	1	20	16	4
Tertiary industries	259	92	167	22	145	9	136	76	60
Wholesale, retail	64	21	43	3	40	2	38	25	13
Services	83	38	45	4	41	3	39	23	16
Miscellaneous	112	33	79	15	63	4	60	28	31
Government services	36	10	26	2	24	—	24	24	—
Private-sector, non-household services	10	4	6	—	6	—	6	6	—
Total	681	353	328	43	285	20	265	173	92

Source: Economic Planning Agency, *National Income Statistics Annual,* 1990.
Note: Producer prices used for production value, gross domestic production, and net domestic production.

Figure 1-4 illustrates this relationship. In order to keep the diagram simple, we have excluded NDP and domestic factor income. Table 1-4 presents GDP, domestic factor income, and other indexes for 1985. This GDP was the result of the labor of 120 million people (of whom 58 million were income-earning workers) who were employed in every sector.

Traditionally, economic analysis has been based on GNP or national income, although the new SNA techniques will probably be used more often in the future. There have always been questions about how suitable these techniques are for measuring the economic performance or "economic welfare" of a country. For example, economic activities that are not mediated by the market—unpaid work in the home or vegetables grown in home gardens—do not show up in production calculations. But if, for example, both a husband and wife work outside the home and someone else is hired to do the housework, the GNP increases by the product of two people. True, housework, like rent on owner-occupied homes, can be imputed, but there are still questions about whether it is appropriate to use opportunity costs to convert housework into a production value.

Another problem is the rise in nominal GNP caused by higher prices. In order to eliminate the influence of price rises, economists use what is called "real GNP," but this creates problems of its own. For example, price rises that are due to improvements in quality are treated just like the nominal rises caused by inflation, so real GNP growth does not reflect gains in quality at all.

There is a more radical criticism as well. GDP, GNP, and other such measures, it is argued, are flawed because they measure only the "goods" in an economy and ignore "bads" like pollution. Economic growth produces both merits and demerits, and the demerits should be subtracted. An example of this school of thought is Hirofumi Uzawa's argument that car traffic carries a heavy social cost (*The Social Costs of Automobiles* [Jidosha no Shakaiteki Hiyo], Iwanami Shoten, 1974).

2. JAPANESE ECONOMIC GROWTH

FROM 1869 TO WORLD WAR II.   Our main focus will be on the period from 1950 to the present—the economic growth that occurred as Japan rebuilt itself out of the devastation of World War II. Nonetheless, some background on the country's prewar economic

TABLE 1-5   International Growth Rate Comparisons (Real GNP)   (%)

	1870–1913[1]	1913–38	1950–60	1960–70	1970–80	1980–85
U.S.	4.3 (2.2)[2]	2.0 (0.8)	3.2	3.9	3.2	2.9
Britain	1.9 (0.8)	1.1 (0.7)	3.0	2.8	2.2	1.9
Germany	2.8 (1.6)	1.6 (1.1)	8.0	4.7	2.9	1.1
Japan[3] A	3.6 (2.5)	4.6 (3.6)	8.0			
Japan[3] B	2.4 (1.3)	3.9 (2.6)	8.0	11.1	4.4	3.9

Notes: (1) For the United States, the average for 1869–78 up to and including the average for 1913; for Japan, the average from 1887 up to and including 1913. (2) Figures in parentheses ( ) indicate the per-capita GNP growth rate. (3) The A figures for Japan were calculated by the Institute for Economic Research group at Hitotsubashi University; the B figures are revised estimates by Kazushi Ohkawa.

history, beginning with the 1868 Meiji Restoration, is also warranted. We will start by comparing Japan's real growth rates with those of other major countries (Table 1-5).

Two primary estimates of Japan's prewar growth rates are available: one made by a group headed by Kazushi Ohkawa at the Institute of Economic Research at Hitotsubashi University; the other, the "Revised Ohkawa Estimates."[3] They differ enormously because they are based on different assumptions about the level of the Japanese economy when it began to embrace capitalism in earnest in 1887. If one assumes, as Ohkawa did in the second set of estimates, that Japan had already developed a great deal of economic strength during the Tokugawa Period (1603–1868) and the early Meiji years, then one arrives at an annual growth rate of 2.4% during the years before World War I—a rate far lower than that in the United States or even Germany.

Recent scholarship suggests that Tokugawa Japan had indeed achieved considerable economic strength and that this enabled the economy to take off in the Meiji era. Looked at from this viewpoint, Japan's pre–World War II growth rates were high, but not exceptional. The truly startling growth periods were after World War I (1914–1918) and, more particularly, in the fifties, after World War II (1939–1945).

[3] These data sets are encompassed in the *Choki Keizai Tokei* (Long-Term Economic Statistics of Japan) published over a period of years by Toyo Keizai Shimposha. A summary in English was published in 1979: *Patterns of Japanese Economic Development: A Quantitative Appraisal* (Kazushi Ohkawa and Miyohei Shinohara, with Larry Meissner; Yale University Press, 1979).

The 1870s Through the 1920s: Japan did not adopt capitalism in earnest until after the Meiji Restoration, almost a century later than the industrialized powers of Europe and North America. It was only in 1871 that the country abolished its warrior–farmer–artisan–merchant caste system. Over the succeeding two years, the government removed restrictions on job choices and many other economic activities and established the principle of private property[4] as Japan prepared to embrace capitalism.

By "capitalism" we are referring to a system that recognizes private property and allows people free choice of jobs and businesses, enabling individual economic units to work independently to maximize their own profits, with supply and demand on the market being the mechanism (Adam Smith's "invisible hand") for making adjustments between the units. We are not referring to "capitalism" in opposition to "socialism."

At the risk of belaboring the obvious, the central challenge to an economy is to decide how and for what purposes it should allocate limited resources and the products thereof. Different economic systems have different answers to this question. Capitalism leaves it up to voluntary decisions by *individual* economic units who are trying to maximize the benefit to themselves. Marxist economics attributes decisive significance to the question of "personal" or "public" ownership of the "means of production": Marxists attribute the *Merkmal* of capitalism to capitalists' ownership of the means of production. Socialism is based on the principles of a planned economy in which the public owns the means of production. In socialist systems, the central planning authorities have the ultimate responsibility for formulating and approving resource allocation plans.

For our purposes, we will not restrict capitalism to this rather narrow definition; but no matter how broadly it is defined, there are still large gaps between capitalism as it exists in the real world and in theory. Real-life capitalism does not rely solely on private economic units and market mechanisms to supply all goods and services. Left to the market, things like national defense and diplomacy, elementary education, and roads would never be supplied at all, or only in inadequate fashion. To prevent these "market failures," the govern-

---

[4]Under feudal law, farmers were only the "occupants" and "tillers" of the land, not its owners. Their ability to buy and sell their crops was limited, as was their choice of what to grow.

ment undertakes to provide certain public and quasi-public goods and to protect infant industries. The degree to which the government intervenes is different for each country and time, depending on a broad spectrum of historical and social factors.

Japan, as we have seen, came to capitalism far later than the rest of the industrialized world. There was no way at the beginning of the Meiji era that it could adopt the philosophy in its pure form. Initially, the government provided incentives and protection for virtually all aspects of the economy.

The 1874 *White Paper on Industrial Promotion*, written by Minister of the Interior Toshimichi Okubo, provides a philosophical defense of this practice at its most extreme:

> The strength of most countries depends on the wealth of their people, and the wealth of the people depends on the availability of goods. The availability of goods is generally said to stem from the industriousness of the people, but the source of this is none other than the degree to which they are led and encouraged by government officials.

Faced with the threat of foreign capitalism, the Meiji government found that it had to use state protection and encouragement to build the modern industry and infrastructure that it required. Some of the policies adopted included those outlined as follows.

(1) To encourage the development of modern industries, the government abolished organizations with traditional feudal privileges, such as the guilds. In their place, companies (joint-stock companies, limited partnerships, etc.) and banks were introduced. This was a key part of "industrialization" policy, and it enabled the government to tap for modernization purposes the private capital that rural landholders and urban merchants had accumulated. It also had an educational effect, giving the Japanese people their first taste of modern capitalism.

The Fiscal History of the Meiji Era (compiled by the Meiji Fiscal History Editorial Board), expressing the dominant view among Japanese economic historians, emphasizes the period's financial reforms: "From its inception, the primary economic policy of the Meiji government was to collect financial resources and encourage industrialization." There is probably no need to review here the importance to later economic development of the monetary and financial systems that were set up at this time. We should, however, emphasize that by putting a monetary and financial system in place, the Meiji government made "credit creation" possible. Whether this resulted in Japan in the credit-creation-driven economic development talked about by Joseph Schumpeter in *The Theory of Economic Development*, we will have to leave for later researchers to decide.

(2) The government decided to put "important industries"— mining, iron manufacturing, shipbuilding, and silk reeling—under "direct management." However, when typical bureaucratic inefficiencies and rising fiscal burdens became apparent, it sold these industries to private entrepreneurs at bargain prices. This process of divestiture began around 1882.

(3) The government in 1869 deregulated the movement of people and commodities (including the most important, rice) beyond their home fiefs, and followed up by building and managing the telegraph, post, and railway systems that would provide Japan with the modern means of telecommunications and transport that it required to defend its borders and develop its industrial base. Initially, the government owned and operated all of the trunk railway lines, but fiscal constraints forced it to permit private ownership of railroads beginning in 1877. This decision enabled Japan to complete a nationwide rail network by 1900.

(4) In trade matters, the Meiji government adopted protectionist policies, which were viewed as a necessary component of a "wealthy nation; strong military" program. At the time, two products— raw silk and tea—accounted for roughly half of the country's exports; cotton thread, cotton cloth, and sugar accounted for about half its imports. Since the government had surrendered the right to set customs duties autonomously to the advanced countries under the treaties of amity and commerce concluded before the Meiji era began, its strategy was to try to improve the quality of export products and provide financial incentives to exporters, while at the same time fostering and subsidizing the spinning and sugar industries, which would enable import substitutions and thereby hold down imports. One result was that exports overtook imports in the spinning and weaving industry by about 1897. In the years that followed, cotton cloth was to replace raw silk as Japan's major export.

(5) The Meiji government financed these programs with a unified national tax code (1873), the chief component of which was land taxes. The money it raised by taxing land enabled it to promote

capital accumulation and industrialization, a formula that was later to become known as "accumulation through land tax."

Opinions are mixed about the significance of the land-tax reform. One school of thought says that it established a "modern tax code"; another, that it was just a repackaging of feudal rents and therefore a "quasi-feudal holdover." We will not delve into this controversy too deeply here, but we should point out two things. First, the land tax did indeed have a modern form. All remittances were in cash, and uniform rates were exacted throughout the country. (However, the tax itself was enacted before the first Diet was convened in 1890 and therefore lacked legislative approval, one of the basic requirements for a "modern" tax. In fact, the tax was itself one of the chief causes of agitation for a popularly elected legislature.) Second, the tax was enacted by a poor government "for the purpose of maintaining revenues at their traditional levels." Unfortunately, the people were expecting Meiji political reforms to lighten their burdens and so felt betrayed when the tax was announced. Tax protests broke out all over the country, and the government cut rates from 3% to 2.5% in 1876.

As can be seen from Table 1-6, the land tax was an important source of financing for Japan's modernization drive. Indeed, between 1875 and 1910, the land tax and the banks were the principal means of tapping the capital that had accumulated and of marshalling it to the cause of modernization. The only other major financial source

TABLE 1-6   Land Taxes and Tax Revenues   (Units: ¥1 million, %)

Year	Land tax	Income tax	Total direct taxes	Liquor tax	Total indirect taxes	Total national tax income
1875	50 (85)		50 (85)	3 (4)	9 (15)	59 (100)
1877	39 (82)		39 (82)		8 (18)	48 (100)
1900	47 (35)	6 (5)	61 (45)	50 (38)	73 (55)	134 (100)
1905	80 (32)	23 (9)	130 (52)	59 (24)	121 (48)	251 (100)
1910	76 (24)	32 (10)	143 (45)	87 (27)	174 (55)	317 (100)
1931	64 (9)	145 (20)	295 (40)	189 (26)	441 (60)	736 (100)
1939	49 (2)	889 (36)	1,624 (65)	267 (11)	871 (35)	2,496 (100)

Notes: (1) Figures in parentheses ( ) indicate percentage of total national tax income. (2) National tax income shown for years in which the tax system was revised.
Source: Japan Development Bank Capital Investment Research Center.

was bond flotations, but this revenue was used mostly to cover war costs.

The policies we have discussed so far were the work of politicians like Toshimichi Okubo and Shigenobu Okuma, and there were several twists and turns that Japan would have to take before it was set firmly on the path to economic development. In 1877 the Satsuma Rebellion took place, a full-fledged revolt of disaffected samurai led by Takamori Saigo. The rebellion was quelled, but it brought inflation in its aftermath. In 1881, government changes resulted in Okuma's losing his seat in the Cabinet; Masayoshi Matsukata, who became minister of finance, enacted strongly deflationary policies that stabilized the economy. And in 1882, the Bank of Japan Act gave the country a central bank.

Japan's strategy had been to use the land tax to accumulate capital, but the Matsukata deflation placed heavy burdens on farming communities, and particularly on small, subsistence-scale farms. (Deflation meant that farmers were getting less for their crops without any corresponding relief from their land taxes.) The result was a "concentration of land" that polarized farmers into a two-tiered structure.

The land tax played a major role in Japan's economic development, but it was not the only factor in capital accumulation. The establishment of joint-stock companies and of the private banks which were founded to finance their own construction and other projects was also instrumental in tapping and allocating the funds that Japan needed.

Prewar Japanese historians tended to emphasize the differences between Matsukata's fiscal policies and those of his predecessor, Okuma, and they usually gave Matsukata higher marks. In general, Matsukata emphasized stability, for instance, while Okuma emphasized growth. But Okuma also anticipated many of the policies for which Matsukata is given credit. When the rampant inflation that followed the Satsuma Rebellion threatened to destroy all that his industrialization drives had achieved, Okuma planned to switch course and issue bonds overseas to raise the money to retire all of the extra currency that had been printed. He also joined in calling for the establishment of a central bank and a convertible currency. In that, he was not far from Matsukata's policies of currency stabilization, bank reform, and specie accumulation. Still, where Matsukata advocated a gradual retirement of inflated currency, Okuma opted to issue bonds and accomplish the task in one fell swoop. This, coupled with his friendliness with more radical reformers like Yukichi Fukuzawa, was what earned Okuma the mistrust of the ruling class and eventually precipitated his fall. For all the praise that Matsukata receives, it was his policy of gradual currency retirement that brought on the prolonged economic contraction Okuma had so feared.

Japan has had two other bouts of deflation in modern history: that presided over by Junnosuke Inoue in 1925, and that initiated by American banker Joseph Dodge immediately following World War II. The high deflationists tend to be regarded highly, while expansionists like Okuma, Korekiyo Takahashi, and Tanzan Ishibashi are looked down on. Granted, it was inevitable that the expansionary policies of Okuma and Ishibashi would give way to the contractions of Matsukata and Dodge; still, it was Okuma's "industrialization" program and Ishibashi's "priority production plan" that established the foundations for the economic development that later took place.

It was a rocky road, but by 1887 or so, and particularly after the Sino-Japanese War (of 1894–1895), Japan was firmly established as a capitalist country. Its economy continued to develop in spite of a war with Russia (1904–1905) and, later, World War I. Prior to World War II, however, the Japanese economy had only one spurt of truly rapid growth—during the interwar period of the twenties. It was at this time that the heavy and chemicals industries grew up and urbanization made inroads.[5]

POSTWAR RECONSTRUCTION. Japan's defeat in World War II brought monumental changes. The economy was devastated, and both the social and political structure had been changed radically. As in any abrupt break with the past, some things were held over and others were jettisoned. How to evaluate this process is one of the chief questions of history. In this book, we will confine ourselves to the changes that affected Japan's economic development and, more particularly, those that are integrally related to what Japan has become today.

The occupation of Japan and the policies adopted by the occupying authorities were, by and large, the work of the United States.

---

[5] More detail is presented in Takafusa Nakamura, *The Japanese Economy: Its Growth and Structure (Nihon Keizai: Sono Seicho to Kozo)*, 3rd ed. (University of Tokyo Press, 1993). The relevant portions of this volume were published in English translation as *Economic Growth in Prewar Japan* (Yale University Press, 1983).

This helped Japan avoid the kind of partition that Germany was subjected to, but it also meant that the country was governed indirectly, if not directly, by the occupying forces, which controlled the Japanese government by issuing orders and memoranda rather than taking direct control. During the early part of the Occupation, the focus was on disarming Japan and transforming it into a democracy that "would never again be a threat to world peace." We will begin, therefore, by looking at the impact of demilitarization and democratization on the Japanese political, educational, and economic systems.

First there were the political reforms. The Occupation forces purged public officials and disbanded nationalist organizations. In 1946, the Constitution was amended in line with the principles of respect for democracy, pacifism, and respect for basic human rights. Legal reforms abolished the nobility, granted women suffrage, expanded and strengthened assurances for basic human rights, renounced war, and prohibited the rebuilding of the military. The women's suffrage movement in Japan traces its history back only to the Taisho era (1912–1926), so considering the fact that it took women until 1918 to get the vote in Britain and until 1920 to get it in the U.S., it is one of history's unexpected ironies that suffrage was granted to Japanese women in 1945. Article 9 of the Constitution, which renounces war and forbids Japan from developing offensive military capacity, was obviously in line with the basic Occupation policy of ensuring that the country would "never again be a threat to world peace." This stance is also clearly visible in the spirit of the preamble to the Constitution. It is a principle that Japan can point to with pride.

Second was the democratization of education. In about 1931, Japan's primary and middle-school education began to be tainted with and eventually taken over by militarism. When the country was defeated, "democratic education" replaced "militaristic education." Japan adopted the "six-three-three system" (six years of elementary school, three of middle school, three of high school), with the first nine years compulsory and a wide range of post-secondary courses available to a broad spectrum of students.

Third were economic reforms, of which the most important was agrarian reform. This was not originally part of the Occupation guidelines; rather, it was initiated on the Japanese side. The initial plans for agrarian reform were criticized both by the Japanese people and by the Occupation administration for not going far enough. They ended up being revised to mandate compulsory government purchase of all land owned by absentee landlords and all farm plots in excess of one hectare. This land was then sold back to the tenant farmers. These reforms marked the end of the "quasi-feudal" system of landlords and sharecroppers that had been put in place with the early Meiji land tax and built up in subsequent agricultural slumps. The resulting small family farm system caused Japanese agriculture to tread a different path from the "capitalist agriculture" pattern of large farms and hired hands.

The second pillar of economic reform was labor. As the heavy-industry and chemicals sector expanded during World War I, the number of people employed by companies increased. The success of the Russian Revolution in 1917 was a spur to the Japanese labor movement: unions were formed, and labor disputes became more prevalent. "Labor–management accord" was the slogan of the thir-ties, but as the war approached, the labor movement was suppressed to the limit. The Allied Occupation saw the legitimization of the labor movement as one of the keys to democratization, so it enacted three major labor laws: the Labor Union Law, the Labor Standards Law, and the Labor Relations Coordination Law. These laws gave workers the right to organize, negotiate collectively, and engage in disputes with management. They also set up an integrated, systematic framework for worker protection.

The third pillar of economic reform was the dismantling of the *zaibatsu* and the establishment of anti-trust laws. One "opinion" that was to have a marked influence on the way Japan was dealt with after the war was the idea that Japanese *zaibatsu* were just as much be-hind the country's adventurism as the military, that they violated the freedom of other domestic companies, and that their influence there-fore needed to be eliminated. This view resulted in the breakup of the *zaibatsu* and the enactment of policies designed to promote free competition by eliminating excessive concentrations of economic power. Not only were the grand old *zaibatsu*—Mitsui, Mitsubishi, Sumitomo, and Yasuda—split up; so also were newer concerns that had emerged during the high-growth, heavy-industry phase of the twenties. Interlocking shareholdings were disclosed and sold off, members of *zaibatsu* families and officials at related concerns were barred from management positions, and the "Law Forbidding Private Monopolies and Ensuring Fair Trading"—Japan's anti-trust law—was passed in 1947.

Prewar Japan was, as far as can be seen, quite happy with the *zaibatsu*. A Japanese proverb advocates "taking shelter under the largest tree," and there is an ingrained idea that "bigger is better." Public criticism of monopolies was generally weak, and cartels were viewed in a positive light as a way to expedite negotiations. Nor was there much of a consumer movement to take issue with price cartels. Things like the *kome sodo*—a rebellion against a cornering of the rice market—were the exception rather than the rule. Added to this was the fact that prewar Japan severely repressed democratic dissent. The upshot was that the dismantling of the *zaibatsu* and the laws forbidding excessive concentration of economic power or monopolies were rather foreign and hard to understand for the general Japanese public. Nonetheless, getting rid of the *zaibatsu* proved a boon to the country's economy. It spurred competition, especially between companies that used to be members of the same *zaibatsu*, it allowed younger managers to gain control, and it generally revitalized business.

The selling off of *zaibatsu* shareholdings brought a flood of new stock to the markets and, at least temporarily, democratized Japanese stock ownership.

The Occupation's initial policy for Japan was to insure that it "would never again be a threat to world peace," but the policies we have looked at so far were those of American New Dealers, who overcame the resistance of domestic and foreign conservatives to ensure that their ideas were adopted. Later, everything would change. As the Cold War broke out and China fell to the communists, Japan replaced China as the key U.S. base in the Far East, and policy shifted to supporting its economic reconstruction. Nonetheless, the policies of the New Dealers in the Occupation period continue to form the basic framework for the Japanese economy today.

It is hard to be sure just what to call this economic system. However, it was after the reforms of the Occupation era that the Japanese economy seemingly became a "modern" capitalist system, and developed further into what some have termed a "mixed system." By "mixed system" we are referring to a system in which private-sector economic activity based on the idea of private property forms the foundation of the economy, but wide-ranging government intervention is permitted in order to make up for the shortcomings this entails. The government in such systems owns a considerable amount of fixed assets and is responsible for a considerable amount of the GDP. Today, most advanced industrial nations are probably "mixed systems."

TAMPING DOWN POSTWAR INFLATION.   Japan lost much of its fixed capital and resources during the war. Its capacity in mining and industry dropped to 53% of 1937 levels, agriculture to 60%, and textiles to just 6%! It was impossible to say when, if ever, the country would be able to recover. The demand side, however, was strong to the point of being inflationary. The people had been forced to live at subsistence level for a prolonged period of time, and wanted to make up for the shortages of food, clothing, and shelter. They had also been subject to "forced savings" through rationing and shortages. Even if they had wanted to consume, they could not, which gave them huge amounts of bank deposits and savings and government bond holdings. No sooner had the war ended than the government began to redeem debts and pay extraordinary military expenses, which combined with a too-early loosening of price controls to spur rampant inflation. The only option left to the government was to clamp down again with emergency financial measures like changing from "old yen" to "new yen" and freezing deposits. None of these measures was able to halt the inflation, however.

At the risk of digression, I myself was employed at the Bank of Japan the first year after being demobilized from the army. My appointment was as "a secretary of the Bank of Japan at a salary of ¥75 a month." That was the standard starting salary for new college graduates before the war. But one of my colleagues found that octopuses were being sold on the black market in the Kanda district of Tokyo for ¥75 each, and we spent a lot of time joking about how we were only worth as much as a lousy fish! This story illustrates how out of control inflation had become by that time. People were withdrawing their bank deposits so fast that the government had to freeze deposits in order to keep banks afloat. In fact, some maintain that the freeze on deposits had nothing to do with inflation-fighting at all, but was solely to protect the banks.

There were two schools of thought regarding the inflation of this time. The first was championed by Tanzan Ishibashi, the finance minister in the first cabinet of Shigeru Yoshida, who argued that it was not "true inflation" as defined by Keynes in *The General Theory of Employment, Interest and Money* (demand in excess of supply under full employment conditions) because resources were idle, much of the population was unemployed, and there was still room to increase production. The way to deal with it therefore was not to suppress demand but to increase production. To do so, Ishibashi advocated 1) using the Reconstruction Bank to channel funds to priority industries, and 2) adopting "priority production plans" that would encourage production of coal and steel. On this basis he proposed to reconstruct the economy. (Priority production, however, did not actually get under way until the Yoshida cabinet had given way to the Katayama cabinet, and the Katayama cabinet to the Ashida cabinet, in 1947 and 1948.)

Ishibashi told the Diet: "The chief purpose of national finances is to provide jobs for our people and reconstruct our industry—to drive the national economy toward 'full employment'. . . Starvation pricing [price rises that come about because nothing is available and the people are starving] will only be ended when we start to produce and distribute goods again" (quoted in Takeo Suzuki, *Modern Japanese Fiscal History* [*Gendai Nihon Zaiseishi*], Vol. 1; University of Tokyo Press, 1952).

The other school said the price rises really were inflation and that the only way to counter them was to suppress demand. This idea was concurred in by the Occupation forces and was by far the more readily accepted. Its leading proponent was Joseph M. Dodge, an American banker who came to Japan in 1949 as an advisor to the Occupation. His policy became known as the "Dodge Line," and it called for scrapping Reconstruction Bank financing and price differential subsidies[6] and enforcing a balanced budget for both the "general" and "special" accounts.

While this was happening, the exchange rate was standardized at ¥360 to the dollar, a rate which held for over twenty years, until the 1971 Smithsonian Accord boosted the yen's value to ¥308.

Table 1-7 shows how the Dodge Line succeeded in stabilizing prices by closing the gap between official prices and free and black market prices, and paving the way for a rapid lifting of price con-

---

[6]The practice of setting official (ration) prices of goods lower than production prices and making up the difference with subsidies, thereby spurring production. (Similar policies are being used by China today.)

TABLE 1-7   Postwar Inflation (1934–36 average = 1.00)

	Wholesale prices (annualized growth)	Consumer prices	Free and black-market prices vs. official prices (consumer goods)
1945	3.5 (1.51)		
1946	16.3 (4.65)	50.6	8.3
1947	48.2 (2.96)	109.1	5.1
1948	127.9 (2.66)	189.0	2.9
1949	208.8 (1.63)	236.9	1.8
1950	246.8 (1.18)	219.9	1.3
1951	342.5 (1.39)	255.5	1.1

Source: Takafusa Nakamura, *Economic History of the Showa Period* (Iwanami Seminar Books, 17).

trols. Nonetheless, it was a stringency measure, and it was feared that the effects on the Japanese economy would be profound.

Luckily for Japan, the Korean War came along in 1950. The country was able to capitalize on the wartime boom by supplying the U.S. military at these favorable exchange rates. It was this more than anything else that set the stage for Japan's recovery from the ashes of defeat and its growth into an economic powerhouse.[7]

[7] Inflation does not necessarily mean that all wages and prices rise uniformly. When wages and prices for manufactured goods rise more slowly than prices in general, people's real incomes contract, causing them to forgo consumption and spending. The government, however—the principal creator of fiscal inflation—can boost its expenditures before the rest of the country by distributing subsidies and building infrastructure. That is why inflation is often called a kind of tax which developing countries regularly use as a means to promote infrastructure creation and economic growth. Some have therefore wondered if perhaps the postwar Japanese inflation was not an intentional "inflationary tax" that was used to promote reconstruction. This line of reasoning gets further support from the fact that once inflation had been squelched, the enormous debt the government had been carrying (the debt was, after all, Japan's biggest postwar "problem") was effectively reduced to zero. While we would not deny that the thought had perhaps crossed the government's mind, it is hard to believe that it intentionally adopted inflationary policies. There are good reasons for believing it did not: inflation is a tax that hits the weakest members of society hardest; the government replaced the currency and froze deposits in an effort to forestall bank failures; and Japan endured marked social upheavals during the time that the old pricing system was being destroyed and a new pricing system built and stabilized. Furthermore, no evidence has been discovered that would suggest that the government intentionally stoked the inflationary fires. (*Showa Fiscal History: End of the War Through Stabilization, Vol. II: Government Debt* [*Showa Zaiseishi: Shusen kara Kowa made; Dai 11 kan: Seifu Saimu*], Tokyo Keizai Shimposha, 1983).

3. ECONOMIC GROWTH THEORY AND JAPAN

In the first section we saw that a country's output depends on its technology, capital, and labor force. Written mathematically, this is expressed as the following production function:

$$Y = F(K, L, T), \tag{5}$$

where Y stands for real GDP or GNP as an expression of output, K for the amount of capital available, L for the amount of labor available, and T for technological levels. F denotes that this is a function in which output Y is dependent on K, L, and T. It is clear from the equation that an increase in K or L will produce a corresponding increase in output. Likewise, higher levels of technology T will also raise output. Thus, the economic growth rate (which we will hereinafter write "$\Delta Y/Y$"), as indicated by the GDP or GNP growth rate ($\Delta GDP/GDP$ or $\Delta GNP/GNP$), is a function of rate of capital growth (capital accumulation rate) $\Delta K/K$, growth rate of labor $\Delta L/L$, and rate of technological progress $\Delta T/T$:

$$\Delta Y/Y = f(\Delta K/K, \Delta L/L, \Delta T/T).$$

But unlike the other two factors, the capital accumulation rate is clearly endogenous. This is not necessarily so for technological progress or population growth. For example, one could make the case that technological progress depends on the investment in research and development or that the population grows in response to GDP or national income, but this happens only up to a point. Once GDP or national income exceeds a certain level, the growth rate of population starts to decrease, so these factors are neither completely exogenous nor completely endogenous. Traditional growth theory, however, treats the rates of population growth and technological progress as exogenous variables, and concentrates instead on capital accumulation.*

---

* The oldest and most famous treatise on population and economic development is Thomas Malthus's *Essay on the Principle of Population*, published in 1789. Malthus argued that once living standards rise beyond the subsistence level, population expands geometrically while food production only increases arithmetically. The law of diminishing returns comes into play, and living standards back downward. Therefore, he concluded, the standard of living of the masses cannot be improved. It was this that led British philosopher Thomas Carlyle to dub economics the "dismal science." Malthus's insights were neither entirely wrong nor entirely right. It is often the case in the developing world that economic progress is impeded by sharp population growth, but Malthusian principles cease to apply in industrialized countries.

The simplest and best-known growth theory is that proposed by Roy Harrod and E. D. Domar, who postulate that the capital co-efficient (capital output ratio = K/Y) is fixed—that the amount of capital required for one unit of production is determined by the technology used and does not change. Expressing K/Y in terms of v, we can rewrite the production function from Equation (5) as

$$Y = K/v. \qquad (6)$$

We can divide existing capital K by v because

$$\frac{\text{Existing capital}}{\text{Capital required for 1 unit production}} = \text{Output.}$$

Strictly speaking, Equation (6) is derived from the following equation:

$$Y = \min[K/v, L/\mu],$$

in which μ stands for the amount of labor required to produce one unit of output; "min" indicates that Y is determined by the smaller of K/v or L/μ. If Y = K/v, then it is capital and not labor that functions as a constraint on output—the amount of capital stock available will determine how much is produced. If there is a surplus of labor but a shortage of capital, an increase in labor in and of itself will not produce a corresponding increase in production capacity.

Going back to Equation (6), we can express increases as

$$\Delta Y = 1/v \cdot \Delta K. \qquad (7)$$

In this equation, the increase in existing capital (ΔK) is none other than realized investments, that is, investment backed by the same amount of intended saving. Therefore,

$$\text{Investment} = \text{Savings} = \Delta K.$$

Because of this relationship ($\Delta K = S = I$), we can substitute I for ΔK in Equation (7) to arrive at:

$$\Delta Y = 1/v \cdot I$$

If we then assume that savings increase or decrease in proportion to income, then $S = sY$, where constants s stands for the saving ratio. Since $S = I$, we have $\Delta K = sY$. Substituting this into in Equation (7), we find:

$$\Delta Y/Y = s/v. \qquad (8)$$

TABLE 1-8   Average Capital Coefficient, Investment Rate, and Economic Growth

		1951–55	1955–60	1960–65	1965–70	1970–75	1975–80	1965–70 U.S.	1965–70 W. Germany
Average capital coefficient	A	2.2	2.5	2.9	2.9	7.1	6.3	4.4	5.3
	B	1.0	1.3	1.5	1.6	3.6	3.1		
Investment rate	A	16.7	21.2	28.2	32.6	34.4	32.3	14.1	25.0
	B	8.0	11.2	14.9	17.8	17.5	16.0		
Economic growth rate		7.6	8.5	9.8	11.2	4.8	5.1	3.2	4.7

Note: A indicates total fixed asset formation; B, capital investment by private-sector corporations.
Source: Created from data in Economic Planning Agency, National Income Statistics Annual.

Or, in plain language, the growth rate of GNP depends on the savings ratio *s* and the required capital coefficient *v*. This is none other than Harrod's famous postulate of the "warranted rate of growth."[8]

Equation (8) expresses an economy in which lack of capital rather than of labor constrains growth. The growth rate is therefore defined in terms of the savings ratio (*s*) and the capital coefficient (*v*).

In Table 1-8 we have tried to apply this relationship to postwar Japan. Instead of using the saving ratio, however, we have used the investment ratio. Saving is always equal to investment *ex post*, so it is acceptable to substitute the investment ratio for the saving ratio. However, because "investment" includes inventory investments and overseas investments as well as fixed capital formation, strictly speaking, the saving ratio is not the same as the investment ratio in the table. Note also that the average capital coefficient in the table was calculated back from the investment ratio and the growth rate. Table 1-8 clearly indicates that a *low capital coefficient* and *a high saving ratio* were responsible for the high growth rates achieved by the Japanese economy from the mid-fifties through about 1970.

Low capital coefficient: Table 1-9 contains capital coefficients, capital-labor ratios, and average productivity statistics from 1955 onward. The capital coefficient clearly rose gradually after the war, but until 1970 it was far lower than that for any other industrialized country. Let us look at why it was so low and how Japan was able to maintain it at those low levels for so long.

TABLE 1-9   Average Capital Coefficient, Capital-Labor Ratios, and Average Productivity

	1955	1960	1965	1970	1975	1980	1985	1988
Average capital coeff.	0.92	0.85	0.87	0.92	1.26	1.36	1.61	1.79.
Capital-labor ratio	89.6	113.2	166.2	277.1	463.9	605.6	834.8	1017.0
Average productivity	97.0	133.0	190.7	301.9	367.7	446.2	518.5	568.8

Note: The units for capital-labor ratio and average productivity are ¥10,000. Old SNA figures used for 1955 and 1960; new SNA figures in 1980 prices used for the rest.
Source: Created from Economic Planning Agency, *National Income Statistics Annual.*

[8] Note that if $1/v = \sigma$ (the reciprocal of the capital coefficient = the output coefficient), then $\Delta Y/Y = \sigma s$.

One often cited reason for Japan's low postwar capital coefficient is the relative lack of capital in the country in comparison to labor—a low capital-labour ratio (K/L).

We can decompose the capital coefficient (K/Y) into two components, the capital-labor ratio and labor productivity, as follows:

$$K/Y = K/L \times L/Y$$

or,

Capital coefficient = Capital-labour ratio ÷ Labor productivity.   (9)

When the Japanese economy began to take off, the capital-labor ratio was low, and this was a prime reason why the country's capital coefficient was also low.

That, however, does not tell the whole story. Investments soon began to pick up, and Japan accumulated capital far faster than its work force grew, but the capital coefficient remained low. What happened, we can presume, is that capital per person, which embodied technical progress, raised labor productivity, effectively offsetting any rise in the capital-labor ratio, allowing Japan to maintain its low capital coefficient. Table 1-9 clearly supports this view.

In short, the capital-labor ratio grew more than three-fold between 1955 and 1970, but average labor productivity also grew by almost the same rate, resulting in little change for the average capital coefficient. In the seventies, however, the capital-labor ratio began to grow faster than labor productivity, which produced a sharp upturn in Japan's capital coefficient. As we will see in more detail later on, technological progress during the high-growth period was embodied in the capital coming into the economy, which boosted labor productivity even as capital-labor ratios were rising. Japan therefore needed less capital per unit production—or, to put it another way, efficient utilization of its capital played a major role in promoting economic growth.

High accumulation rate: The most important factors determining the "capital accumulation rate" are the "propensity to invest" and the "propensity to save." In the model we have looked at so far, we have assumed that all savings are invested: $\Delta K = I = sY$, which indicates a "strong desire to invest." This combines with a high propensity to save to produce a high rate of accumulation.

During the period we are looking at, Japan did indeed have higher growth rates than other countries.[9] Its corporate net savings and personal savings rates were both well ahead of the rest of the industrialized world, and this has been often pointed to as an important factor underpinning the country's growth.[10]

The question of why Japan's propensity to save was so high has perplexed many economists. One theory has it that workers' wages grew mostly in the form of "bonuses" and other irregular income and this served to boost the savings rate. However, the fact that Japan's personal savings rate continued to be high even after growth stabilized undermines this thesis. Miyohei Shinohara therefore looked for the cause in the "conservationism" of the Japanese people. More recent studies have tried, with some success, to apply the "life-cycle theory" to Japan. This thesis says that Japan has such high savings rates because the average age of its population is young and its productivity growth rate is high. Japan, however, stands apart from other industrialized countries for its higher savings rate among the elderly, too. Because of this, the country's personal savings rate did not decline as much as expected when the population began aging in the seventies.[11]

Now let us consider the "strong desire to invest." While Japan was closed off from the rest of the world during World War II, the march of technology continued, especially in the United States. This generated a large technological gap and, in consequence, a heavy backlog of technology to be imported. Most of this technology was "technology embodied in capital," which meant that Japan had to invest in order to raise productivity through new technology rather than just increasing the scale of its facilities.

The dissolution of the *zaibatsu*, meanwhile, boosted competition across the spectrum, including competition between former *zaibatsu* allies, and banks and government agencies were able to encourage

---

[9] Ryutaro Komiya, "Postwar Japanese Capital Accumulation Rates" (Sengo Nihon no Shihon Chikusekiritsu) in *Modern Japanese Economic Studies* (*Gendai Nihon Keizai Kenkyu*) (University of Tokyo Press, 1975).

[10] Investments are only realized when there are underlying savings. Otherwise, the result would be "excessive investments," which would merely serve to drive up prices (or, in an open system, spur excessive imports).

[11] "Personal savings" in Japan includes the savings of non-incorporated self-employed workers. The savings rate is different for the self-employed from what it is for the general population, so the percentage of self-employed people in the population will have an impact on the overall personal savings rate.

corporate investments through risk-sharing that lessened some of their investment risk. For example, if excessive investments by a company with strong middle- and long-term potential pushed the firm into insolvency and made it likely to go under, banks would weigh the losses from bankruptcy against the firm's future potential. If it were found to have sufficient potential, the bank would prop it up with generous loans and perhaps put some of its own people on the company's board of directors. The government and the Bank of Japan were also generous in their lending to banks in order to keep them from failing, with the result being that banks, the government, and the Bank of Japan shared the risks of corporate investments. Then, once the economy took off, "investment bred more investment." Domestic markets developed (even in rural areas, thanks to agrarian reform and rice-price supports), and the advantages of mass production began to be seen.

At least, that is the theory, but it assumes that labor does not function as a constraint on growth. In reality, however, economic development fosters employment, so L/μ, the second variable in our "$\min[K/v, L/\mu]$" clause, begins to dampen expansion: labor becomes a constraint. But μ, the amount of labor required per unit production, is the reciprocal of labor productivity. The result (under the Harrod theory) is that the economic growth rate is determined by the growth rate of the work force (which we will call n) and the "rate of technological progress embodied in labor" (which we will call t). The real growth rate is therefore $n + t$, which is known as the "natural rate of growth."

Let us assume that the Japanese economy has hit the labor constraint ceiling. The real growth rate cannot surpass $n + t$, so if s/v (the savings ratio divided by the capital coefficient) is larger than $n + t$, the following holds true:

$$\text{Actual growth rate } (\Delta Y/Y) \leq \text{Natural growth rate } (n + t) < s/v. \quad (10)$$

We can therefore conclude:

$$v\Delta Y < sY. \quad (11)$$

The right side represents savings; the left, the increase in the capital required for production, which is the equivalent of investment. Equation (11) therefore represents an economy in which savings outpaces investment. This kind of economy is likely to see excesses on the supply side, which is why it is often termed a "low-pressure economy."

By contrast, if s/v is less than the actual growth rate ($\Delta Y/Y$), then

$$v\Delta Y > sY. \tag{12}$$

Investment (the left side) is greater than savings, which produces excess demand and a deterioration of the country's balance of payments.

This is called a "high-pressure economy." In these terms, Japan was a high-pressure economy during its growth period, though growth did cause the labor supply to tighten and eventually reach a "crunch."

The Harrod–Domar theory assumes no substitution between labor and capital, and on that basis hypothesizes that the capital coefficient is fixed. But obviously there is in fact a degree of substitution between capital and labor over both the long and the short terms. If the cost of using capital ("rent") increases, entrepreneurs will use labor instead; if wages rise, they will use capital. The neoclassical production function takes this substitutability into account, which is why it can be used to estimate the degree to which different production factors *contribute* to economic growth.

To create a production function that takes the substitutability of factors into account, we can use either Equation (5) above or Equation (13) below:

$$Y = A(t)f(K, L). \tag{13}$$

In this equation, $A(t)$ stands for technology, and a change in it is known as "neutral technological progress." This is because the neoclassical model assumes that A changes over time independent of K and L.

The Cobb–Douglas production function[12] provides a good starting point, and from it we can derive:

---

[12] The Cobb–Douglas production function is

$$Y = A(t) K^\alpha L^\beta \tag{a}$$

where $\alpha + \beta = 1$. From this we can calculate the growth rate $\dfrac{dY}{dt}/Y$; all we need to do is take the logarithmic differential of Equation (a):

Output (GDP) growth rate = Rate of technological progress
                         + α × Capital accumulation rate
                         + β × Rate of labor increase   (14)

where α is the capital share and $\beta = (1 - \alpha)$ is the labor share.

Let us assume that real GDP is growing at an average of 10% a year, the capital share is 0.3, and the labor share 0.7. If labor grows by an average of 2% a year, and capital by 10%, the contribution of capital to the 10% annual growth rate will be 10% × 0.3 = 3%; and the contribution of labor, 2% × 0.7 = 1.4%. That leaves 5.6% unaccounted for, and it is this amount that is usually attributed to technological progress. (These values are roughly equivalent to those calculated by Hisao Kanamori for the real growth rate of the Japanese economy between 1955 and 1968.)

But these estimates give a rate of technological progress of 5.6%, or over half of the annual growth rate. That does not agree with either the Harrod–Domar model or the common wisdom of the time that "high investment leads to high growth."

Answering these doubts will require a more detailed analysis of the contributions of labor and capital. For this we will use techniques developed by Robert Solow, Edward Denison, and their followers and look at how they have been applied to Japan by Yutaka Kosai and Seiichi Toshida.

Solow, applying the embodiment hypothesis, presumed that "newer, stronger technology is embodied in new capital goods." As Table 1-10 shows, the contribution of capital was indeed high, and that matches the perceptions of most observers. The contribution of capital is higher here than in the Kanamori estimates because there had been a change in the nature of capital itself. Technological progress had been embodied in capital and was calculated as part of capital's contribution.

One more point that can be made from the analysis of growth factors in Table 1-10 is that during the high-growth period the residual

---

$$\log Y = \log A(t) + \alpha \log K + \beta \log L.$$

Then, if we consider Y, K, and L all to be functions of time, we find:

$$d\log Y/dt = d\log A(t)/dt = \beta \cdot d\log K/dt + \beta \cdot d\log L/dt.$$

If we express the growth rate as G(Y), then

$$G(Y) = G(A) + \alpha G(K) + \beta G(L).$$

TABLE 1-10   Factors in Economic Growth

	1960–65	1965–70	1970–75	1975–79
Growth rate	9.7	11.1	4.7	5.3
Labor	0.6	1.0	−0.2	1.3
No. of workers	(1.7)	(1.8)	(0.4)	(1.2)
Working hours	(−1.0)	(−0.5)	(−1.7)	(0.7)
Quality of labor	(0.4)	(0.6)	(0.9)	(0.2)
Capital	7.8	8.2	4.8	2.3
Capital stock	(11.2)	(12.7)	(11.1)	(6.4)
Quality of capital	(6.5)	(5.4)	(1.2)	(0.0)
Rate of technological progress	1.3	1.9	0.1	1.7
Labor share	56.2	54.7	60.3	64.0

Source: Yutaka Kosai and Seiichi Toshida, *Economic Growth* (*Keizai Seicho*) (Nihon Keizai Bunko, 1989).

attributable to technological progress ("neutral technological progress") above and beyond that embodied in capital was still a high 1.3–1.9.

Two factors were at work: 1) this figure includes a shift of resources from fields with low productivity (e.g. agriculture) to those with higher productivity (e.g. manufacturing); and 2) it includes the benefits from "economies of scale" or mass production. If we compare this to the analysis above, one of the more interesting things we find is that much of the reason for the general decline in Japan's productivity growth today stems from the fact that relatively more people are employed in the low-productivity agricultural sector than in other industrialized countries.

When we add the "portion attributable to better-quality capital" and the "portion attributable to better-quality labor" in Table 1-10 to the "remainder attributable to technological progress," we arrive at a figure of 4.3% for the period 1960–1965 and 4.6% for 1965–1970. In other words, 44% and 42% of the respective growth rates for these periods can be explained by technological advances.

The conclusion, therefore, is that while much of the rapid growth of the fifties and sixties undeniably stemmed from high investment rates, those investments created more "technological progress embodied in capital," which greatly improved productivity. This too was major factor in Japanese development.

In fact, the embodiment of technological progress is so important to understanding Japan's high-growth period that it deserves fuller treatment.

In traditional neoclassical theory, technological progress is assumed to have a uniform effect on all capital during each time period considered. In actuality, however, technological progress only affects new investments (including replacement investments), not existing machinery and facilities. The capital that exists at any one time consists of new and old machinery and facilities, or "capital of different *vintages*." New capital, which is said to be "malleable" to technological progress, embodies new technology, and so is assumed to have higher productivity. Therefore, the higher the percentage of total capital accounted for by new investments or new-vintage capital, the greater the ratio of "effective capital" (which takes productivity into account) to material capital. In other words, when there is a high percentage of new investments, capital is modernized, which leads to rapid technological progress and consequently enables physical capital to be more effective in boosting production. This is because 1) an increase in investment in physical capital will boost the capital-labor ratio and consequently raise labor productivity and 2) the technological progress embodied in capital will improve productivity.

When the vintage of capital is taken into account (these kinds of models are called "vintage models"), one realizes that it is not just net investment that has an impact on economic growth but gross investment, which includes replacement investment. Replacement investments reduce the vintage of capital, which has the effect of boosting productivity.

One reason Japan emerged from its high-growth period with greater international competitiveness than the United States was that its capital was of younger vintage.[13]

As we have already noted, Japan's industrial structure changed significantly during the growth process. Table 1-11 charts these changes using Colin Clark's three industrial classifications (primary industries: agriculture, forestry, and fishing; secondary industries: mining, manufacturing, and construction; tertiary industries: wholesale, retail, services, utilities, telecommunications, finance, transportation, etc.).

[13] This idea was first developed by Robert Solow. For details, see Ryuzo Sato's *Theory of Economic Growth* (*Keizai Seicho no Riron*) (Kēisō Shobō, 1968).

TABLE 1-11   Percentage of National Income by Industrial Sector

	1955	1960	1965	1970	1975	1980	1985	1989
Primary industries	23.0	14.9	11.2	7.7	5.5	3.5	3.0	2.4
Secondary industries	28.5	36.3	35.9	38.3	37.6	36.3	34.4	36.5
(Manufacturing)		(29.2)	(27.9)	(30.2)	(27.4)	(26.2)	(26.8)	(26.3)
Tertiary industries	48.5	48.9	52.9	54.0	56.9	60.1	61.5	61.1

Source: Bank of Japan, International Statistical Comparisons.

TABLE 1-12   Production Volume for Major Products

	1955	1960	1965	1970	1975	1980	1985	1990
Crude steel (millions of tons)	9.41	22.14	411.17	93.30	102.30	111.40	105.28	110.34
Ships (millions of gross tons)	0.82	1.73	5.36	10.47	17.74	7.30	9.35	n.a.
Automobiles (millions of vehicles)	0.02	0.165	0.696	3.18	4.58	7.04	7.64	9.95

Source: Ministry of International Trade and Industry, *Industrial Statistics.*

The tendency for less of the population to be engaged in primary industries the more an economy develops is known as Petty's Law (after the seventeenth-century economist Sir William Petty). Japan was no exception. During its high-growth period, while the population engaged in primary industries declined, the working population in secondary industries, especially manufacturing, increased. The proportion of the economy accounted for by secondary industries did decline in 1965, but this was because of a recession that year. The low productivity of primary industries can be seen from the fact that in 1960, 30% of the population was employed in agriculture but generated only 14.9% of Japan's income; in 1970, 17.4% of the population was in agriculture and generated only 7.7% of total income.

Finally, Table 1-12 provides production figures for representative products. In 1970, Japan produced 93.3 million tons of crude steel, up almost 10-fold from 1955. Likewise, ship production was up almost 13-fold, and automobile production up 16-fold. That same year (1970), Japan ranked third in the world in crude-steel production (second in 1980), first in ship production, and third in automobile production (first in 1980). This gives some idea of the dramatic increase in Japan's output during the growth spurt.

4. ECONOMIC GROWTH AND ECONOMIC POLICY

According to neoclassical theory, there is little room for policy to influence growth rates except insofar as it affects technological progress; there is no room at all for interference in the form of monetary or fiscal policy. Economists have been leaning more and more toward the neoclassical school in recent years, and as a result have been unwilling to give much credit to policy at all.

The neoclassical school holds that unemployment will take care of itself if the automatic adjustment mechanisms of the market are allowed to do their job. If government tries to cut unemployment before the market is ready, it causes prices to rise. When prices rise, expectations of price rises (or "expectations of inflation") are created and the situation quickly degenerates into stagflation, the simultaneous presence of inflation and unemployment.

Keynesians argue that involuntary unemployment (what is left over when voluntary and frictional unemployment are subtracted) is the result of a lack of "effective demand." To reduce unemployment, therefore, it is necessary to increase effective demand, and in this way policy can influence growth rates. This is the philosophy that was advocated in the United States under the Kennedy administration, and it is at the heart of the "neo-classical synthesis" advocated by Paul Samuelson, James Tobin, and others.

Keynes and the Keynesians thought that by increasing government spending, lowering taxes, and providing easier access to money, governments could boost effective demand, which then would reduce unemployment. Taking this a step further, all the government has to do is change its fiscal and monetary policy mix in order to influence the country's growth rate.

Let us assume for the sake of simplicity that price levels remain constant. For Keynesians, the level of effective demand is determined at the point where savings from national income is equal to investment. Point Yf on Figure 1-5 represents national income under full employment conditions; line SS, society's aggregate propensity to save; line I_0I_0, society's aggregate propensity to invest. Effective demand is at point E_0, so full employment is achieved. Note that with

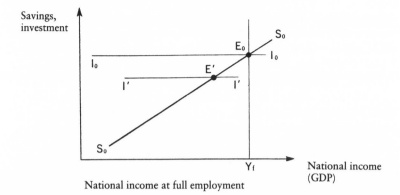

FIGURE 1-5　Fiscal and Monetary Policy Mix and Capital Accumulation (1)

investment as shown in line $I'I'$ effective demand is determined to correspond to point E', which is below full employment levels.

Assume that point E_0 has been achieved and that the government, wanting to raise the growth rate, adopts a combination of easy money and austere budgetary policies. Other things being equal, private investments will increase as a function of declining interest rates—the lower the interest rates, the higher is investment. Thus, as can be seen in Figure 1-6, line II will shift upward.

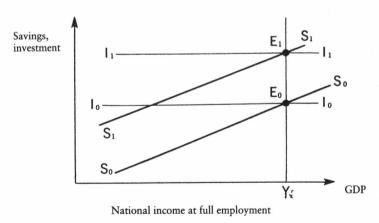

FIGURE 1-6　Fiscal and Monetary Policy Mix and Capital Accumulation (2)

By the same token, government austerity policies (reductions in government consumption expenditures, increases in tax receipts, etc.) will raise government savings, shifting line SS upward as well. As a result, the equilibrium point achieved under full employment E_1 will be higher than point E_0. Investments realized at point E_1 will be higher than those realized at E_0 by a corresponding amount. In short, a higher capital formation rate can be achieved *with* a combination of easy money and government austerity than *without*.

The growth rate ($\Delta Y/Y$) can be decomposed as follows:

$$\frac{\Delta Y}{Y} = \frac{\Delta K}{\Delta Y} \cdot \frac{\Delta K}{Y} = \frac{\Delta Y}{\Delta K} \cdot \frac{I}{Y} = \text{Reciprocal of the marginal capital coefficient} \times \text{Rate of capital accumulation.}$$

That is why an easy money/government austerity policy mix is thought to boost growth rates by raising savings (accumulation) rates. (See the Supplement on page 56 for more detail.)

However, two prerequisites must be fulfilled in order for this policy mix[14] to be feasible: 1) private-sector investments must be sensitive to interest rates (have a large interest-rate elasticity); and 2) fiscal measures must have the potential to increase society's savings rate (or "social thriftiness"). (Government savings and private savings cannot be substitutable. Higher government savings must not cause private savings to drop, and lower government savings must not cause private savings to rise.)

Milton Friedman and others have criticized Keynesian policies by arguing that policies that bring the monetary rate of interest below the natural rate of interest determined by the savings/investment relationship end up only accelerating inflation over the long term and therefore do not lower real interest rates at all. In short, they do not promote growth—they do not "deepen" capital. As we will see later on, the influence of the neoclassical synthesis has waned in recent years, at least in part because of a worldwide bout with inflation. Nevertheless, the ideas of Keynes and his followers seem adequate to explain what happened in Japan during its growth phase.

---

[14] Using lines IS and LM in Figure 1-7, this policy mix is equivalent to a shift from E_0 to E'. Under easy money conditions, interest rates decline from r_0 to r_1, while the combination of government spending cutbacks and higher taxes shifts line IS to I'S'. GDP does not change, so under these conditions lower government spending and private-sector consumption will cause an increase in private-sector investment.

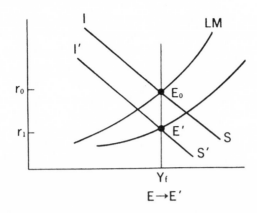

FIGURE 1-7

With the background established, let us turn to postwar Japanese fiscal and monetary policy.

The first landmark in fiscal policy was the Dodge Line with its emphasis on fiscal soundness. The Dodge policies demanded that the government balance both its general account and special account budgets. This brought severe deflationary pressure on Japan, which the government tried to alleviate with easy-money policies. Easy money was, however, a last resort to counteract the deflationary pressures of the Dodge Line and not an intentional attempt to spur growth. Still, this policy mix was the model upon which later governments navigated Japan through the high-growth phase.

With their advocacy of fiscal responsibility and prohibitions against bond issues, the Dodge policies forced Japan to pay as it went rather than rely on bonds and borrowings. There were some exceptions, of course. Article 4 of the Fiscal Policy Law allowed the government to issue bonds for public works projects or contributions to international institutions (for example, the IMF or the World Bank), so the occasional "Construction Bond" or "Investment Bond" was floated. The government could also issue short-term bills to smooth out its cash flow provided they were redeemed during the same fiscal year they were issued, since this meant they were not included in the definition of "bonds" in Article 7 of the law. The only other exceptions were government-guaranteed bonds, which also are public bonds in the broad sense of the term but nevertheless were permitted. Japan was able to keep to the "no bonds" rule all the way until 1965, and did not start floating government debt in very large quantities until the oil crisis of 1975.

This emphasis on fiscal soundness combined with stiff constraints on military spending to prevent the government budget, particularly consumption expenditures, from ballooning.

Though Carl S. Shoup, an American economic advisor during the Occupation, had established the principle of a comprehensive income tax, postwar Japan adopted a number of measures to encourage saving. Opinions are divided, however, as to their effect. Likewise, a number of investment incentives were built into the corporate tax system.

In finance, Japan adopted an "artificially low interest rates" system in which interest-rate ceilings were set by government fiat. This was based primarily on deposit interest rates, though subsidized loans were also made available on a priority basis to strategic industries. These artificially low rates made possible the investments that played such an important role in economic development, especially for capital-using industries in which investments would not otherwise have been feasible. The technology chosen by entrepreneurs is, as is generally acknowledged, influenced by the relative cost of rent (the price paid for the use of capital) and wages. When rent is high in comparison with wages, entrepreneurs will opt for technology that conserves capital, whereas if it is low in comparison with wages, they will opt for capital-intensive technology. No matter how good the technology itself is, if there is too much of a gap between its relative price and its degree of capital intensity, corporations will, so far as they are rational, refuse to use it. Artificially low interest rates are instrumental in facilitating the introduction of capital-intensive technology because they change the relative costs of wages and rent.

It is hard to say just how much *in toto* these fiscal and monetary policies contributed to growth. It is even harder to give a definitive answer about whether or not tax breaks designed to encourage saving actually fulfilled their purpose, and if so, how much they accomplished.

Above and beyond its fiscal and monetary policies, Japan also adopted a set of industrial policies that were designed to promote exports and foster import substitution industries. Again, opinions are divided as to how much was achieved by these industrial policies designed to protect infant industries and protect and encourage exports and import substitution.

Miyohei Shinohara is one who doubts the efficacy of policies to protect export industries and foster import substitutions. He argues that the fact that the yen was undervalued in comparison to the dollar did more to promote exports and discourage imports than did any protectionist policy.[15] In 1955, purchasing power parity was in the ¥450–490 range, so that the yen was overvalued at ¥360; but in the process of catching up with the West, purchasing power parity declined and the yen became cheap at ¥360.

This period saw a stream of economic plans: the "Five-Year Plan for Economic Independence" of 1955 (Hatoyama government), the "New Long-Term Economic Plan" of 1957 (Kishi government), the "Plan to Double the National Income" of 1960 (Ikeda government), and many others.[16] Higher-than-anticipated growth made all of these plans obsolete within a few years after they came out. They were an important factor in Japan's growth in that their existence gave entrepreneurs a reason to be optimistic, but many (for example, Tsunehiko Watanabe) argue that rather than being indicative of where the economy was going, they were merely decorative, a way of showing the rest of the world that Japan had an economic plan.

My opinion is that the economic plans played a considerable role in Japan's economic development because they gave entrepreneurs the confidence to undertake risky new ventures. We should not forget, however, that there were other things that also facilitated corporate risk-taking, not the least of which were stable exchange rates and the willingness of banks to forge steady relationships with firms and come to their rescue should a crisis loom. These policies or systems of sharing corporate risks were equally important in fostering confidence.

BUT WHAT ABOUT JAPANESE "INDUSTRIAL POLICY"? Japan's economic development has naturally attracted international interest, and as researchers search for causes, they inevitably focus on the industrial policies of the Ministry of International Trade and Industry

---

[15] For a detailed survey of both sides of the argument see Shozaburo Fujino's *The Dynamics of the International Currency System and Japan* (*Kokusai Tsuka Taisei no Dotai to Nihon*) (Keiso Shobo, 1990).
[16] The "Middle-Term Economic Plan" of 1965, the "Plan for Economic and Social Development" of 1967, and the "New Plan for Economic and Social Development" of 1970 (all issued under the Sato government).

(MITI). There is a myth that MITI's "industrial policy" was the key to Japan's growth.

The first line of argument we should look at in this connection is that advanced by Chalmers Johnson in *MITI and the Japanese Miracle* (Stanford University Press, 1982). According to Johnson, one should not look for the causes of Japan's growth in the unique temperament of the Japanese people, nor in the oft-repeated fallacy of the excellence of the Japanese bureaucracy or the effectiveness of its industrial policies. Johnson points to other reasons why Japan, which started down the road of capitalism far later than many other developed countries, was able, through a process of trial and error, to succeed in creating a development-oriented system.

Johnson notes that if there is a broad consensus on policy objectives, a planned system can be better suited than an American-style market-oriented system to achieving them. American-style economic systems emphasize rules and procedure, anti-trust legislation being the prime example. The government actively avoids dealing with such questions as which industry or company should be fostered, preferring to let the market decide instead. By contrast, Japanese-style "developmental states" emphasize goal-setting and prioritization. An elite, highly trained bureaucracy decides which industries and companies should be protected and encouraged. Financial instruments, taxes, and investment coordination are all used to give firms the incentives they need to meet government targets. Industrial policy was therefore part of the plan-oriented economic system arrived at by the late-starting and resource-poor Japan through a process of trial and error. It is thus natural that the style and role of this industrial policy should change as Japan's economy grows. In the process of moving closer to a market-oriented system, the emphasis in policy will be forced to switch from "effectiveness" to "efficiency." Even today, it is harder for the Japanese to understand the concept of efficiency for the system as a whole than to understand arguments about the effectiveness of this or that policy. This is largely because of the way the Japanese economy has been organized since the Meiji Era.

There is another school of thought that is skeptical about the efficacy of Japanese-style industrial policy; its leading proponents are Hugh Patrick and Ryutaro Komiya. It is rare, they argue, for the public to accept the intentions of bureaucrats at face value. Companies with firm long-term plans often had the power to go after their goals directly (or at least obliquely) even if it meant opposing government intentions, so it is doubtful how effective Japanese industrial policy really was.

This school of thought grants that the government created an environment conducive to growth, but it maintains that the "industrial policy" theory overstates the role that the government played.

Yet a third group tries to understand industrial policy from a theoretical perspective.[17] The main contention here is that the setup costs involved in establishing new industries are more than private companies can bear, so government policy intervention at this point had a significant impact in determining Japan's trade and industrial structure.

Two cases often cited as proof that postwar economic, and especially industrial, policies had little influence in determining later Japanese industrial structures are Kawasaki Steel's decision to ignore government guidance urging it to halt construction on its Chiba plant, and the government's failure to enforce restrictions on entry into the petrochemicals industry. But these sorts of exceptions are hardly enough to prove that policies had no impact at all. As long as industrial policy is based on the principle of *inducing* corporations to go where the government wants them to go rather than *forcing* them to do so, it is natural and indeed unavoidable that there will be companies that ignore them.

As Tsuruhiko Nambu[18] says, it is the nature of industrial policy to be effective during the initial stages of setting up an industry. As such, it has considerable impact. We will return to this point in the section on changes in the economic structure, where we will look at its relationship to the Heckscher–Ohlin theory that a country's industrial structure is determined by its endowment of resources.

My opinion is that policies giving priority to exports and heavy industry clearly had some effect in determining Japan's industrial structure during the high-growth period. But over the long term, market conditions had more impact, chief among them the depreciation of the yen due to the productivity gains of the high-growth period,

---

[17] See, for example, Motoshige Ito, Kazuhara Kiyono, Masahiro Okuno, and Kotaro Suzumura's *Economic Analysis of Industrial Policy* (*Sangyo Seisaku no Keizai Bunseki*), (University of Tokyo Press, 1988). English edition published by Academic Press, Inc., 1991.

[18] "The Effectiveness of Industrial Policy" (Sangyō Seisaku no Yukosei), in Hirofumi Uzawa, ed., *The Japanese Economy: The Course of Accumulation and Growth* (*Nihon Keizai: Chikuseki to Seichō no Kiseki*) (University of Tokyo Press, 1989).

the availability of stable, cheap oil supplies, and the country's natural resources endowment. It was these factors more than policy that gave rise to an industrial structure that favored exports. In this, I agree with Nambu that "the only time industrial policy was able to dominate was during the very early stages of the high-growth period."

SUPPLEMENT: THE THEORY OF EFFECTIVE DEMAND

At the heart of Keynesian economics is the idea that "effective demand" levels are determined so that the total demand for final goods equals the total supply. (The discussion below assumes price levels to be constant, eliminating the need to distinguish between real and nominal figures.)

$$\text{Demand for final goods} = C + i + g$$

$$\text{Supply of final goods} = Y = C + S.$$

Equilibrium conditions are expressed as:

$$Y = C + i + g. \tag{a}$$

If

$$\text{Consumption } (C) = \alpha + c\,(Y - t) \tag{b}$$

$$\text{Investment } (i) = i(r) \tag{c}$$

$$\text{Government expenditures } g = \bar{g} \tag{d}$$

$$\text{Taxes } t = \bar{t} \tag{e}$$

$$\text{Interest rates } r = \bar{r}, \tag{f}$$

then equilibrium for Equation (a) is

$$Y = \alpha + c\,(Y - \bar{t}) + \bar{g} + i(\bar{r}). \tag{g}$$

Therefore,

$$Y = \frac{1}{1 - c}\,\{\alpha + \bar{g} - c\bar{t} + i(\bar{r})\}. \tag{h}$$

We can also write Equation (a), which expresses the equilibrium between the supply and demand for (final) goods, like this:

$$Y - C = i + g. \tag{i}$$

In this case, Y − C stands for savings and i + g for investment. Making substitutions from Equations (b), (c), (d), and (e), we find:

$$Y - c(Y - \bar{t}) - \alpha = i(\bar{r}) + \bar{g}.$$

The value for Y is, as above:

$$Y = \frac{1}{1 - c} \{\alpha + \bar{g} - c\bar{t} + i(\bar{r})\}.$$

The effects of increases in government expenditures g and tax cuts are, respectively:

$$\Delta Y = \frac{1}{1 - c} \Delta g \qquad\qquad\qquad (j)$$

$$\Delta Y = \frac{-c}{1 - c} (-\Delta t). \qquad\qquad (k)$$

In Equation (k), −Δt stands for the decrease in taxes. If easy money policies lower interest rates r, then investments i increase. If this change is considered Δi, then effective demand increases by the amount

$$\Delta Y = \frac{1}{1 - c} \Delta i. \qquad\qquad\qquad (l)$$

We can divide government expenditures (government purchases of goods and services) into investment expenditures g_I and consumption expenditures g_C. Doing so turns Equation (i) into:

$$Y - C - g_C = i + g_I$$

or

$$\underbrace{\{(Y - \bar{t}) - c\,(Y - \bar{t}) - \bar{\alpha}\}}_{Private\ Savings} + \underbrace{\{\bar{t} - \bar{g}_C\}}_{\substack{Government \\ Savings}} = i + g_I$$

Figure 1-8 contains a graph of this relationship.

$$\text{Social savings} = \underbrace{[(Y - t) - \alpha - c\,(Y - \bar{t})]}_{Private\ Savings} + \underbrace{(t - g_C)}_{\substack{Government \\ Savings}}$$

$$\text{Social Investments} = \underbrace{i(r)}_{Private} + \underbrace{g_I}_{Government}$$
$$\underbrace{}_{Investments}$$

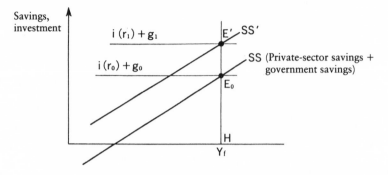

FIGURE 1-8

FIGURE 1-8

Equilibrium for the goods market is therefore achieved when

$$[(Y - t) - \alpha - c(Y - \bar{t})] + (t - g_C) = i(r) + g_I.$$

Tax hikes and reductions in government consumption will raise "social saving," which pushes line SS upward. Easy money and an increase in public investments will raise line $i + g_I$. If the scale is increased while a fiscal balance is maintained, then $\Delta g = \Delta t$, and from Equations (j) and (k) we can conclude:

$$\Delta Y = \frac{1}{1 - c} \Delta g + \frac{-c}{1 - c} \Delta t = \frac{1 - c}{1 - c} \Delta g = \Delta g \qquad (m)$$

Effective demand will increase by an amount equivalent to the increase in government spending. In this case, therefore, the fiscal multiplier is 1. If, however, the money supply is an exogenous given and interest rates are determined endogenously, an increase in effective demand with a constant money supply will boost interest rates, which will have the effect of lowering private investments, resulting in a multiplier of less than 1.

5. GROWTH RATES SLOW

In the seventies, and especially the latter half of the decade, many industrialized countries, including Japan, saw their growth rates drop. Table 1-5 provides a comparison. Japan saw its real growth rates cut in half, from 11% during the sixties to 4.4% during the seventies and to 4% during the first half of the eighties. Likewise, Britain and West

TABLE 1-13 Factor Analysis of Japan's Real Annual Growth Rates

	Real growth rate	Productivity of all factors	Labor contribution	Capital contribution	Private-sector capital investment as % of GNP	Annualized capital investment growth rate (%)
1970	10.2	4.5	0.8	4.9	17.4	19.3
1971	4.3	-1.8	0.3	5.8	16.3	-2.5
1972	8.4	1.9	-0.6	5.8	15.3	2.2
1973	7.6	0.5	1.4	5.7	16.3	14.2
1974	-0.8	-3.5	-1.8	4.5	15.7	-4.2
1975	2.9	1.2	-0.8	2.5	14.3	-6.1
1976	4.2	-1.4	2.2	3.5	13.7	-0.2
1977	4.8	0.6	1.5	2.7	13.1	-0.4
1978	5.0	0.7	1.5	2.7	13.0	4.5
1979	5.6	1.1	1.6	2.9	13.9	12.9
1980	3.5	0.1	0.8	2.6	14.5	7.9
1981	3.4	1.0	0.5	1.9	14.6	3.8
1982	3.4	0.6	1.0	1.8	14.3	1.3
1983	2.8	-0.5	1.5	1.8	14.1	1.7
1984	4.3	1.1	1.4	1.8	15.1	11.7
1985	5.2	3.1	0.6	1.5	16.1	12.1
1986	2.6	0.8	0.6	1.2	16.4	4.4
1987	4.3	1.6	1.2	1.5	16.7	6.7
1988	6.2	2.6	1.5	2.2	18.1	14.8
1989	4.7	2.0	0.5	2.2	20.1	16.6
1990	5.6	2.8	0.5	2.4	21.5	12.4
1955–68*	10.0	5.6	2	1.4	—	—

Note: Asterisk (*) indicates estimates from Hisao Kanamori.
Source: Economic Planning Agency, *Economic White Paper 1991, National Income Statistics Annual 1992.*

Germany experienced dramatic declines in their performance during the fifties and sixties. As can be seen from Table 1-13, Japan's real average annual growth rate remained a low 4.1% during the period 1973–1983, during which the two oil crises occurred. Let us look at some of the reasons that have been suggested for these dramatic slowdowns:

(1) The first hypothesis holds that this was a transition period. Throughout the high-growth phase, rising production created more jobs and ended up spurring an increasingly serious labor shortage. Labor replaced capital and foreign exchange reserves as the biggest constraint on growth. While the upper limits of Japanese growth were demarcated by the natural growth rate (n + t), savings remained high and the (marginal) capital coefficient small. The result was that Japan was transformed into an economy in which

$$\frac{s}{v} > n + t > \frac{\Delta Y}{Y}$$

was likely to hold true—in which, equilibrium rate > natural rate > actual rate of growth. To go back to an earlier metaphor, Japan in the seventies went from a high-pressure economy to a low-pressure economy in which private investments were lower than savings and deflation was a real possibility. In order to maintain equilibrium, it was necessary to supplement demand through public investments. The leading proponent of the transformation theory was Osamu Shimomura, who during the high-growth period had been extremely bullish about Japan's development potential. The problem with this hypothesis, however, is that it denies the possibility of substitutions among production factors.

(2) The second hypothesis, proposed by Miyohei Shinohara and others, was that Japan had reached the downward phase of a ten-year investment cycle. The first oil crisis hit the Japanese economy just when it was in the middle of the downward part of the middle-term cycle that had begun in 1970, prolonging the downturn for an additional two years and forcing Japan to wait until 1977 for the trough. (This ten-year wave was said to be a product of the average life of capital equipment.) Whatever this theory may say about Japan, however, it is marred by its inability to explain the general stagnation that occurred around the world.

(3) A third hypothesis blames the increased cost of imported oil in the wake of the oil crises. Within this school, there are two or

three different views about the mechanism by which these effects made themselves felt.

One view holds that higher imported oil prices weakened the terms of trade, and therefore dampened growth rates. Weaker terms of trade mean that if, for example, a country had earlier needed to export one automobile in order to import one unit of oil, it now needed to export two or maybe even more. This is the same as a transfer of income from oil-importing to oil-producing countries, and its impact is greater, the higher a country's dependence on imported oil. In 1974, oil imports accounted for 4.6% of Japan's GNP, and this theory holds that higher oil prices cost the country 3.1% GNP growth that year. However, this was a one-time occurrence and did not have a prolonged or continuing impact.

Another group of economists emphasizes the supply-side effects. Higher fuel and raw materials prices had an impact on production and lowered growth rates, they maintain.

The most famous evidence for this is the analysis done by Michael Bruno and Jeffrey Sachs, who concluded that under certain conditions a rise in raw materials prices will, like a regression in technology or "negative technological advancement," serve as a constraint on the supply of goods. When the relative price of oil rises, consumers cut back on the amount they use, but not by as much as the rise in relative prices. Higher oil prices therefore raise intermediate input costs, which forces cuts in real wages and interest rates if the economy is to operate under its current capital–labor ratio. In short, it forces incomes down. This is exactly the opposite of what happens when technological progress causes real wages and interest rates to rise. The more downwardly rigid real wages are, the higher is the resulting unemployment. The converse of this is true as well: the more elastic wages are, the lower unemployment is. The oil crises produced massive unemployment in many European countries because the labor unions fought hard to prevent decreases in real wages. Japan and West Germany were able to get through the crisis without a great deal of unemployment because their real wages were more elastic.[19]

But regardless of their effect over the short term, over the middle and long term, higher oil prices prompted a switch from technolo-

---

[19] See Michael Bruno and Jeffrey Sachs, *Economics of World Stagflation* (Harvard University Press, 1985).

gies requiring high fuel consumption to those better able to conserve fuel. This technological progress transformed the industrial structure from one oriented toward *high energy consumption* to one that was *energy-saving* or *technology-intensive*. Owing in part to its high dependence on imported oil, Japan made rapid strides in developing energy-saving technology and invested large sums of money in getting this technology into factories. Because it was able to make this transformation relatively quickly, it was able to achieve higher growth than other developed countries in 1978 and 1979, though growth rates were still lower than they had once been. When the second oil crisis hit in 1979 and 1980, growth rates slowed again, but Japan's economy was able to grow fairly steadily in comparison to the rest of the world.

(4) The fourth hypothesis emphasizes the impact of government efforts to deal with the oil crises. After the first crisis, countries had to battle with "homemade inflation." As a result of these bitter experiences, they opted for strict controls when the second crisis rolled around rather than the accommodative policies that had been tried the first time. This undeniably resulted in a prolonged slump.

During the first crisis, soaring oil prices worsened the terms of trade and brought on a recession. Governments tried to counter this by stimulating the economy through higher public spending and the adoption of monetary policies that permitted prices to rise to reflect higher oil costs. The result of these accommodative policies was to cause *imported inflation* to become *homemade inflation*. The recession was light, but price rises were sharp. When the second crisis came along, the authorities responded instead by reining in the economy, creating stagnation instead of inflation.[20]

---

[20] Figure 1-9 provides supplementary information on hypotheses 3 and 4. The vertical axis in the figure represents price levels; the horizontal axis, GDP. Assuming the amount of available capital to be constant, the horizontal axis will correspond to the amount of employment in the economy. If we assume money wages, technology levels, imported fuel prices, and exchange rates to be constant, the gross demand curve AD will slope downward and the short-term aggregate supply curve AS will slope upward. Where these lines intersect, point E_0, determines income and price levels. If E_0 is on vertical line Y_f, which represents income level under full employment, its income level is equivalent to full-employment income. Let us start with point E_0 in this equilibrium condition and then raise fuel and raw materials prices. According to Bruno and Sachs, higher costs have the same effect as negative technological progress, so the aggregate supply curve AS_0 will shift upward and to the left. All other conditions being constant, equilibrium will move to point E', price levels will rise to point P', and income will drop to point Y'. But aggregate demand is a function of how dependent a country is

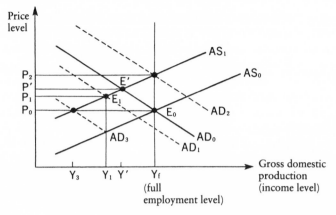

FIGURE 1-9

(5) A fifth hypothesis is that changes which occurred around 1970 in the structure of the world economy itself brought on an "age of uncertainty" that had just as much of an impact on Japan as on other countries. In *The Crises of Keynesian Economics* (1974), John R. Hicks says:

> The historian . . . may well come to reckon the third quarter [of the twentieth century], now nearly completed, as the age of Keynes. . . . It does, however, remain an open question how far this

---

on imported fuel. If the country is very dependent on imports, so much so that worsening terms of trade drain off massive amounts of income to other countries, the aggregate demand curve will shift downward and to the left as AD_1 has, and the new equilibrium point will be E_1. To sum up, over the short term, higher raw materials and fuel prices cause price levels to rise from P_0 to P_1, income levels to decline from Y_f to Y_1, and unemployment to rise.

If governments try to avoid unemployment by adopting "accommodative policies" (for example, easing up on credit), the AD curve shifts up and to the right as shown by AD_2, causing price levels to rise to P_2. When this kind of price rise creates expectations of inflation, money wages rise, but this increase in money wages shifts the AS line upward, which means even higher prices and accelerating inflation. This is what is known as "homemade inflation."

What if the authorities adopt stringent controls to try to hold down prices? If wages are flexible, prices stabilize and there is no unemployment. But if wages are downwardly rigid, then massive unemployment (as shown by point Y_3) and a profit squeeze result, causing the economy to stagnate. We will look at this in more detail in Chapter 6. See also Bruno and Sachs, *Economics of World Stagflation.*

success [the economic boom] was due to Keynesian policies. . . .
The combination of more rapid technical progress (surely a fact)
with the socialist tendencies which increased demand for collective
goods (also a fact) could have produced such a boom without the
added stimulus of Keynesian policies. It is still unclear how much
is attributable to the one and how much to the other. There can
yet be no doubt that the boom was associated, in the minds of
many, with the Keynesian policies.

Hicks argues (and the Japanese economy seems to support him)
that while there is little direct correlation between Keynesian policies
and the quarter-century worldwide boom, it is nonetheless true that
during this boom most countries in the world were able to act with
confidence in their economic future, which was one of the things that
served to prop up the boom. This confidence was destroyed, however, when the Vietnam War triggered a seemingly endless outflow of
dollars—an oversupply that generated inflation on a global scale,
undermined confidence in the dollar, took the dollar off the gold
standard, destroyed the IMF-led system, and forced the world onto a
system of floating foreign-exchange rates. Floating rates have a great
deal of merit, but they also have the disadvantage of increasing uncertainty about the future.

The inflation that was generated as a part of this process—often
attributed to Keynesian policy—undermined government officials'
confidence in their ability to manage their economies and produced a
"slump" in thinking about economic policy. This in turn caused the
public to lose confidence in government authorities, which further
amplified uncertainty.

The late seventies and early eighties were thus a unique time.
Historians may come up with a better name for it, but for our purposes, we will dub it the "age of uncertainty."

Before we turn our attention to the boom that continued from
1985 to 1990, let us look at some of the quantifiable characteristics
of the period from 1974 (following the first oil crisis) through 1985
(the year of the Plaza Accord that sent the yen skyrocketing).

The two hikes in oil prices brought about sharp rises in prices and
wages, which in turn caused private capital investments to slow and
the ratio of capital investments to GNP to drop to 13% in the late
seventies and hover at 14% through the early eighties (see Table
1-13). Some investments were made in energy-saving technology in an

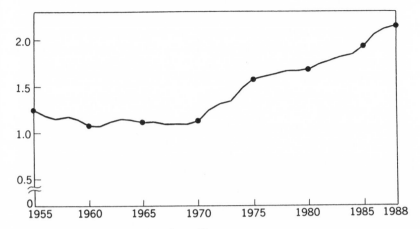

FIGURE 1-10   Average Capital Coefficient
Note: Capital coefficient = Capital stock/(GNP – public demand), 1980 prices.
Capital stock for all industries, term averages. Discrepancies with Table 1-9 are due to
the use of different denominators.

effort to counter higher oil prices; however, these investments did not
lead to labor productivity gains in the short term. The result was, as
can be seen from Figure 1-10, that the capital coefficient continued unabated in the rise that had begun in the early seventies. During the
high-growth period, it stood at around 1.1; by the late eighties it had
reached 2.1. This effectively destroyed the two pillars that had supported Japanese growth during the sixties: the low capital coefficient
and the high accumulation rate. Factor analysis of the real growth
rate shows that neutral technological progress, which had previously
made the largest contributions to growth, now contributed less than
did capital.

6. THE AGE OF UNCERTAINTY

In 1985, there was a fundamental change in the "high dollar, high
interest, high oil price" framework that had defined the world
economy ever since Ronald Reagan became president of the United
States in 1981. The Japanese economy naturally changed, too.

What touched it off was a meeting of the finance ministers and
central bank chairmen from the Group of Five economic powers (the

U.S., Britain, France, West Germany, and Japan) at the Plaza Hotel in New York City. During the meetings, the U.S. agreed to abandon its high-interest/strong-dollar policy in favor of more coordinated policies among all members of the group. This became known as the Plaza Accord, and two of its immediate effects were to correct the yen's undervaluation in comparison to the dollar and to send oil prices tumbling.

For Japan, the appreciation of the yen lowered import prices and raised export prices. On the one hand, this caused imports to increase and exports to decline; but on the other, it improved Japan's terms of trade. The capital investments that drove the recovery of 1984–1985 were mainly the result of higher exports, so when the yen began to surge, capital investment stalled (see Table 1-13), and the economy, just after an upturn, took a temporary dip. This did not last long, however. The higher yen and pressure from overseas forced Japan to invest in transforming itself from an external-demand-driven economy to a domestic-demand-driven economy. This transformation involved a wave of deregulation, which spurred more capital investment and spending on research and development. On top of this investment demand, Japanese monetary authorities succumbed to pressure both at home and abroad to "cooperate with other countries" and cut interest rates. Easy credit convinced firms to invest even more, especially on equipment replacement that they had been putting off. And because low interest rates work to the advantage of long-term investment, they stimulated areas like resort development and construction, which caused land prices to rise and eventually resulted in the formation of a speculative bubble. We will look at this more in the chapter on finance.

The 1990 *Economic White Paper* analyzes the factors driving capital investments and concludes that during the eighties they differed from one year to the next. If there was anything at all that they had in common, it was sharp changes in technology, which spurred early equipment replacement and increased the need for new and independent investments. Added to this were larger investments in labor-saving equipment to counteract the labor shortage and pressure to reduce working hours. Increases in capital investments naturally meant an increase in capital stock, which eventually resulted in a "stock adjustment"—a situation in which an excess of stock serves to limit capital investment growth. This hints that stagnation may be in store, though it might be argued that the sharp increase in the capital coefficient during the late seventies and eighties mitigates against a stock adjustment because technological innovations mean that more capital is required per unit production, so an increase in investments alone is not enough to bring about a surplus in production capacity.

In May 1989 the Bank of Japan finally raised the prime lending rate to nip in the bud the inflationary tendencies due to serious labor shortages, and thereafter raised the rate at intervals. At first these tight-money policies seemed to have little effect, but by the beginning of 1990 the speculative bubble of land and stock prices had burst; share prices plummeted to about 60% of their highest level, and 1992 land prices too began to decline. These drops in asset prices hit hardest the firms and financial institutions which had heavily expanded securities investments and lending for real-estate purchases during the low-interest-rate period, thereby increasing uncertainty about the future.

Given these fundamental changes in the economic framework, it is hard to forecast what is in store for Japan. But this much is certain: the Japanese economy can no longer afford to ignore the rest of the world, nor can the world economy afford to ignore Japan. We have truly reached a new stage of development.

2
MONETARY POLICY

1. THE ROLE OF FINANCE

Let us begin by looking at the role of finance in an economy. Generally, people point to three functions for the financial services industry: 1) to supply payment instruments and facilities; 2) to spur economic activity by lending the excess funds of economic units running surpluses (including temporary surpluses) to those running deficits; and 3) to provide households and other economic units with the financial assets that are generated by the lending process. Figure 2-1 diagrams this relationship.

Funds flow either directly from units running surpluses to units running deficits or indirectly through financial institutions. Of the latter, indirect financing, some will go through banks (monetary intermediaries), and some through other, non-monetary intermediaries.

As can be seen from Figure 2-1, financial intermediary institutions *transform* the primary securities (bills, corporate bonds, public bonds, stocks, etc.) issued by deficit units which want to raise funds into indirect securities that are less profitable but more liquid, are more easily divisible, or are more stable in value than primary securities. Doing so enables financial intermediaries to absorb idle funds and promote their smooth distribution throughout the economy. The reason financial institutions are able to undertake these transformations is that they enjoy "economies of scale." Funds tend to concentrate in institutions, and if they do so on a sufficient scale, it enables institutions to invest short-term funds in long-term projects. Since money continuously flows into and out of the institution and part

69

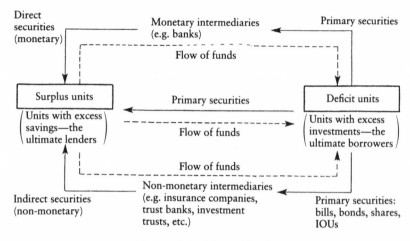

FIGURE 2-1   Flow of Funds

always remains in the form of deposits, it is necessary only to keep part of that money on hand and invest the rest. There is an asymmetry of information between the lenders of funds and the borrowers, which from the standpoint of information puts lenders at a disadvantage. In order not to be defrauded by borrowers, lenders must check the borrower's credit, gather and analyze information on the project's future potential, and monitor progress after the loan has been made. These activities are known as the *production of information*, and it is here that economies of scale come into play. Instead of leaving it up to the ultimate lender—the depositor—financial institutions take care of producing information about borrowers, which enables them to cut the costs associated with lending.[1] Whether or not the indirect securities it issues are monetary in nature determines whether the institution is a "monetary intermediary" (bank) or a "non-monetary intermediary" (insurance company, trust bank, etc.).

In contrast to banks, securities companies have the responsibility to support the issue and sale of the primary securities instruments (bonds, stock, etc.) issued by the ultimate borrowers of funds through

[1] There is also an "asymmetry of information" between banks and depositors. Strictly speaking, depositors need to monitor whether or not banks are performing their fiduciary responsibilities in good faith, but as long as the interest on deposits is fixed in advance and deposits are insured, there is no need for depositors to check or monitor the bank's credit.

underwriting and dealing, and to facilitate the circulation of securities by mediating the buying and selling of primary securities owned by the lenders or investors that reduce the spread between the selling price and the buying price.

Depending on the funds and assets they trade, financial markets are classified as either short- or long-term markets, and as either capital (stocks and bonds) or money markets. Furthermore, markets may be either open or closed (an example of the latter being the interbank market) depending on whether or not there are limits on who can participate. We will not delve into these classifications in detail here, however.

The financial assets generated in the course of lending funds from surplus units to deficit units are owned by households and corporations and, as we saw in Chapter 1, form part of the national asset balance. The ratio of financial assets to "real" assets is a useful quantitative index of the relative importance of finance to a country's economy. It will vary according to how dependent the economy is on external funding, how large a proportion of its financial assets are indirect, how rapidly its productivity increases, and how much asset prices fluctuate.

Table 2-1 compares financial assets to GNP rather than real assets, giving figures for both Japan and the United States. At the beginning of its postwar growth phase, Japan's ratio of financial assets to GNP was 2.12, which was about half of the 4.01 ratio posted by the United States. But the ratio grew from there, overtaking the U.S. in

TABLE 2-1   Balance of Financial Assets as a Percentage of GNP

| | Japan | | U.S. |
	Financial assets	of which shares	Financial assets
1955	2.12	0.13	4.01
1960	2.80	0.21	4.21
1965	3.53	0.22	4.45
1970	3.66	0.38	4.18
1975	4.33	0.41	4.01
1980	4.90	0.51	4.31
1985	5.92	0.76	4.68
1987	6.74	1.46	4.89

Source: Economic Planning Agency, *Economic White Paper 1989.*

1975 when it reached a multiple of 4.3 (4.3 times the GNP). When share prices took off in the late eighties, the ratio soared even higher.

The American ratio of financial assets to real assets has tended to be lower than Japan's, but, as we shall discuss later, that is because the U.S. is less dependent on external funding and indirect finance. When land is excluded from real assets, one can see a sharp increase in the ratio during the second half of the eighties. This is, first, the result of new financial products, which created a multi-level flow of funds, and, second, of the appreciation in share prices. This accumulation of financial assets helps expand the stock market and other secondary markets.

2. OVERVIEW OF THE JAPANESE FINANCIAL SYSTEM

Japanese financial institutions comprise the Bank of Japan (the central bank) and other public and private institutions. The latter include both monetary and non-monetary financial intermediaries. Securities companies, which broker trades on the securities markets, are also financial institutions. But unlike financial (credit-granting) intermediaries, securities companies do not issue indirect securities in the form of debt securities on themselves; they merely broker trades. Even when they underwrite securities, they do so for the purpose of selling them at a later date.

THE CENTRAL BANK.   Central banks usually have three functions: 1) issuing currency; 2) acting as a "banker's bank;" and 3) acting as the government's bank.

The Bank of Issue: Today's central banks are generally given a monopoly on currency issues. In the past, this was not necessarily the case. The "national banks" of Meiji Japan or of the U.S. until the thirties, for example, were allowed to issue their own notes. Later, countries found it advisable to give the central bank a monopoly on note issues in order to prevent inflation through overissuing. In Japan, this was codified first in the Convertible Bank Note Act of 1889, and then in Article 29 of the Bank of Japan Act of 1942.[2]

---

[2] Not everyone agrees with this. Friedrich Hayek, for example, argues that deregulation of currency issues so that all banks could issue their own notes would spur competition and that good money would drive out bad.

The Bank of Japan was established in 1882. Its initial purposes were to sink the large quantities of non-convertible paper money (including some national bank notes) that had been floated to finance the quelling of the Satsuma Rebellion; to fight inflation by issuing convertible bank notes; and to establish a monetary system that would foster public confidence in paper money. It was given a monopoly on bank note issues at this time.

Initially, notes were issued under an "elastic limit system," but this was gradually modified to an "elastic maximum limit system" that directly prescribes the maximum amount of notes the Bank can issue. "Elastic" in this case refers to the fact that the Bank of Japan is allowed under the law to exceed its limit under certain conditions.

As we will see later on, there are no real differences between bank notes and Bank of Japan deposits, so it is fairly meaningless to place limits only on bank note issues and ignore the other—even more so because the maximum is raised virtually every year anyway. Many in Japan argue that the limit should be done away with all together, as indeed has been done in most countries. Having switched from the gold standard to a system of managed currency, the central bank should be allowed to use the policy weapons in its arsenal to keep the money supply at optimal amounts as indicated by various economic indexes (prices, employment, etc.).

The Banker's Bank: Central banks function as reserve banks, which means they hold all of the reserves that private financial institutions are required to keep, and function as lender of last resort should private institutions find themselves with liquidity problems (lack of cash or central bank deposits). As the lender of last resort, central banks will discount bills, provide loans, and allow current account overdrafts in order to keep institutions solvent. Supplying liquidity, however, is not the same as "rescuing" a bank. Rescues occur when banks, through defaulted loans or other reasons, are unable to make their payments; when a bank has liquidity problems, its assets are sound but it is temporarily short of money. Still, the ability to receive an infusion should liquidity be short is a form of "insurance," and implicit in this is the danger of "moral hazards." Preventing these moral hazards is part of the rationale for having the central bank conduct regular inspections of private institutions.

Postwar Japan has been criticized for being excessively protective of its banks. The Bank of Japan has often stepped in with measures that go far beyond shoring up temporary liquidity gaps. In its zeal to avoid bank failures, it has rescued many institutions whose defaulted assets placed them on the verge of bankruptcy. Even if we grant that deposit-taking institutions form an important link in a country's economic system and need to be protected, Bank of Japan-style protection allows bank managers to take the easy way out, and efficiency is sacrificed as a result. In the United States, the Federal Reserve system, which functions as the central bank, has been more restrained in granting money to deposit banks in trouble than has the Bank of Japan.

Banker to the Government: The central bank is the government's banker. It handles all payments and receipts for the treasury. It also underwrites short-term government securities issued to smooth out the treasury's cash flow.

By providing these services, the central bank fulfills its obligations to "stabilize prices," "facilitate financing," and "maintain order in the credit system." (Article 1 of the Bank of Japan Law terms this "regulation of the currency, control and facilitation of credit and finance, and maintenance and fostering of the credit system.") Granted, the bank has sometimes given priority to other policy objectives (for example, high growth), but in the postwar period as a whole, and especially in recent years, it has placed greatest emphasis on price stability.

As in other countries, the Bank of Japan's relations with the government and the legislature have not always been friendly. Whatever harmony may appear on the surface, there has been tension underneath. The government and the legislature have a natural bias toward expansion, since it is in their interest to emphasize production and employment. The central bank, on the other hand, is a "chronic worrier," a "virgin fearful that a man may be hiding under her bed"—or at least that inflation is hiding there! The Bank of Japan, however, is far less independent than the U.S. Federal Reserve. The authorities that oversee it can give the bank "business orders" and can fire its officials. One result has been to make it rare for conflicts over financial policy administration between the Bank of Japan and the government (Ministry of Finance) to reach the surface. Many argue that the Bank should be made more independent so that financial policies remain neutral, but others respond that a more independent central bank would only make it harder to coordinate financial and fiscal policy.

UNIQUE ASPECTS OF THE JAPANESE FINANCIAL SYSTEM. Let us look at some of the things that set the Japanese financial system apart from those of other countries.

Public Financial Institutions: We should begin by noting the wide variety of public financial institutions in Japan. There are any number of lending institutions, for example, that are funded with postal savings accounts and the surplus funds from postal insurance, welfare pensions, and national pensions. Among them are the People's Finance Corporation; Housing Loan Corporation; Agriculture, Forestry and Fisheries Finance Corporation; Export-Import Bank of Japan; and Japan Development Bank. The funds they handle are enormous, and in recent years, some of them (for example, the Japan Development Bank) have also been financed through government-guaranteed bonds.

Barriers between Banks and Securities Companies: Like the United States, postwar Japan adopted rules forbidding banks and securities companies from engaging in each other's businesses. This prohibition is found in Article 65 of the Securities and Exchange Law, which the Occupation administration modeled on America's Glass–Steagall Act when it revised the law in 1948. There are three major reasons for keeping banks out of the securities business: 1) to prevent additional risks in bank operations and thereby protect depositors; 2) to prevent conflicts of interest; and 3) to prevent the concentration of power that would allow banks to dominate markets (giant financial institutions, it is argued, would have a greater ability to develop monopolies and use them to dominate industry).

The Specialization of Financial Institutions: The third characteristic of Japanese finance is that markets are compartmentalized by the principle of division of labor and that each market has its own specialized institutions: long-term lenders are separate from short-term lenders, trust banks from ordinary banks; there are specialists for foreign exchange, and others for small business lending (the *sogo* banks[3] and credit associations).

The roots of this pigeonholing go back to the early Meiji Era, when it was thought desirable to separate lenders of short-term funds (commercial banks) from lenders of long-term capital (agricultural and industrial banks). Meiji regulators considered it unsound for commercial banks, which accepted short-term funds in the form of

---

[3] Most of the *sogo* or "mutual" banks converted to "ordinary" bank status in 1989.

demand deposits, to finance long-term capital investments (which they called "quiet capital"). Doing so would produce a mismatch in the maturities of their assets and liabilities. After the war, regulators wanted to protect and foster small businesses and thought it wise for certain institutions to specialize in lending to them. This was set into law in 1952, when a chronic shortage of funds convinced regulators that the traditional divisions of labor should be kept and reinforced. They therefore proceeded to classify the way funds were used and create specialized institutions for each field, giving them the responsibility for using money effectively within their area of expertise.

That case is harder to make now. In the high-growth phase that followed, Japan began to accumulate financial assets, and when growth slowed down in the mid-seventies, the country began to record chronic surpluses rather than chronic shortages.[4] In the process, it became apparent that Japan's specialist institutions were unable to deal swiftly with an ever wider range of financial needs. We will discuss that in greater detail later on. First let us look more closely at how the Japanese financial system worked during the growth spurt of the sixties and early seventies.

3. THE DEVELOPMENT OF THE JAPANESE FINANCIAL SYSTEM

FROM THE OCCUPATION TO THE SEVENTIES. As is apparent from Figure 2-2, the largest surplus sector through the mid-seventies was the personal sector, and the largest deficit sector the corporate sector. There were several other things that characterized this period:

(1) By far the largest flow of funds was from the personal sector to the corporate sector.

(2) Indirect financing—flows of funds through financial institutions—accounted for an overwhelming majority (80–90%) of the whole. (This can be seen from Table 2-2.) Of this, 70–75% was loans and advances, indicating how dependent companies were on financial institutions for their investment funding.

Akiyoshi Horiuchi divides this period into two halves, with the line dividing them coming around 1965. Horiuchi notes that secur-

---

[4]This is the same as the transformation from a "high-pressure" to a "low-pressure" economy, or as John Hicks terms it, from an "over-draft economy" to an "autonomous economy."

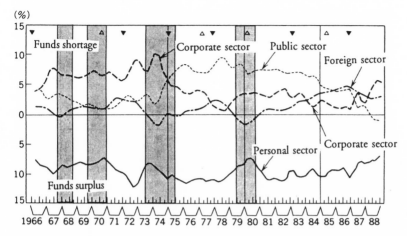

FIGURE 2-2   Surpluses and Shortages of Funds by Sector (as a Percentage of Nominal GNP)
Notes: (1) Seasonally-adjusted, 3-term weighted moving average (weighting 1:2:1). (2) Tight-money periods indicated with shading (and so throughout). (3) △ indicates peak of cycle; ▲ indicates trough (according to Economic Planning Agency figures, and so throughout).
Source: Bank of Japan, *Economic Statistics Monthly.*

ities, particularly stocks, accounted for a comparatively large proportion of total fund-raising during the first half, but lost their position to bank lending in the wake of the upheavals that occurred on Japan's markets in the mid-sixties.[5] Up to that point, the traditional corporate financing method of using bank borrowings for investments and then later issuing stock with which to pay back loans and consolidate capital structures seemed the most functional.

(3) Banks accounted for a relatively large share (40–50%) of total finance. There are four reasons usually given for this: i) households and individuals had still not accumulated many assets and so leaned more toward deposits with the safety and liquidity they provided; ii) the government adopted policies that favored deposits; iii) borrowings from financial institutions were more flexible and therefore more

[5] See Akiyoshi Horiuchi and Kojiro Sakurai, "Development of Financial and Capital Markets" (Kin'yu Shihon Shijo no Tenkai) in Hirofumi Uzawa, ed., *The Japanese Economy: The Course of Accumulation and Growth* (*Nihon Keizai: Chikuseki to Seicho no Kiseki*) (University of Tokyo Press, 1989).

TABLE 2-2   Flow of Funds Through (Broadly Defined) Financial Markets   (Top half: ¥100 billion; bottom half: %)

	1955–59 (avg.)	1960–64 (avg.)	1965–59 (avg.)	1970–74 (avg.)	1975–79 (avg.)	1980–84 (avg.)	1985	1986	1987
(1) Financial institutions	16.4	44.7	95.6	246.4	408.2	501.0	542.8	724.6	883.9
Banks etc.	11.8	33.5	64.8	167.3	241.8	264.2	280.0	371.8	472.8
Other private-sector institutions	1.7	4.7	13.0	30.3	47.6	77.6	84.6	171.5	242.2
Public financial institutions	2.9	6.5	17.8	48.8	118.8	159.2	178.2	181.3	168.9
(Loans)	14.2	39.0	76.6	209.0	273.4	354.8	381.8	438.4	595.4
(Securities)	2.2	5.7	19.0	37.4	134.8	146.3	160.9	286.2	288.5
(2) Domestic securities investments by the domestic non-financial sector	2.6	8.6	5.0	16.7	37.6	67.3	27.1	–58.5	–5.1
(3) Foreign capital markets	0.7	3.0	2.5	8.7	9.3	18.6	42.0	3.1	26.8
Total	19.8	56.2	103.0	271.8	455.1	586.9	611.9	669.2	905.6
(1) Financial institutions	82.9	79.5	92.8	90.7	89.7	85.4	88.7	108.3	97.6
Banks etc.	59.8	59.5	62.9	61.6	53.1	45.0	45.8	55.6	52.2
Other private-sector institutions	8.5	8.3	12.6	11.2	10.5	13.2	13.8	25.6	26.7
Public financial institutions	14.7	11.6	17.3	17.9	26.1	27.1	29.1	27.1	18.7
(Loans)	71.8	69.3	74.3	76.9	60.1	60.4	62.4	65.5	65.7
(Securities)	11.1	10.2	18.5	13.8	29.6	24.9	26.3	42.8	31.9
(2) Domestic securities investments by the domestic non-financial sector	13.3	15.2	4.8	6.1	8.3	11.5	4.4	–8.7	–0.6
	(24.4)	(25.4)	(23.3)	(19.9)	(37.9)	(36.4)	(30.7)	(34.1)	(31.3)
(3) Foreign capital markets	3.8	5.3	2.4	3.2	2.0	3.2	6.9	0.5	3.0
Total	100.0	100.0	100.0	100.0	100.0	100.0	100.0	100.0	100.0

Notes: (1) The "(Loans)" and "(Securities)" rows contain totals for the loan or securities portion of financial sector holdings and loan or securities investments by the domestic non-financial sector. (2) Financial institution securities holdings include BoJ holdings. Financial institution securities holdings and domestic securities investments by the domestic non-financial sector include commercial paper holdings. (3) The statistics are not necessarily continuous due to changes in statistical methods. (4) "Banks etc." includes trust banks and insurance companies etc.

Source: Bank of Japan, Applied Table of Flow of Funds Accounts; Bank of Japan Research Monthly, June 1988 issue.

attractive to companies than bond issues; and iv) banks functioned as the "lenders of last resort" for companies, and stable client relationships gave them an advantage in information production.

(4) Markets were highly compartmentalized. There were the deposit market, the long-term money market, the short-term money market, the bond markets (issuing and trading), the stock markets (issuing and trading), the small business financing market, and a number of others besides. Interest rates on each of these markets were artificially determined: the long-term prime rate, the short-term prime rate, the bank debenture yield (two- and five-year), the time-deposit interest rate, and so on. Between this segmentation and artificial rate determination, it was impossible for borrowers to arbitrage rates between different markets.

When both interest rates and funds are allowed to move freely, interest-rate arbitrage will cause the long-term yield on funds of equivalent risk (except for maturity) to become equal to the average of expected short-term rates.[6] For example, say the annual interest on a long-term bond with a maturity of ten years is R_{10}. And, for the sake of simplicity, let us assume that this is simple interest rather than compound. We will call the expected yield on short-term bonds in the first year r_1, that in the second year r_2, and so on through r_{10}, short-term interest in the tenth year. We can express this mathematically as

$$R_{10} = \frac{r_1 + r_2 + \ldots r_{10}}{10}. \tag{1}$$

If, however,

$$R_{10} < \frac{r_1 + r_2 + \ldots r_{10}}{10},$$

then people will avoid long-term bonds and invest in short-term bonds instead. This will cause long-term yields to rise and short-term yields to fall until the two sides of the equation are again equal. Conversely, if the yield on long-term bonds is higher than the average expected yield on short-term bonds, people will buy long-term rather than short-term bonds, driving long-term rates down and short-term rates up until once again both sides of the equation are equal. A

---

[6] We have assumed risk-neutral investors here, who are able to focus on expected values and ignore risk.

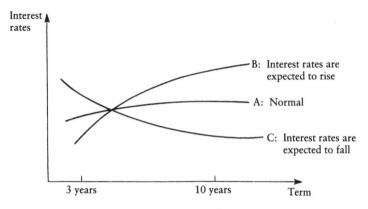

FIGURE 2-3   Term Structure of Interest Rates

more general way to write Equation (1) is:

$$R_n = \frac{r_1 + r_2 + \dots r_n}{n}.$$

Figure 2-3 contains a diagram of the term structure of interest rates that illustrates this concept. If the expectation is that interest rates will rise in the future, the line slopes upward; if the expectation is that they will decline, the line slopes downward.[7] The lines on Figure 2-3 are known as "yield curves," which fluctuate to reflect expected changes in short-term interest rates due to variations in business conditions.

In postwar Japan, however, interest rates were set artificially so that long-term rates were always higher than short-term rates. This enabled banks to turn an easy profit by accepting short-term funds (demand deposits) and using them to buy long-term assets, for example by discounting three-month or six-month bills or making one-year loans. When interest rates are deregulated, the spread between long and short rates may contract; in extreme cases such as that shown in Figure 2-3, there may actually be a negative spread.

(5) The financial services industry tended to be more heavily regulated than other areas. In addition to normal financial regulations,

---

[7]For example, if the expectation is that interest rates will rise, and $r_1 = r_2 = r_3 = \dots = r_9 < r_{10}$, then $R_{10} > r_1$. Conversely, if $r_1 > r_2 = r_3 = \dots = r_{10}$, then $R_{10} < r_1$.

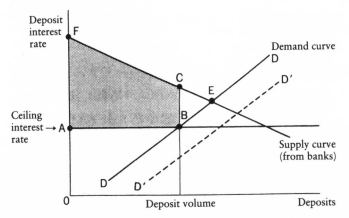

FIGURE 2-4   Relationship Between Deposit Volumes and Deposit Interest Rates
Note: Banks have filled the condition that they maximize their profits when they supply deposits at the point on the supply curve where interest rates and deposit volumes intersect.

"foreign exchange controls" were in effect until 1980, interest rates were kept artificially low, and "bond float coordination" in the new issues market amounted to a rationing of funding. The ceiling on deposit rates, in fact, has not been entirely lifted even today. When rates are completely free, interest is determined by the relative demand for and supply of deposits, just as prices are determined for any other product. As Figure 2-4 illustrates, all things being equal, there will be more demand for deposits the higher the interest paid on them. Conversely, when interest rates are high, banks will cut their supply of deposits. What is important to note, however, is that the orientation of supply and demand curves is opposite that for conventional products. If the upper limit on deposit interest is set lower than point E, where the supply and demand curves intersect, the amount of deposits available will be determined by demand, as illustrated in Figure 2-4. This will give banks windfall profits, as shown by shaded area ABCF. The more deposits they can attract, the greater their profits will be, so a fierce battle for deposits ensues.

(6) Managed trade and foreign exchange enabled the government to pursue independent financial and fiscal policies without having to worry that changes in interest rates would cause capital to drain

overseas or come surging into Japan. In short, the government had great latitude in using its policy tools to promote domestic equilibrium. In this, Japan differs sharply from West Germany. By deregulating capital comparatively quickly, West Germany robbed itself of a powerful inflation-fighting tool. When it tried to raise interest rates to hold down prices, capital flooded in from overseas, which offset any effect its monetary policies would have had.

(7) It was easy for government authorities to control the economy. Corporations, as we saw in (2), were forced to depend on loans from financial institutions, so all the authorities had to do was exert pressure on institutions to make the entire economy fall into line. The Bank of Japan was also known for its "window guidance," the practice of directly regulating bank lending to corporations. This was a particularly good way to have quick impact.

CHANGES SINCE 1975. In 1971, Richard Nixon announced that the United States would no longer be converting gold to dollars, and the world sailed into the age of floating interest rates. The yen rose against the dollar as a result, and the economy stalled. In Japan, this became known as the "Nixon Shock." With the economy stagnant, tax revenues were unable to cover expenditures in 1971 and 1972, forcing the government to boost its bond issues from traditional levels in the hundreds of billions of yen to well over a trillion yen. Once that barrier had been broken, trillion-yen bond issues became an annual occurrence, though until the oil crisis hit in 1973, tax revenues were actually growing faster than expenditures. OPEC put an end to that forever. When the growth rate slowed in the mid-seventies, the government began to run up large deficits that brought fundamental changes in the financial climate.

(1) Figure 2-2 illustrates how in 1975 the public sector replaced the corporate sector as the largest deficit sector in the economy. For the next decade or so, the gap between them continued to widen. The corporate sector's deficits declined while the public sector's grew. Until it was overtaken by the foreign sector in the mid-eighties, the public sector was Japan's largest deficit producer. What this amounted to was a change in the flow of funds. During the high-growth period, most of the money went from the personal sector to private corporations; after 1975, it moved from the personal sector to the public sector.

(2) The public sector covered most of its deficits with bond issues,

which brought about a large increase in the proportion of funds raised through securities. Between 1960 and 1974, securities issues accounted for only about 22% of the funds raised each year. In 1975, this proportion jumped to 37%, and it did not drop until the 1990s.

(3) Declining capital investments reduced the private sector's need for funds, which consequently cut corporate deficits and in some cases gave companies surpluses.

(4) The personal sector maintained its high savings rates even after growth slowed in the mid-seventies, leading to further expansion in personal and household assets.

(5) Advances in telecommunications and transportation produced a rapid internationalization of people, goods, and money. The 1980 revisions to the Foreign Exchange and Foreign Trade Control Law further integrated Japan financially with the rest of the world.

Let us consider what these changes meant for the workings of Japan's financial sector.

(1) The biggest problem faced by Japanese finance was how to absorb all the bonds being issued by the government. That was, in fact, one of the main reasons for liberalizing interest rates. Until the mid-seventies, there were *de facto* restrictions on market sales of government bonds, partly because financial institutions underwrote and held only small amounts of them. These restrictions had to be relaxed and eventually scrapped in order for the markets to absorb the influx of new government issues. The upshot was that the markets were free to set prices for government bonds as they thought best, which essentially liberalized interest rates. This period saw the launch of "medium-term bond funds" (*chukoku funds:* investment trusts that held portfolios of free-interest government bonds) and similar free-interest commodities. The funds were so popular they threatened to lure customers away from banks—"disintermediation" is the technical name for the phenomenon—so banks were forced to launch free-interest commodities of their own in order to maintain their position within the system. Negotiable certificates of deposit and interest-free large time deposits soon appeared. Figure 2-5 shows what happens when medium-term bond funds, free-interest products that compete directly with deposits, are introduced into the schema of Figure 2-4. Depositors withdraw their money from banks and invest it in bond funds instead, so the demand for deposits drops from DD to D'D', causing the volume of deposits to decline from

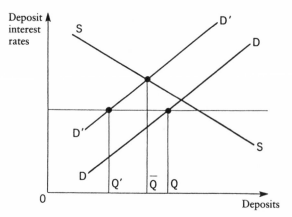

FIGURE 2-5   Changes in Deposit Volumes Resulting from Deregulated Interest Rates
Note: Deposits switch to free-interest products such as medium-term bond funds (disintermediation).

OQ to OQ′. If interest rates are deregulated, however, that decline can be mitigated to OQ̄ rather than OQ′.

The impact of deregulated interest rates was to prove far-reaching. Today, formal deregulation is complete for everything except small term deposits and demand deposits.

(2) As individuals, households, and corporations accumulated more assets, and as pension funds and institutional investors increased, more of the money circulating within the system began to look for profitability as well as safety, which meant that much of it was now very sensitive to interest rates. This aided the shift from regulated to free-interest products, which in turn spurred further deregulation.

(3) As Japanese finance became more internationalized (especially after the 1980 revisions in the Foreign Exchange Law), Japanese companies, financial institutions, and individuals had more latitude to raise and invest their money on foreign markets. When funds could be raised more cheaply and more flexibly overseas, many companies decided to go overseas for their fund-raising. Likewise, when the returns were better on foreign assets, more institutional investors began shifting their money to foreign markets.

Financial institutions fled the heavily regulated domestic markets for the relative freedom of other countries; so did bond issuers—and for the same reasons. Japan's financial markets began to be hollowed out, and complaints began to be heard of a Japanese "over-presence" on foreign markets.

(4) The issue of massive government debt spurred the development of the secondary market for bonds—a new market to trade bond and stock futures[8] and to launch new securities like certificates of deposit and commercial paper. This trend became known as "the securitization of finance."

THE OUTLOOK FOR THE FUTURE. The public sector ran Japan's biggest deficits from the mid-seventies to the mid-eighties; since then, however, public debt has declined rapidly and deficits in the foreign sector have emerged in its place. This is tantamount to an outflow of capital. Other trends expected to continue include: 1) greater internationalization and globalization of finance; 2) demand for a wider range of financial services and securitized financial commodities; and 3) advances in data transmission technologies.

Since the seventies, expanding international trade has caused finance to become more internationally integrated. When the United States began to post large current account deficits after the second oil crisis (1977–1979), it became the world's largest importer of capital, which wrought significant changes in the international financial climate. First, the direct investment component of international capital movements declined in favor of the securities investment component—more particularly, the bond investment component. Second, the relaxation (and in some cases scrapping) of national regulations on capital movements spurred active arbitrage between financial commodities. These changed expectations brought about frequent, large, and instantaneous movements of capital across national borders. Third, less regulated, more integrated markets developed new needs and new technologies and commodities to deal with them. These new developments in turn furthered globalization.

But deregulation and internationalization have not been all good. On the one hand, they have expanded banks' and other institutions' range of activities and given them more latitude in their portfolio

[8] Futures enable investors to hedge their risks. An investor who sells a future (a contract to deliver securities three months or six months in the future) at the same time as buying bonds can avoid the capital loss that would have occurred if market interest rates had risen. Selling at a set price ahead of time insulates the investor from losses due to price declines in the underlying security.

selections (or, to put it another way, given them more latitude in their portfolio *risk* selection); on the other, a lack of experience with new technologies and products has resulted in losses from imprudence and spurred an increase in the moral hazards involved with public risk-sharing systems like deposit insurance. (The prime example of this is increased lending to high-risk real-estate ventures.) People soon began to perceive the need for unified international standards that would place enough of a limit on banks' portfolio selections to maintain order in the credit system. Thus, in 1987, central bank heads from around the world adopted the uniform capital adequacy standards proposed by the Bank for International Settlements (BIS). This is one example of a trend that we will be seeing more of in the future. As finance becomes more globally integrated, countries are revising their systems and changing their practices in a search for regulations that can be applied uniformly around the world. Globalization has pushed us a step beyond the traditional concept of "reciprocity" to seek fair competitive conditions for all countries. When the institutions of one country use heavy protection of their domestic markets as a springboard to growth overseas, the world complains—and more loudly and stridently than ever before. For Japan, this will increase the pressure to scrap its system of compartmentalized specialists and limited market entry in favor of a system that conforms more to international trends.

The consumers of financial services also would like to see the compartmentalized system go. Having accumulated more financial assets, customers want more and different services, and the compartmentalization of finance is standing in their way, preventing them from taking advantage of products and services that cross industry lines.

Meanwhile, the securitization of finance is erasing in practical terms many of the differences between the banking and securities industries. One example is the bank practice of packaging credits as securities and selling them piecemeal. Not only are the divisions between banking and securities increasingly meaningless; if institutions were allowed to compete in each other's sectors, it would promote greater efficiency, new products, and better services.

Recent reports by the Financial System Research Committee and the Securities and Exchange Council have recommended that banks and securities companies be allowed to compete head-to-head in a wide range of business, arguing that such a move would bring

Method Form	Direct	Indirect
Loans	(1)	(2)
Securities	(3)	(4)

FIGURE 2-6   Financial Categories

Japan's system in line with international standards, promote competition, and make the economy more efficient.

A Financial Reform Act based on these recommendations has been approved, and changes were beginning to materialize in 1993. In the real financial markets, the pace of change is unabated, or even picking up. Let us assume that we can divide finance by method into "direct finance" and "indirect finance" and by form into "loans" and "securities." Loan-style finance is "negotiated": the borrower and the lender discuss and agree on the terms of each transaction, which makes it easy to build permanent customer relationships between them. Securities transactions, however, are formalized. There are markets that trade the securities created, making it easy to transfer credits to other parties. This is an important difference. Figure 2-6 illustrates the four different classifications that can be conceived. Category 1 is most important when an economy is in the initial (or primitive) stages of development, but at present it is virtually nonexistent in Japan. By contrast, classification 2 was the country's dominant form of finance in 1975; and in the eighties, categories 3 and 4 began to take over. Whether or not 3 gains a bigger share of Japanese finance, as it has in the United States and Britain (in fact, this was the condition assumed by both Keynes and the monetarists when they developed their theories), will depend on the kind of financial policies Japan adopts. It will be an interesting process to watch.

4. THE MONEY SUPPLY MECHANISM AND FINANCIAL POLICY

MONEY AND ITS TYPES.   Money is commonly used as a means of payment; whether it is made of metal or paper or something else is really very unimportant. As long as people can use it to trade goods and services or pay debts and other people will accept it without delay, it does its job: in the end, money is what people believe is money. If the government of Japan were suddenly to declare that the country's money would no longer be yen but special drawing rights, SDRs would not immediately become money. What would determine the success of the decree is how much *confidence* people had in it, whether they were able to think of SDRs as money. Money that has lost people's confidence is little more than scraps of paper.

In Japan, certain coins issued by the government, Bank of Japan notes, and demand deposits are recognized as money. The coins (including "subsidiary coins" minted before the Currency Law was revised) and Bank of Japan notes are called "cash money," the demand deposits issued as liabilities on banks[9] are called "deposit money," and time deposits are called "quasi-money." However, private banks are required to deposit reserves with the Bank of Japan, and the deposits they hold with it can be exchanged for Bank of Japan notes at any time; so, in reality, they are no different from Bank of Japan notes themselves. Cash and these deposits are termed "high-powered money." Subtracting the amount of money banks hold in reserve against payments of demand deposits from total "high-powered money" gives the amount of cash (or "cash money") in circulation. When demand deposits (or "deposit money") are added to this, it is called M_1; when quasi-money is added, it is called M_2; when certificates of deposits are factored in, it is called $M_2 + CD$. As should be clear from this discussion, high-powered money (H) consists of bank payment reserves (R) and cash money (C) in circulation. Therefore

$$H = C + R, \tag{2}$$

and from this it is clear that

$$M_1 = C + D, \tag{3}$$

where D stands for "deposit money." If the left side of the equation read M_2 instead of M1, D would stand for demand deposits plus time deposits, but the basic relationship would not change.

Table 2-3 uses these concepts to chart Japan's money supply for

---

[9] However, banks' demand deposit balances include checks that have been written but not yet deducted from accounts. When calculating the money supply, they must be subtracted to arrive at a net figure.

TABLE 2-3   Japan's Money Supply   (Unit ¥1 trillion)

Year end	Cash[1]	Deposits with monetary autho-rities	High-powered money	Reserves held by deposit money banks	Cash money	Deposit money	M_1	Quasi-money	M_2+CD
1975	13.3	1.5	14.8	3.3	11.5	38.4	49.9	75.4	125.3
1980	20.3	2.6	22.9	5.5	17.5	52.1	69.6	137.4	209.0
1985	27.0	2.7	29.7	6.3	23.4	65.6	89.0	217.8	314.9
1989	40.4	4.1	44.5	7.9	36.7	77.8	114.5	343.2	470.0
1990	43.0	4.8	47.9	10.6	37.3	82.4	119.6	375.4	505.0

Note: (1) Coins and bank notes, including those issued before the revisions to the Currency Law.

the five-year period beginning in 1975. At the present time, the most important money supply index for Japanese prices and business conditions is not M_1 but M_2 + CD.

From Equations (2) and (3) we can deduce

$$M/H = (C + D)/(C + R),$$

which can be rewritten as

$$M = \left[\frac{C/D + 1}{C/D + R/D} \right] \cdot H. \tag{4}$$

In Equation (4), R/D stands for the reserve ratio and C/D, the ratio of cash to deposits. Today's banks, however, practice *fractional reserve banking*, which means that they keep part of their deposits in cash or cash-substitutes (for example, central bank deposits) as reserves, and invest the rest in loans and the like. In addition, banks are obligated by law to keep a fixed percentage of their deposits as a "legal reserve," in cash or central bank deposits. Since legal reserves do not earn any interest, banks normally keep only the reserves they are required by law to have. The rest of their money they invest. Because of this, a rise in the legal reserve rate—the percentage of deposits that banks are required to keep on hand as reserves—will cause a decline in the money multiplier $\left(\frac{C/D + 1}{C/D + R/D} \right)$. The opposite will cause an increase.

Changes in legal reserve rates are called "reserve requirement operations" because they exert influence on M.

TABLE 2-4   Monetary Authorities Account[1] (End of 1989) (Unit: ¥1 trillion)

	Assets		Liabilities		
	Foreign assets (short term)	8.8	Outstanding cash currency	40.4	H
	Credit granted to government	13.2	Deposits	4.1	
A	(of which government bonds)	(10.2)	Government deposits	2.2	
	Credits to deposit money banks	15.7			
	Other net assets	9.0			
		46.7		46.7	

Note: (1) Account integrates the Bank of Japan and foreign exchange funds.
Source: Bank of Japan, *Economic Statistics Annual.*

Equation (4) makes it clear that if the money multiplier, which is a coefficient of H, is constant, the size of M will change in proportion to that of H. Even if the money multiplier is not constant, so long as changes in the money multiplier are not completely offset by changes in H, the monetary authorities can manipulate H to change the size of M. Let us look at H manipulations more closely.

High-powered money (cash and reserve deposits, the basis for M_1 and $M_2 + CD$) is in reality a liability on the monetary authorities.

Prior to 1943, Bank of Japan notes were convertible. Printed on them was a statement that they could be exchanged for an equivalent amount in gold or silver coin, and they contained the official seal of the governor of the Bank of Japan. It was therefore apparent to all that they represented a debt or obligation of the Bank. In 1943, the statement about being able to exchange them was removed and Bank of Japan notes became nominally inconvertible, which lessened their association with an obligation of the national government. But in real terms there has been no change. As Table 2-4 shows, Bank of Japan notes are entered on the liabilities side of the balance sheet as debt notes issued by the government against its assets. This balance sheet represents the accounts of the monetary authorities, an integration of the Bank of Japan accounts and the foreign exchange fund calculated by the IMF method. From the balance sheet we can see that H is

$$H = A - \text{Government deposits, etc.}$$

H is manipulated by controlling private lending (credit to private financial institutions), credit granted to the government (by government bond holdings and the like), and gold and foreign exchange holdings (by trading on the foreign exchange markets).

TOOLS FOR CONTROLLING FINANCE.   "ODR policies" attempt to influence credit to deposit money banks (current account overdrafts, etc.) by changing the official discount rate, the interest at which the monetary authorities lend money to private institutions. "Open market operations" are an attempt to influence the credit granted the government or private sector through central bank trading of public bonds and short-term government securities and bills on the open markets.

Much central bank bond trading, however, is negotiated between the bank and financial institutions. This had particularly been the case traditionally in Japan, where almost all Bank of Japan buying or selling of bonds was based on individual negotiations with institutions. Many people therefore choose to lump open market operations with negotiated trades and call them "bond operations."

Central banks also trade currencies on the foreign exchange markets, a process which is called "intervention" in these markets. By providing a means by which the central bank can adjust its reserves of gold and foreign currency, intervention gives it a tool for controlling the supply of high-powered money.

This is the basic arsenal that central banks have at their disposal when they want to manipulate H. ODR policies, bond operations, and legal reserve rates are the three main tools of monetary policy, though there are others that are known as "selective" or "qualitative" policy tools: changes in the margin requirements for financing stock trades or the collateralization requirements for consumer credit; and legal or administrative means of supplying funds to target sectors (or, conversely, preventing money from getting to them). Japan has used these sorts of selective policy tools in the past to clamp down on lending to the real-estate industry.

Then there is "moral suasion"—direct regulation, "window guidance," and lending ceilings that are used to control increases in the lending of private institutions, but are not coercive. Institutions do not have to follow moral suasion if they do not want to, but since the Bank of Japan is their lender of last resort, it is hard to ignore.

All of these tools for controlling the money supply have been developed because there was a close relation between the money supply and economic activity (production, employment, prices). By con-

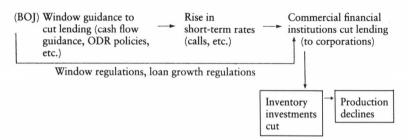

FIGURE 2-7   Impacts of Monetary Policies and How They Spread

trolling the money supply, the government controls prices and production.

Or at least that is the argument, and it is one that has raged between monetarists and Keynesians for much of this century. Monetarists emphasize the direct impact on the economy of the money supply; Keynesians maintain that the money supply is only able to influence economic activity through the medium of interest rates. Another idea, advanced by the late John R. Hicks, Joseph E. Stiglitz, and Alan Blinder, is that in an economy where many corporations face credit restraints and information is imperfect, financial policies influence economic activity not through the money supply or interest rates, but through changes in the amount of funding (or credit) available. The money supply changes only after the fact.

As we have seen, in postwar Japan, corporations were heavily dependent on loans from banks and other financial institutions (this is called "over-borrowing"), and banks, particularly the large commercial banks, were heavily dependent on Bank of Japan loans and call market funds. The ideas of Hicks and his colleagues therefore describe the situation in Japan very well, especially when it is remembered that the Bank of Japan's chief means of control were ODR policies, lending restraints at its overdraft window ("cash-flow guidance"), and window guidance. Figure 2-7 illustrates this relationship.

The Bank of Japan had two channels of control: the indirect route, in which it used its overdraft window to drive short-term interest higher and thereby dampen market institutions' ability to lend money to corporations and individuals; and the direct route, in which market institutions were given direct orders about their loan growth.

Opinions are divided as to which was more effective. However, it seemed to be not so much the money supply itself as the availability of funds (principally loans from private financial institutions) that clearly had the most profound impact.[10]

But the Japanese financial structure is changing. The emphasis is shifting from the "indirect finance" of bank lending to the "direct finance" of securities. Assuming this trend continues, Japanese financial policies will, like financial policies in the West, be forced to pay more attention to the money supply and, more especially, to interest rates. In point of fact, the global integration of recent years has produced a major shift in policy emphasis toward more coordination with international interest rates. We will look at this in more detail in the section on Japan's place in the international economy.

[10] In July 1991, the Bank of Japan abandoned window guidance and announced that it would rely only on market interest rates to control finance.

3
PUBLIC FINANCE

1. FUNDAMENTAL IDEAS OF THE POSTWAR ERA

The years since World War II have seen governments become more involved in their economies and the size of their budgets expand. This has been just as true for the Western democracies as for the Soviet Union and Eastern Europe. Part of it stems from the popularity of "cradle-to-grave" social welfare in places like Britain and Scandinavia, but perhaps even more is attributable to the surge in defense spending during the Cold War. Stuck in the middle, with little in terms of welfare or defense commitments, Japan was better able than most to maintain a relatively small government.

During the war, its enormous military spending weighed heavily on Japan, but defeat lifted this burden—and, one would have thought, paved the way for a contraction in public finance. Unfortunately, this was not to be the case. Japan's public expenditures were, in fact, even higher after the war than during. The country had war reparations and the costs of the Occupation to pay, it needed to rebuild its economy, and it also had to spend money to counteract spiraling inflation (see Table 3-1). As we touched on briefly in Chapter 1, it was not until 1951 that Japan was able to rein in its public finance to comparatively conservative levels. That was the year that Joseph M. Dodge, the American banker working with the Occupation, forced an emergency contraction in spending.[1] Ever since, the pri-

---

[1] Dodge came to Japan in 1949 as the public finance advisor to the Supreme Commander for the Allied Powers (SCAP). His job was to enforce a "nine-point economic sta-

TABLE 3-1   Japanese Government Expenditures   (¥100 million)

	Total General and Special Accounts[1]	Government agencies	Total Expenditure General Acct. of Central Government, Ordinary Accts. of Local Government
Fiscal 1944	84.7		24.1
1945	99.8		26.8
1946	153.5		144.3
1947	406.0		305.4
1948	1,038.5		741.2
1949	1,573.9	1,317.5	1,144.8
1950	1,812.8	987.5	1,249.6
1951	1,601.4	447.9	1,418.5

Note: (1) Arithmetic totals used until 1945, net figures thereafter.
Source: History of the First Hundred Years of the Ministry of Finance, Supplement.

mary goal in Japanese fiscal policy has been to maintain "sound public finances." For the most part, the country was successful in doing that all the way through the late sixties, though there were several factors that made this easier than it otherwise might have been. The economy was growing fast enough that it was a fairly straightforward task to keep public expenditures low as a percentage of GNP (or GDE). Economic growth brought higher revenues, principally from taxes, part of which could be put toward expanded outlays and the rest toward cuts in the tax rate. And, of course, Japan needed to pay very little for its defense.

2. THE ROLE OF PUBLIC FINANCE

Most commentators point to three functions that government spending is to fulfill in national economies: 1) the *allocation function* (smoothing out the distribution of resources), 2) the *distribution function* (smoothing out the distribution of income), and 3) the *stabilization function* (smoothing out economic cycles).

bilization program." Having just helped to overcome the German monetary crisis, Dodge forced Japan to adopt a balanced budget and extremely tight monetary policies. He also scrapped the multiple rate system in favor of a single, standard exchange rate. He is noted for describing the Japan of the time as "riding on two legs of a hobby horse: subsidies and American economic supports."

THE ALLOCATION FUNCTION. In principle, capitalist economies leave the distribution of resources to market mechanisms, but there are times when market mechanisms fail to do the job completely and a "market failure" occurs. It is the government's role to remedy those failures by allocating needed resources in a more appropriate manner. This includes providing goods and services that are important to society but are not supplied or only partially supplied by the market; and eliminating "bads" (as opposed to "goods") that are undesirable from a social standpoint but are oversupplied by the market. In short, the government needs 1) to provide public goods and 2) quasi-public goods, and 3) to eliminate or suppress "bads" (such as environmental pollution).

For example, society requires diplomacy, defense, and judiciary services, and their benefits extend to everyone regardless of whether they have paid for them. It is therefore neither desirable nor in most cases possible to discriminate in their distribution between those who have and have not paid. The police cannot turn a blind eye if Family A's house is robbed, for example, even if Family A does not pay its taxes; and even if the police did, Family A still benefits from the safer streets that other people are paying to provide. Such benefits cannot be confiscated from free-riders. If they are acting "rationally," therefore, people will not go out of their way to pay for services like this. Why should they when they can get a free ride? The market mechanism has failed.

Such goods and services in which market mechanisms do not work are called "public goods." There are also "quasi-public goods," which (unlike defense and diplomacy) could be provided by the private sector, but would not be supplied in sufficient quantities if left entirely to the market. Examples include education and fire departments. Higher educational levels bring great benefits both to individuals and to society as a whole, and these benefits do not necessarily belong only to specific people. That is why the individuals being educated and their guardians do not bear all of the costs by themselves. Were education left up to market mechanisms, it would indeed be supplied, but at levels that fall short of what is socially desirable. Goods like this that have large "external merits" need to be supplied or subsidized by the government in the same way that purely public goods are.

There are also goods and services in which the economies of scale are so great (the law of diminishing costs) that were they left to the market they would soon result in "regional" or "natural" monopolies. Examples are electricity and water. The government needs to regulate or become involved in these areas in order to eliminate the potential damage that monopolies could do. In extreme cases, this involvement might even take the form of state-run enterprises.

Finally, there are times when the uncertainties of a project are too great for private companies to take the risks. These areas demand government subsidies. The classic example is space exploration and development.

THE DISTRIBUTION FUNCTION. When left entirely to market mechanisms, there are no guarantees that income will be distributed in a manner that is socially desirable. The "socially weak"—the elderly, single-parent families, and the handicapped—are threatened. It is impossible to say what, in all times and all places, constitutes a socially "fair" distribution of income, which is entirely a value judgment; but it is not so difficult to identify levels of poverty that most people find unacceptable—a minimum standard of living or "civil minimum" that the majority can agree on. One function of public finance has been to keep people above this level. (We should note, however, that the government creates a new set of problems if the "civil minimum" is too high, since this can sap people of their desire to work.)

Another function of public finance is to compensate for unfair distribution of income or wealth through tools like taxation policy.

Still another government responsibility is to provide subsidies and encouragement for minimum levels of insurance against illness and accident, and pensions for old age, though the prime responsibility for these lies basically with individuals. In the past, people in Japanese communities tended to look out for and support one another, but in the process of urbanization that function has been largely lost, and more of the responsibility for "mutual aid" has been handed over to the government.

THE STABILIZATION FUNCTION. Since the dawn of the modern era, it has been government's responsibility to alleviate swings in the economy and achieve and maintain stable prices and high rates of employment. Public spending goes hand in hand with regulation of the money supply and interest rates as a means of doing this. The global inflation after the oil crises of the seventies, however, cast doubts on the public sector's ability to achieve gains in this area. Monetarists and supply-siders maintain that whatever short-term effects they may have, discretionary public spending policies at best have almost no long-term impact on real economic activity (production, employment, etc.) and at worst could be a cause of volatility.

The supply-siders also argue against income redistribution (guarantees of minimum living standards, progressive income taxes, and the like), saying that they have a negative impact on the desire to work and save and are therefore detrimental to economic development. This was one of the core policy ideas in the United States under the Reagan administration, and was imported to Japan and became a leading concept in the administrative reforms undertaken in the eighties.

Keynesian discretionary spending was also attacked from a different angle by James McGill Buchanan and Richard E. Wagner, who argue that it does not work in democracies. Legislators, they maintain, will work to maximize their own interests, and their main interest, of course, is keeping their posts—being reelected. They will not, therefore, support policies that are unpopular with the voters in their districts. As a result, democracies see their deficits expand and the threat of inflation increase. In enacting policies, Buchanan and Wagner conclude, it is necessary to take into account the damages from "government failures" as well as "market failures." Far from being democratic, there is no denying that Keynesian policies stem from an elitist, "Harvey-road" economics.

Of these three functions, the allocation function is the one that has longest been considered an entirely governmental province. It was only after economies began to develop that the distribution function came into play, and then only in the form of "anti-poverty measures" that were enacted because it was important to keep laborers healthy in order to maintain reproduction levels. Gradually, however, income redistribution also came to take a role as an important aspect of social policy. The stabilization function was not recognized as a government responsibility until after the Great Depression of the thirties.

As government took on more responsibilities, the scale of public finance naturally rose. The tendency of public spending to expand as economies develop was termed by Wagner "the *law of increasing state activity*." Japan has been no exception. During the Taisho era (1912–1926), public spending accounted for 12–13% of peacetime

TABLE 3-2 Government finance

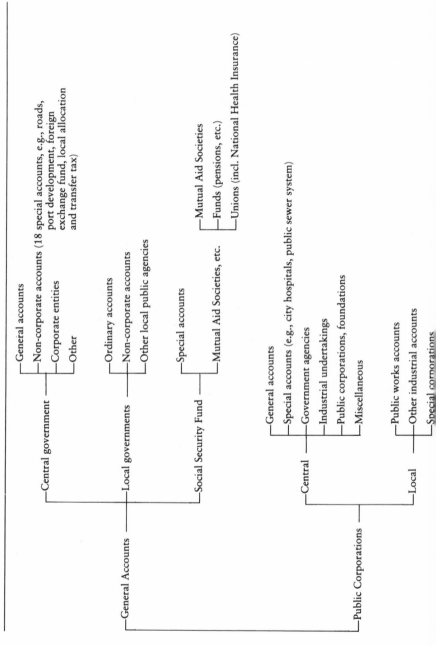

GNP. During the postwar growth period, however, it rose to about 19%, a level it maintained until the late sixties when it surged to 30%. It has since tended to decline.

3. SIZE AND PURPOSES OF GOVERNMENT EXPENDITURES

Table 3-2 contains a detailed breakdown of the agencies in Japan that provide public services; Table 3-3, a breakdown of how much is spent by whom. Note that the spending by public corporations is, with the exception of that posted to the government's "special accounts," generally funded through the Fiscal Investments and Loans Program (FILP).

To discover how much the government actually spends on the private sector, however, we will first have to correct for double accounting. Some of the money in the "general accounts" of the central government is "allocated" to local governments (the equivalent of 32% of all revenues from income taxes, corporate taxes, and liquor taxes; 24% of consumption taxes; and 25% of tobacco taxes). In addition, one fifth of the revenues from the consumption tax, which is administered by the central government, all of the local road taxes, and half the revenues from petroleum taxes are "transferred" from the center to local entities. The central government also provides subsidies to local agencies for specific purposes, which are expenditures from the national treasury but accounted for as expenditures from local public finance plans. The values in the "Net Central and Local Spending" column in Table 3-3 are corrected to eliminate redundancy.

Table 3-3 illustrates clearly the trend we discussed earlier: during the high-growth period of the sixties, Japanese public spending was equal to about 19% of GNP, but after the oil crises, it broke the 20% barrier and rose to almost 30% before declining to about 25% under recent "administrative reform" campaigns.

Now let us look at where all this money goes. Table 3-4 divides government expenditures into "final government consumption," "gross capital formation," and "social security transfer payments." It contains the nominal percentages of GNP accounted for by each category, as well as international comparisons. From this we can discern three major characteristics of Japanese government expenditures:

Public Finance

TABLE 3-3   Scale of Japanese Public Finance (Expenditures) (Unit: ¥1 billion)

Accounting year	Central govt. general accounts	Local fiscal ordinary accounts	Net total central & regional fiscal accounts	Fiscal investments & loans	As percentage of gross national expenditures (%)
1966	4,459	5,026	7,377	2,085	19.0
1967	5,113	5,725	8,466	2,497	18.3
1968	5,937	6,725	9,916	2,783	18.1
1969	6,918	8,034	11,657	3,181	18.0
1970	8,188	9,815	14,091	3,799	18.8
1971	9,561	11,910	16,914	5,009	20.4
1972	11,932	14,618	20,748	6,038	21.5
1973	14,778	17,474	25,193	7,413	21.6
1974	19,100	22,888	32,745	9,038	23.7
1975	20,861	25,654	37,260	10,561	24.5
1976	24,468	28,907	42,796	11,218	25.0
1977	29,060	33,362	49,842	13,414	26.2
1978	34,096	38,347	57,857	14,021	27.7
1979	38,790	42,078	65,321	16,175	29.0
1980	43,405	45,781	70,986	18,104	29.0
1981	46,921	49,165	76,496	19,410	29.5
1982	47,245	51,133	79,771	20,604	29.3
1983	50,635	52,307	84,741	20,705	29.8
1984	51,481	53,870	85,706	19,612	28.3
1985	53,005	56,293	88,906	20,491	27.7
1986	53,640	58,717	92,175	21,536	27.6
1987	57,731	63,220	99,014	27,595	28.3
1988	61,471	66,402	104,264	29,523	27.9
1989	66,312	62,772	98,439	32,271	24.7
1990	66,237	67,140	106,933	34,572	24.9

Source: Ministry of Finance, *Fiscal Statistics.*

(1) Japanese public finance is smaller than that for any other indus-
    trialized country (surprisingly, it is also a relatively small part of
    the economy in the United States).
(2) Two of the main reasons Japanese public finance is so much
    smaller than that in other countries are: 1) final consumption ex-
    penditures for areas like defense and education are lower, and 2)
    Japan has traditionally had lower social security transfer pay-
    ments. The latter, however, will in all likelihood be changing: as
    the population ages, social security payments are projected to
    rise sharply.
(3) Finally, in contrast to its low consumption, the government
    of Japan spends large sums of money for gross capital

TABLE 3-4 International Comparisons of the Scale and Composition of Public Finance (as Percentage Nominal GNP)

	Government final consumption	General government gross capital formation	Social insurance transfer payments	General government gross expenditures
Japan				
1934–36	15.5	3.2	1.6	(20.3)
1965	8.2	4.6	4.4	
1970	7.5	4.6	4.7	(20.3)
1975	9.8	5.3	7.8	
1980	10.0	6.1	10.2	
1985	9.7	6.6	11.1	(27.4)
1987	9.4	5.3	11.6	(33.8)
U.S.A.				
1970	19.1	2.5	7.7	(32.6)
1985	18.1	1.6	10.9	(36.6)
Britain				
1970	17.5	4.8	8.6	(39.7)
1985	21.0	2.0	13.7	(47.6)
W. Germany				
1970	15.8	4.4	12.7	(39.0)
1985	19.8	2.2	16.0	(47.3)

Source: For Japan: Economic Planning Agency, *National Income Statistics Annual*; for others, OECD, National Accounts.

formation—the building of roads, bridges, and port facilities, and the improvement of living environments. This indicates the rapid pace at which the country has formed its social capital.

Table 3-5 shows trends in the central government's spending mix, which provides a general picture of the country's priorities. The first two columns in the table show the percentages on the general accounts that are earmarked for debt servicing (payment of interest and principal on government bond issues) and transfers to local governments. The servicing of bond issues is a non-discretionary spending item for the government; bonds are obligations that must be fulfilled. The central government also has very little choice in its transfers to local governments, since it has promised them 32% of revenues from the three major sources (income taxes, corporate taxes, and liquor taxes). The only policy choices the central govern-

TABLE 3-5   Composition of General Accounts Budget   (%)

Fiscal year	1934–36	1955	1965	1970	1975	1980	1985	1988
Debt service	( )	4.4	0.6	4.4	4.9	12.5	19.5	20.3
Transfers to local governments	16.9	13.9	19.6	20.9	20.9	17.3	18.5	19.2
General accounts	83.1	81.7	79.8	74.7	74.4	70.2	62.0	58.2
Social security	0.7	10.5	14.1	14.4	18.5	19.3	18.2	18.3
Pensions	7.6	9.0	4.6	3.8	3.6	3.9	3.4	3.3
Education, science	6.6	13.2	13.0	11.3	12.0	10.6	9.2	8.6
Local govt. finance	0.3							
Defense	44.8	13.6	8.2	7.2	6.2	5.2	6.0	6.5
Public works	7.4	16.5	20.0	17.7	13.7	15.6	12.1	10.7
Economic cooperation		1.0	0.4	1.1	0.9	0.9	1.1	1.2
Small business		0.3	0.6	0.6	0.6	0.6	0.4	0.4
Energy				0.5	0.4	1.0	1.2	0.8
Food management			3.0	4.8	4.3	2.2	1.3	0.8
Miscellaneous	14.3	16.8	14.5	12.7	12.6	10.0	8.2	7.0
Reserves	1.4	0.8	1.4	1.4	1.4	0.8	0.7	0.6
	100	100	100	100	100	100	100	100
Total	22.8*	9,915*	3.66	7.95	21.29	42.59	52.50	56.70

* In units of ¥100 million.
Source: Takao Takeda et al., eds., *Outline of Japanese Public Finance* (Tokyo: University of Tokyo Press, 3rd. ed., 1987); Fiscal Policy Research Group of the Okura Zaimu Kyokai, *Outlook for the 21st Century.*

ment can make, therefore, concern how to spend the remainder. As the table shows, before the war, much of the budget went to servicing the massive quantities of debt that the government had floated. Between the end of the war and 1965, however, there was a decline in the percentage of the budget going to bond servicing. The oil crises of the seventies marked a turning point. Starting in about 1975, there was a sharp rise in the balance of government bonds outstanding, which in turn caused servicing costs to balloon. Today, about 20% of the budget goes to cover debt payments. Transfers to local governments, however, have since 1965 remained a fairly stable 17–20% of the budget, though they have varied somewhat in reflection of economic conditions (which cause increases or decreases in revenues from the three main taxes).

That leaves general expenditures. Between 1952, the year the San Francisco peace treaty was signed, and 1955, the largest share went to public works at 16.5%. Note, however, that military spending did not disappear, as some people are inclined to rather naively assume. The costs of the Occupation and, after the peace treaty, of defense accounted for 13.6% of the budget, which made it the second largest spending item, slightly ahead of education and science. Public works continued to garner the largest share of general expenditures until about 1970, when they were overtaken by social security payments. This emphasis on public works was quite natural. During the war and the period preceding it, little was spent on new flood control projects, roads, or bridges, and those in existence were poorly maintained. (I can remember having to go through all sorts of contortions when it rained and snowed in those years, to keep my shoes clean until I reached a paved road, and it was quite common for cars to become stuck in the mud even in the big cities.) When the war ended, there was strong pent-up demand for infrastructure spending, and such spending was indeed necessary for the development of the economy. Then, after highways were constructed in the sixties and early seventies, infrastructure gave way to social security spending as attention turned to providing better medical care, pensions, and welfare for the people of Japan. The bond issues of the late seventies, however, brought greater servicing costs. Wanting to wean itself from its dependence on deficit finance, the government embarked on a program of "rebuilding the national finances without tax increases," which it accomplished through across-the-board cuts in general expenditures. As Table 3-5 illustrates, the percentages of the budget allocated to different areas have been virtually fixed ever since, the two exceptions being defense spending and foreign aid programs.

For many years, Japan operated under the "incremental principle of budgeting." Last year's budget formed the basis for this year's, with the only question being how much to add or subtract for particular spending areas. This, however, fostered sectionalism among the ministries and agencies competing for their share of the pie, which was only aggravated by groups of legislators catering to special interests. Theoretically, it would have been best to build the budget from the ground up each year; it being impossible in real life to put together an entire government budget from scratch in such a short period of time, however, standard across-the-board cuts were the only viable alternative for rebuilding national finances. Unfortunately, prolonged reliance on across-the-board cuts created problems of its own—for example, for small towns and villages that depended heavily on disbursals from the central budget—and detracted from the efficiency of the budgeting process. Across-the-board cuts have also fossilized the budget, which in turn is creating serious distortions in resource allocation which will have to be dealt with soon. In fact, adding more flexibility to resource allocation is one of the chief challenges facing Japanese budgeters.[2]

4. TAXES AND BOND ISSUES

There are three main sources of funding for government expenditures: taxes, bond issues, and social insurance premiums. Additionally, the government can also draw on profits from state companies, revenues from the sale of government assets, and contributions by the Bank of Japan. The sale of government assets includes monies generated by the flotation of stock in NTT, the telecommunications monopoly, and income from sales of national land. The Bank of Japan also contributes its net profits (income minus costs) to the national coffers, where it is accounted for as "miscellaneous income." In the past, net income from the tobacco and alcohol monopolies was also included in the budget as "monopoly income," but this ended with the establishment of Japan Tobacco, Inc., and its privatization in April 1985. Money from these areas is now subsumed under "tax revenues."

The total of taxes and social security contributions is called the "national burden," and the ratio of the national burden to national income is called the "national burden ratio." The tax burden has tended to increase. In the late sixties (the high-growth period), it stood at just over 18%, but by the late eighties had risen to 25% and in 1990 was at 28% (see Table 3-6). The social security burden also began to rise in the seventies, and is now over 10%. The result has been to drive up the national burden from a level of about 22% in the sixties to 25% in the seventies, over 30% in the eighties, and close to 40% for the early part of the nineties.

---

[2] A telling statement was made by Takashi Inoue, a member of the Upper House, of the Diet, to the *Asahi Shimbun* on July 6, 1991: "All that is well and true, but it's impossible to change the shares allocated to different ministries and agencies. They all have their backers." The newspaper concluded that "this 'sectionalism' directly impinges on the fortunes of different agencies and the ability of legislators beholden to special interests to capture votes; it is the source of governmental ossification."

TABLE 3-6   Tax and Social Security Burden on National Income   (%)

		Tax burden	Social insurance burden	Total (national burden)	(for reference) General government surplus/GNP
Japan	1970	18.9	5.4	24.3	1.8
	1985	24.1	10.1	34.2	−0.8
	1988	27.5	10.5	38.0	2.2
USA	1970	28.0	6.5	34.5	−1.4
	1985	25.7	8.7	34.5	−4.1
	1988	25.7	9.1	34.9	−3.5
Britain	1970	41.3	7.9	49.2	2.4
	1985	41.2	9.1	50.4	−2.7
	1987	41.1	11.3	52.4	0.3
W. Germany	1970	29.1	16.0	45.1	0.7
	1985	30.8	20.9	51.7	−1.1
	1988	29.6	20.6	50.2	−2.1

Source: Bank of Japan, International Statistical Comparisons, etc.

One of the reasons that Japan was able to keep its national burden ratio lower than that of other countries is that government expenditures were lower, especially for social security benefits. Changes in the country's demographics will bring this to an end, as the aging population drives pension payments up sharply. Under the current system, the social security burden will reach 14.0–14.5% by 2000 and 16.5–18.5% by 2010, according to estimates published by the Ministry of Health and Welfare. That is one of the reasons there is a great deal of interest in revising the Pension Law today.

As we have already noted, the principle governing Japanese public finance has been that spending must be funded from sources other than bond issues or borrowings. The country's experiences with inflation during and directly after the war caused it to include a clause in Article 4 of the Public Finance Law to that effect. However, the Law itself allows an exception: the exemptions clause to Article 4 says, "Notwithstanding these provisions, bonds may be issued and money may be borrowed up to a ceiling approved by vote of the Diet when said monies are used to fund public works, investments, or loans." As a result, the government has from the beginning been able to float "construction bonds" and "investment bonds" (to raise funds, for example, to cover Japan's contribution to the IMF, World Bank, or Asian Development Bank).

Article 5 mandates that debt financing be done through the markets: "No bond issues may be underwritten by the Bank of Japan, nor may any borrowings be made from the Bank of Japan except in special cases and within limits determined by vote of the Diet."

However, the prohibition against bond issues and the mandate to finance debts through the markets only apply to issues that are carried over beyond the fiscal year in question. They do not apply to Ministry of Finance securities and interim financing used to smooth out the treasury's cash flows. (Article 7 states: "When necessitated by revenues to or disbursements from the treasury, the government may issue Ministry of Finance securities or seek interim financing from the Bank of Japan.")

Japan's Constitution also touches on the budget. Article 86 says, "The Cabinet shall prepare and submit to the Diet for its consideration and decision a budget for each fiscal year," obligating the government to adhere to a single-year budgetary process. Article 85 also marks a departure from past practice with its provision that "no money shall be expended, nor shall the State obligate itself, except as authorized by the Diet." Compare that to the prewar Meiji Constitution, which gave the state permission to take such fiscal means as necessary "by Imperial edict . . . should there be emergency demand for purposes of public security."

In spite of all the stipulations that expenditures should in principle be met with revenues other than those from bond issues or borrowings, Japan was forced to issue a deficit bond during fiscal 1965 to cover a shortfall in its revenues caused by a slump in the economy. The issue was made under the "special exemptions" to Article 4 of the Public Finance Law and required enaction of a special law of its own. It was to be the first of many such exceptions. "Construction bonds" have been an annual practice ever since.

In 1974, Japan experienced its first year of negative growth since the war. The primary cause was the oil crisis of the previous year, which sent prices soaring and production tumbling. With tax shortfalls of ¥770 billion in fiscal 1974 and ¥3,879 billion in fiscal 1975, the government floated ¥3,480 billion in bonds including "special-exception bonds." With the taboo broken, large bond issues were floated each and every subsequent year. Soaring prices and rising wages drove up the government's costs, while higher oil prices and salaries cut into corporate profits and thereby diminished the country's tax revenues.

This continued until fiscal 1990. The campaign to "rebuild the national finances" forced the government to rein in its expenses, but revenue growth was not always strong enough to make up for the revenue shortages. All it took was a couple of years of sustained growth to push tax revenues up, which combined with cost-cutting efforts to end dependency on deficit financing. Though the goal of replenishing the public coffers has been achieved, Japan still has an outstanding debt of ¥170 trillion, and most expect that figure to continue rising for the foreseeable future. That gives the country large debt service obligations. The challenge for policy makers will be to find ways to minimize new additions to the national debt and lessen the government's dependence on bond issues over the medium term while meeting demands from at home and abroad for higher public spending.

THE PROBLEMS WITH BOND ISSUES.   Critics of public bond issues usually point to the following five "detrimental effects":

(1) *Crowding out:* Public bond issues drive up interest rates and thereby crowd out private-sector investment.

(2) *Inflation:* Governments trying to avoid the crowding out phenomenon easily come to rely on increasing their money supply, which sets the stage for "fiscal inflation."

(3) *Fiscal ossification:* A higher bond balance means higher interest payments (debt service), which breeds rigidity in public finance, impeding it from performing its traditional functions.

(4) *Irresponsibility:* Bond issues mask the true costs of government programs, which could easily result in a loss of "fiscal discipline." Because tax revenues are needed to pay the principal and interest on the debt, bonds are really a "forward contract on future tax payments." The burden on the public has therefore been increased, just as it would be with a tax hike, but it does not *feel* any heavier. Public spending already lends itself to those who would reap the benefits of others' burdens while paying no taxes themselves. Bonds being a contract against future tax revenues, no one perceives their own burdens to have increased, though their benefits have. That makes it even easier to spend money.

(5) *Future generations:* Bond issues are an attempt to pass on costs to future generations.

There are answers to some of these criticisms:

(1) Economic conditions at the time determine whether or not crowding out actually occurs. When the economy is in decline, private-sector investment contracts, so there is no crowding out.

(2) Whether or not bonds breed inflation depends on whether or not excess currency is issued to aid their absorption. As long as bonds are absorbed by the markets and the central bank does not lose its monetary discipline, bond issues themselves will not cause inflation.

(3) So long as human beings are rational, they will not be fooled by appearances, so there is little risk of their losing their fiscal discipline. Japan during the eighties is a case in point. Far from becoming fiscally irresponsible, the government set itself a goal of rebuilding the national finances and worked to make the necessary spending cuts.

The argument over whether or not bond issues pass on burdens to future generations, however, is not so simple. Indeed, it is a long-running debate. If domestic bonds are issued, they result in no net increase or decline in domestic resources. Even if later generations are taxed to make the payments, the same generation that pays the debt also receives payment for it, so later generations are not particularly disadvantaged—or so says the classical argument (and we should note that this argument does not extend to foreign bonds). Critics, however, maintain that bond issues carry with them other burdens for later generations. For example, public bond issues will drive interest rates higher than they otherwise would be. If this dampens private investment, then future generations will inherit less capital than they would have had the bonds not been issued.

My opinion is that it is wrong to overemphasize the drawbacks to public bond issues, but there clearly are limits. When bond issues become excessive—when 20% of all public money must be used to service them—it is harder to find funding for traditional public spending purposes, and that is obviously not a good situation to be in. (We should note, however, that we have not dealt with Ricardo's "equivalency principle" or "irrelevancy theory," which maintains that there is no real difference between covering public spending with taxes and covering it with bond issues.)

TAXES. At the basis of Japan's postwar tax system was the program of reform recommended by the 1949 Shoup mission.[3] The basic results of the recommendation were to establish a self-assessment system and to reconfirm the comprehensive income tax as the central means of government fund-raising. Before the war, indirect taxes—principally the liquor tax and customs duties—had brought in over 60% of Japan's revenues. The Shoup mission reversed that allocation, recommending that personal and corporate income taxes account for 50–60% of government income. With the advent of the high-growth period, direct taxes came to account for over 70% of revenues. That was one of the rationales for cutting income taxes and adopting a general consumption tax that would replace excise taxes on individual commodities.

"Comprehensive income tax" refers to a tax on all the income that has accrued during a period of time—or, to put it another way, the net increase in assets (wealth) that has accrued during a period of time plus consumption during that period:

$$Y = \text{(Wealth at end of term} - \text{Wealth at beginning of term)} + \text{Consumption.}$$

This is known as the "tax base." Generally, comprehensive systems levy taxes on all income above a set minimum, and tax rates are set progressively for purposes of income redistribution. As a result, taxes are also levied on interest payments, dividends, capital gains, and retirement allowances.

There are other ways that tax systems could be arranged. Some maintain that interest income (or, in the broader sense, any income from assets) should not be taxed because pre-savings income has been taxed once already and to tax the interest on those savings is double taxation. Others argue, from the standpoint of tax-bearing capacity, that it would be fairer to base taxes on consumption rather than on income. Expenditure-based taxes, they claim, also have the advantage of allowing tax-payers to choose when they will pay their taxes.

If one assumes that people spend all of the income they have earned before they die, then it makes no difference to the tax base

[3] A group of seven American tax specialists headed by Professor Carl S. Shoup of Columbia University visited Japan in 1949 as part of the Occupation.

whether that money is taxed at the income stage or at the expenditure stage. But practical difficulties in implementing expenditure taxes have dissuaded any country from adopting them so far.

After income taxes, the other main revenue source for the Japanese government is corporate taxes, which are a tax on corporate income defined as:

Corporate revenue − Costs (including interest[4]) =
Corporate income (dividends plus retained profits).

There are two different theories of corporations. One holds that they are real entities in their own right; the other, that they are mere fictions, "juridical persons" that stand for the aggregate of their shareholders. The Shoup mission recommendations followed the latter theory, viewing corporations as fictions. Corporate taxes, therefore, are a matter of convenience in collecting the taxes that should actually be paid by the shareholders, a way of collecting them at the corporate stage just as the government collects withholding taxes. Since corporate taxes are a precollection of individual income taxes, it is necessary to adjust for them when calculating individual income taxes so as to avoid double taxation. That is why the withholding tax on dividends was originally deducted from the individual tax on total taxable income in Japan, thus constituting a tax credit for the individual shareholder. Unfortunately, this point was not well understood by the general public and thus the measures were criticized as favoring dividend income over working income. In the end, the government succumbed to public pressure and changed the system, adopting in its stead the practice of adjusting for only part of the double taxation. Still, these sorts of adjustments are not made at all in the United States. (In fact, the Shoup mission was in part a grand experiment, an attempt to implement in Japan the latest ideas of American academic economists.)

Though it ostensibly has a comprehensive tax system, Japan in fact institutionalized a number of tax breaks that encourage and reward savings. Until 1987, small savings (including those with the post office) were made tax-exempt, as were small-lot government bond purchases and *zaikei* savings plans (earmarked for housing or pensions). This system stayed in force until 1987. Capital gains on stocks

[4] Opinions differ as to the significance and economic impact of excluding interest payable from taxable income. For detailed discussion see Joseph E. Stiglitz, *Economics of the Public Sector* (W.I. Norton), Chapter 23.

are also tax-exempt for practical purposes (rather than taxing capital gains, the government imposed a securities trading tax), and investors can choose to have their dividend income taxed either with the rest of their income or at a flat rate of 35%.

To supplement income tax revenues, Japan used taxes on liquor and tobacco as well as excise taxes on particular commodities (for example, clocks and watches, perfume, and furs). Until 1989, however, it had no general tax on consumption. Funds generated by other special taxes (on gasoline, motor vehicle tonnage, and petroleum) are earmarked for specific purposes—for example, road construction.

Local community governments are allowed to issue bonds. Other sources of local revenue include tax transfers from the central government (local allocation tax, shared tax, as subsidies), property taxes (land and housing tax), consumption taxes (the automobile tax, automobile acquisition tax, and tobacco tax), and income taxes (inhabitants' tax and business tax).

Note that aside from the inheritance tax, the central government gets little in the way of taxes on assets (which are different from property income taxes). The securities trading tax and stamp tax fall into this category, but they generate relatively little revenue. By contrast, property taxes play a major role in funding local governments. At the root of this are two different styles of taxation. The central government levies taxes based on the person's ability to pay, whereas local governments tend to levy taxes based on the benefits the individual receives from the community and therefore emphasize "external standards" (the area of one's land or the floor space in one's house).

Table 3-7 shows the composition of income, consumption, and property taxes used in leading countries (1985). Interestingly enough, property taxes generate roughly the same percentage of revenue for all countries except West Germany.

Referring to Table 3-7, let us focus on the Japanese tax (revenue) mix. We have already seen that direct taxes, particularly corporate taxes, generate much more revenue for Japan than for other industrialized countries and that indirect taxes generate far less revenue (with the exception of the United States). At work here is the fact that the EC countries have all enacted consumption-based value-added taxes; Japan failed the first time it tried to enact a general consumption tax, and while it has one now, its future is by no means certain.

TABLE 3-7 Composition of Major Revenues (National Taxes) (1985; %)

	Japan	U.S.A.	Britain	W. Germany	France
Direct taxes	72.8	89.3	58.2	43.4	38.3
—of which, income taxes	39.4	74.3	37.1	35.2	20.8
Corporate taxes	30.7	13.6	11.2	7.2	8.6
Indirect taxes	27.2	10.7	41.8	56.6	61.7
—of which, liquor taxes	4.9	1.4			
Valued-added tax	0		20.3	31.7	44.6
	(100.0)	(100.0)	(100.0)	(100.0)	(100.0)
Income taxes	65.1	60.4	46.5	55.0	32.1
Consumption taxes	19.0	24.9	37.9	40.1	51.1
Property taxes	15.8	14.7	15.8	4.9	16.9
Non-tax revenue	¥3.4 trillion	$18.5 billion	£15.2 billion	DM 51.2 billion	Fr 106.4 billion
National income (for reference)	¥275.1 trillion	$3,234.0 billion	£202.3 billion	DM 1,420.0 billion	FR 4,669.8 billion

Source: Bank of Japan, International Statistical Comparisons, *Foreign Economic Statistics Annual.*

Finally, we should note that local governments have other sources of revenue besides what they receive from the central government, among them prefectural taxes, municipal taxes, business taxes, property taxes, and prefectural and municipal residential taxes.

WHAT IS A GOOD TAX SYSTEM? Every economic thinker since Adam Smith has had rules for a good tax system. Smith's four maxims were: 1) it should be fair (based on ability to pay); 2) it should be transparent (rather than arbitrary) and therefore should be based on law; 3) it should be convenient to taxpayers (for example, payers of value-added taxes should be able to decide if and when they pay taxes on luxury goods); and 4) the costs of collection should be low.

These are virtually the same principles generally espoused today: 1) fairness, 2) neutrality (does not generate excessive burdens), 3) simplicity, and 4) low collection costs.

Even if they agree on principles, however, people do not generally agree on how best to embody them. One recent trend has been to move away from progressive tax structures to a non-progressive flat tax. The Reagan-era tax reforms in the United States and the Japanese tax reforms of the eighties were products of this trend, which is based on the idea that progressive income taxes, like excessively high aid levels and minimum wages, sap people of their desire to work and save. More study will be required, however, before it can be shown that the tax reforms enacted in Britain or the United States have actually made people work harder and save more.

Another recent point of contention is general sales (or consumption) taxes. The United States does not have a value-added tax, though some states do impose a tax on retail sales. European value-added taxes are "consumption-based, multi-stage, non-cascade levies," which means that the tax is collected at several different stages; however, the end result is no different from a single-stage general sales tax. At first the Japanese government wanted to impose a multi-stage value-added tax, consumption-type, but it ended up having to settle for the current single-stage consumption tax, which is well known for its problems. Critics question the appropriateness of taxing food, for example, and they claim that simplified reporting procedures and the high exemption point for small businesses make the tax unfair. Still, the consumption tax is generally more neutral than traditional excise taxes. In economic parlance, its excess burden

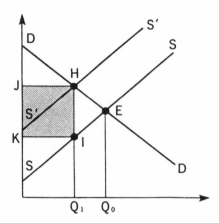

FIGURE 3-1   Partial Equilibrium Analysis of Excess Burdens of Commodities
Taxes

is low. Figure 3-1 illustrates this point by graphing the changes in demand and price for a product when a "specific duty" (an absolute amount per unit of a product sold) is levied. Line SS represents the pretax supply curve; EQ_0, the equilibrium price. When a specific tax is levied, the supply curve shifts upward to $S'S'$, the price shifts from EQ_0 to HQ_1, and the after-tax price received by the seller shifts to IQ_1. The difference between the two, HI, is the amount in per-unit taxes, and triangle EHI represents the "excess burden." The excess burden is the decline in production and trading of a product directly attributable to the tax. It is a dead-weight loss in economic welfare. It does not benefit the seller, the buyer, or the government. In this respect, general sales and consumption taxes are less wasteful than specific duties. When all products are taxed at the same rate, their prices change little relative to each other, so there are no incentives to increase or diminish production and trading. That does not, however, mean that these kinds of taxes are entirely neutral. EC-type value-added taxes, by taxing consumption, end up favoring savings over consumption. Their effect, therefore, is to spur greater savings, which makes them a worthwhile tool for developing countries suffering from low savings rates. Unfortunately, consumption taxes are regressive from the point of view of income redistribution, so they require special provisions for low-income households in order to offset the damage. Examples of ways to make consumption taxes more palatable to low-income households include tax reductions or exemptions for basic necessities, though we should remember that taxes with multiple rates quickly lose their claims to neutrality.

Another issue is taxes on land ownership, which will be outlined only briefly here, since a comprehensive survey of Japan's land problem would require a volume of its own.

Ownership taxes are levied against the owners of land when certain conditions are met. Land prices can be explained in the same way one would explain share prices, because both land and shares are assets. If the asset markets were perfect and traders were free to arbitrage prices, the profits would be the same whether one invested money in land or in financial assets. The profits that accrue from land are equivalent to the revenue obtained by putting the land to work (which we will call "land-use revenue") plus capital gains. Therefore:

$$\frac{\text{Land-use revenue} + (\text{Next term's land price} - \text{Present land price})}{\text{Present land price}}$$

$$= \text{Interest rate.}$$

In this equation, "Next term's land price − Present land price" stands for the capital gains accruing from land ownership. We can rewrite this equation to read[5]

$$\text{Present land price} = \frac{\text{Land-use revenue} + \text{Next term's land price}}{1 + \text{Interest rate}}. \quad (1)$$

[5] From Equation (1) we can derive the relationship:

$$\text{Next term's land prices} = \frac{\text{Land-use revenue} + \text{Land price in term after next}}{1 + \text{Interest rate}}.$$

We can substitute this back into Equation (1) and then repeat the same procedure for the term after next, and so on down the line. Assuming that land-use revenues are unchanging, then:

$$\text{Present land price} = \frac{\text{Land-use revenue}}{\text{Interest rate}}.$$

If the profit from land increases by a factor of α each year, then:

$$\text{Present land price} = \frac{\text{Land-use revenue}}{\text{Interest rate} - \alpha}.$$

If we then assume a land-holding tax rate t, we find:

$$\text{Present land price} = \frac{\text{Land-use revenue}}{\text{Interest rate} - \alpha + t}.$$

In other words, the price of land will be determined by the revenues the land generates, its expected price in the future, and financial factors such as interest rates. Factors that would cause land prices to rise, therefore, include expectations that they will be higher in the future, that credit will become easier, or that the construction of a nearby road will increase the land's use value. Conversely, tighter credit will cause land prices to fall. If the land-holding tax is levied on all land at a uniform rate, and if its impact cannot be passed on in the form of higher product prices, then its effect will be to reduce the numerator of Equation (1), which means lower land prices. If, however, it is levied only against corporate land-holdings and not against property owned by individuals or local governments, its effect might be to spur land transfers. Whatever the case, we would warn against placing too much faith in tax measures alone to solve Japan's land problems.

5. THE FILP

Though the term "Fiscal Investments and Loans Program," or FILP, may not be familiar to most people, there are few in Japan who have not heard of the Export–Import Bank of Japan, the Overseas Cooperation Fund, the Japan Development Bank, or the Housing and Urban Development Corporation. At the very least, there is no one who does not know about the postal savings system. All of these institutions play an integral part in the government's investment and loan programs, which rank with the general accounts budget and the ordinary accounts budget as one of its central economic activities.

Figure 3-2 illustrates how the system works. Simply put, the government uses funds collected through the postal savings, public pension (welfare annuities and national pensions), and postal insurance systems to fund housing and urban development and foreign aid. Most of the money collected by the postal and pension systems first passes through the hands of the Fund Management Division in the Ministry of Finance, where it is pooled with funds from the postal insurance system and the industrial investment special account before being allocated to public corporations and finance companies run by the central and local governments. Examples of these include the Housing and Urban Development Corporation, Japan Highway Public Corporation, Housing Loan Corporation, Export–Import Bank of Japan, and Japan Development Bank. There are others. These institu-

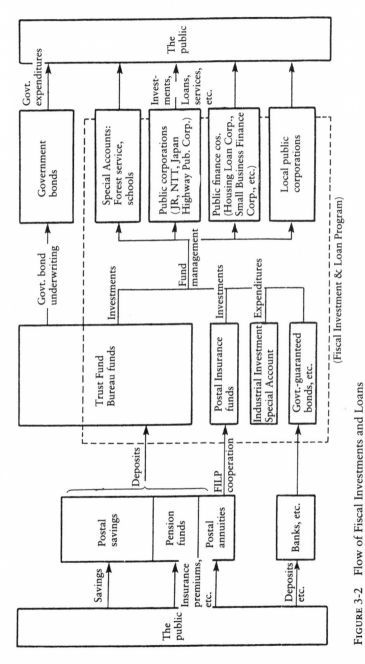

FIGURE 3-2   Flow of Fiscal Investments and Loans

Note: The dotted lines surround investments made under the FILP Plan. Funding for the plan in 1989 was approximately ¥34.5 trillion.

tions then use the money for such purposes as housing development, construction of social-overhead capital, community revitalization programs, small-business lending, and international cooperation. Centralized management was adopted as a way to ensure that funds are used efficiently (by preventing redundant investments, cutting down on administrative costs, and enabling priorities to be set). Each year, the government drafts its Fiscal Investments and Loans Program at the same time it drafts the budget. In fact, the document is so important, it is often referred to as the "second national budget."

In recent years, however, some of the funds in the system have been taken out of the FILP in order to aid in the placement of government bond issues. Some government agencies are also allowed to float their own government-guaranteed bonds in order to cover funding shortfalls in the FILP. The Small Business Finance Corporation, for instance, is a regular issuer of government-backed bonds.

Still, we should emphasize that fiscal investments and loans are different from public finance:

(1) Taxes and public impositions are similar to membership fees for a club. They are an obligation that public power forces one to pay. By contrast, the funds in the investment and loan program are discretionary. Savings deposits and insurance premiums are paid to the post office voluntarily, which from the government's point of view makes them passively received funds.

(2) Funds put into the investment and loan program come back at a profit. At some time, depositors can lay claim to interest and principal, and policyholders to insurance benefits.

(3) But unlike private-sector funds, the money that comes into the system is public in nature, since it has been collected based on the full faith and credit of the government.

This has led some to conclude that the postal savings system is really just a type of public bond issue. But where there are issuing ceilings to public bonds, there are none for postal savings and insurance; all the government does is accept whatever comes in. Also, we should note that public bonds are negotiable, whereas the funds in the FILP are not.

Having been collected under the full faith and credit of the government, this money is public in nature, and the emphasis is therefore on using it to supplement public spending and encourage the provision of quasi-public goods. Policies provide funding for goods that would not be supplied at socially desirable levels if left entirely to market mechanisms and for projects that carry dauntingly high risks or long recovery periods. Sometimes these funds may come at a price, when such is desirable, and sometimes interest-bearing government loans may be coupled with subsidies or interest-bearing private loans. Until the seventies (during the high-growth period), the priority was on establishing key industries (steelmaking, coal mining, electric power production, and shipbuilding); on building up industrial infrastructure (the road system, transportation facilities, and telecommunications network); and on providing more housing. Later, it shifted to developing Japan's industrial and social base. More recently, however, higher volumes of government bond issues have caused more funds to be diverted from the investment and loan program and used to underwrite government debt or provide subsidies to local governments. The investment and loan program can be manipulated much more easily and flexibly than can the budget, so it is often used as a counter-cyclical tool for stabilizing the economy.

The postal savings system and government financial institutions are not universally popular, however. The post office, which provides the bulk of the funding for the investment and loan program, competes directly with private banks for money, while the Japan Development Bank, Export–Import Bank, and Small Business Finance Corporation compete for lending.

The postal savings system dates from the Meiji Era, when it was enacted as a way to provide low-income households with an easy, secure way to save their money. The system was given special tax breaks during and after the war as a way to absorb the excess funds being held by households and thereby prevent inflation. During the postwar period, those tax breaks resulted in a sharp influx of money into the system. As of the end of March 1989, the post office had ¥125.9 trillion in time deposits on its books, compared to less than ¥112 trillion for all of Japan's city (large commercial) banks. This goes far beyond "supplementing the private sector," which is the accepted province of state-run enterprises and has led to repeated calls for the system to be split up and privatized.

Likewise, government lending institutions also compete with the private sector, which has led to demands that they abandon their operations in areas that do not require subsidies. This, however, is no easy task. Reforms will mean overcoming a host of entrenched interests.

4
THE SOCIAL SECURITY SYSTEM

1. HISTORY OF THE JAPANESE SOCIAL SECURITY SYSTEM

Social welfare in Japan goes back only to the Relief Ordinances, or *Jukkyu Kisei*, of 1874. (By that time, England's social security system had been in existence for more than 270 years.) In 1929, the relief ordinances became codified in law as the Relief Law (which took effect in 1932), but it was not until after World War II that Japan began to see a systematic social welfare program as a worthwhile policy goal. The basis for this change was Article 25 of the new Constitution, which states: "All people shall have the right to maintain the minimum standards of wholesome and cultured living."

Directly following Japan's defeat, the central issue in social welfare was how to maintain living standards for the most destitute, so there were few resources left with which to develop an organized social security program. In 1948, however, a "Social Security System Commission" was established, which in 1950 issued a report that provided the blueprint for today's social security system (public assistance, social welfare, social insurance, and public health services) and clearly delineated how responsibilities should be divided between the national government and the general population. This report was to prove the catalyst for the creation of a systematic social security program in Japan.

Right after the war, the focus was on protecting livelihoods, but in 1950, the entire system was overhauled with the enactment of the Livelihood Protection Law, which sought to assure people of minimum standards of living as part of the larger system of social safety nets. The program that developed out of this law paid benefits according to predetermined standards, which it funded from premiums on insurance for old age, sickness, death, disability, and retirement benefits. One of the central goals of "livelihood protection" was to provide insurance and pension coverage for everyone in the country. In the beginning, the top priority was medical care, but with the 1959 institution of the Welfare (non-contributory) Pension System, and the 1961 establishment of the Contributory National Pension System and National Health Insurance System, the goal of full insurance and pension coverage was reached. In 1972, allowances for dependent children were added, and in 1973, medical care for the aged, rounding out Japan's welfare system and bringing it up to the levels of other industrialized democracies.

Japan classifies the components of its social security system into: 1) livelihood protection, 2) social welfare, 3) social insurance, 4) health and sanitation, and 5) unemployment benefits. From 1955 to about 1970, priority went to livelihood protection, unemployment benefits, and health and sanitation, but in the seventies, the weight began to shift in the direction of social welfare, with a corresponding decline in the emphasis on livelihood protection, health and sanitation, and unemployment benefits (the last two in particular). Behind this was the country's sharp economic growth, which allowed it to move beyond the poverty-fighting stage and concentrate on improving welfare. Table 4-1 displays the social security payments made since 1975, including their ratio to national income and a sector-by-sector breakdown. Note that social security benefits have steadily risen as a percentage of national income. In 1970, medical benefits garnered a larger share of the pie than annuities, but annuities gained the lead in subsequent years, as shown in Figure 4-1.[1]

While the high-growth period of the sixties led to both quantitative and qualitative improvements in the social security system, the eighties brought Japan to a turning point. On the one hand, demand for welfare benefits is growing as the population ages and the environment deteriorates; on the other, the shift from "high growth" to "stable growth" has been to the detriment of the public coffers, and there is no longer enough money to meet the demand. The country is now searching for ways to supply quality services as efficiently as

---

[1] Consider old-age insurance and livelihood protection to be included under "medical and non-medical benefits" and retirement pensions to be included under annuities.

Table 4-1   Breakdown of Social Security Payments   (Unit: ¥1 billion)

Fiscal year	1975	1980	1985	1986	1987	1988
Totals	11,673	24,604	35,644	38,589	40,655	42,278
(as % of national income)	(9.41)	(12.34)	(14.01)	(14.60)	(14.88)	(14.48)
Medical insurance	4,924	9,361	9,142	9,718	10,227	10,625
Old-age insurance	—	—	4,057	4,419	4,734	5,058
Annuities	2,095	8,377	14,573	16,403	17,625	18,725
Employment & workers' compensation insurance	1,015	1,558	1,991	2,101	2,100	1,956
Children's allowance	144	178	159	156	156	149
Livelihood protection	676	1,155	1,503	1,471	1,433	1,367
Social welfare	763	1,600	1,561	1,641	1,671	1,717
Public health	423	484	540	544	534	531
Pensions	811	1,701	1,902	1,915	1,936	1,900
Support for war victims	110	191	216	217	240	249

Note: Old-age insurance includes medical and other health-care benefits.
Source: Ministry of Health and Welfare, Minister's Secretariat, Policy Planning and Evaluation Division statistics.

possible. This overhaul of the system, however, is not a problem Japan faces alone. Britain, the United States, and other countries are having to make the same sorts of choices.

2. SOCIAL SECURITY AND INCOME REDISTRIBUTION

Social security is a public safety net designed to protect people in situations in which it is impossible for them to maintain "minimum standards of wholesome and cultured living" if things are left entirely to market mechanisms: old age, sickness, death, disability, unemployment, and retirement. This protection takes many forms. Some of it is public assistance funded through taxes and public impositions; other parts come from social insurance programs funded through contributions. In all cases, however, a *transfer of income* takes place between those who pay the costs and those who receive the benefits. The simplest example is welfare payments, which protect the living standards of the very old, the very young, and the disabled. In these cases, taxes collected through the progressive income tax are redistributed to the "socially weak"—the destitute, old, and young. In medical insurance, the transfer is from the healthy to the sick; in old-age annuities, from the young to the old. The Ministry of Health and Welfare's Policy Planning and Evaluation Division evalu-

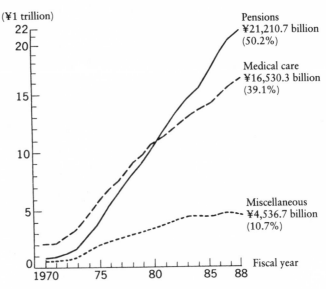

FIGURE 4-1   Breakdown of Social Security Benefit Payments
Source: Ministry of Health and Welfare statistics.

ated the impact of this redistribution in its 1987 *Survey of Income Redistribution.*

(1) It began by using the Gini coefficient,[2] a measure of the inequality of income distribution, to determine the impact of the social security system. The Gini coefficient shows the gap between perfectly equal income distribution and actual income distribution.

[2] Simply put, in the Gini coefficient, the vertical axis represents the cumulative percentage of income; the horizontal, the cumulative percentage of households. Along straight line OA, income is distributed fairly among all households; along curve OBA, there are distortions in income distribution. If, for example, the total income of all households up to 40% was equal to 40% of all income, or the total income of households up to 50% equal to 50% of all income, then income distribution would be straight along line OA—in other words, fair. If, however, the total income of all households up to 40% was equal to only 20% of all income, or even only 10% of all income, then there would be a gap between curve OBA and straight line OA. This is called the "Lorentz curve," and it is used to express the inequality of income distribution. The greater the distance from line OA, the greater the inequality. The ratio of the area (λ) of the shaded part between the Lorentz curve and straight line OA and

TABLE 4-2   Annual Comparisons of Income Redistribution Effect

Year of survey	Initial income	Redistributed income		Income redistribution via social security	
	Gini coefficient	Gini coefficient	Degree of improvement	Gini coefficient	Degree of improvement
1981	0.3491	0.3143	10.0	0.3317	5.0
1984	0.3975	0.3426	13.8	0.3584	9.8
1987	0.4049	0.3382	16.5	0.3564	12.0

Notes: 1) Initial income is defined as the total of worker income, business income, agricultural income, livestock income, asset income, home work income, miscellaneous income, and personal benefits. 2) Redistributed income = Initial income − (taxes + social security premiums) + Social security benefits + Medical expenses. 3) Income redistribution via social security = Initial income − Social Security premiums + Social Security benefits + Medical expenses. 4) Degree of improvement (%) = (Gini coefficient of initial income − Gini coefficient of redistributed income) ÷ (Gini coefficient of initial income × 100).

Source: Ministry of Health and Welfare, *Welfare White Paper*, 1989.

The smaller its value, the smaller the income differential. By comparing the Gini coefficients for "initial income" (income which excludes security benefits and medical expenses, and before deduction of taxes and social insurance contributions) and "redistributed income" (after deduction of taxes and social insurance contributions, and with social security benefits and medical expenses added in), it is possible to gauge how effective social security policies in the *broad sense* have been in redistributing in-

---

the area of triangle OAC—that is, λ/S—is the Gini coefficient. Since it will always be the case that $0 < λ/s < 1$, the closer the value to 1, the greater the inequality.

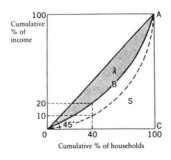

TABLE 4-3   Per-Household Income Redistribution by Income Level

(Unit: ¥1 million)

Initial income level	Total contributions	Total receipts	Redistribution coefficient (%)
Aggregate	88.8	87.1	−0.4
less than 0.5 million	10.2	215.6	3,214.9
0.5–1 million	14.4	129.1	154.9
1–1.5 million	20.3	98.4	63.4
1.5–2 million	28.0	77.1	28.2
2–2.5 million	35.6	60.4	11.1
2.5–3 million	40.9	64.0	8.4
3–3.5 million	49.0	62.8	4.3
3.5–4 million	58.4	66.1	2.1
4–4.5 million	66.0	64.7	−0.3
4.5–5 million	76.4	59.8	−3.5
5–6 million	92.4	75.6	−3.1
6–7 million	113.2	65.4	−7.5
7–8 million	136.2	65.4	−9.6
8–9 million	168.0	75.1	111.0
9–10 million	192.0	100.9	−9.6
10 million or more	364.8	86.7	−18.6

Note: Redistribution coefficient (%) = (Redistributed income − Initial income) ÷ (Initial income × 100).

come. By excluding the impact of taxes, we can gauge the effectiveness of income redistribution by social security policies in the *narrow* sense.

From Table 4-2 it is obvious that the Gini coefficient for initial incomes has tended to rise (i.e., that there is greater inequality), but this has been offset to some extent through taxes and social security benefits. We should point out, however, that the large improvement in the Gini coefficient for 1987 was the result of reforms to the public pension system in 1986 that brought about larger benefit payments.

(2) Table 4-3 gives a picture of per-household redistribution for different income levels. Households with annual incomes of less than ¥4 million receive more than they contribute (in taxes and insurance premiums, etc.), which means that income from households making more than ¥4 million is being redistributed to those making less.

(3) Table 4-4 gives a picture of income redistribution according to

TABLE 4-4 Per-Household Income Redistribution by Age of Head of Household

	Aggregate	Under 30	30–39	40–49	50–59	60–69	Over 70
Number in family	3.41	2.33	3.67	3.93	3.42	3.05	2.91
Initial income (¥1 million)	4.68	3.14	4.48	5.37	6.05	3.84	2.79
Redistributed income (¥1 million)	4.66	2.85	4.14	4.91	5.60	4.65	4.29
Redistribution coefficient (%)	−0.4	−9.3	−7.5	−8.5	−7.4	20.9	53.9
Total contribution (¥1 million)	.88	.47	.74	.97	1.20	.87	.58
Taxes	.54	.24	.40	.57	.75	.60	.39
Social security premiums	.34	.22	.33	.39	.44	.27	.19
Total receipts (¥1 million)	.87	.17	.40	.51	.75	1.68	2.09
—of which, pensions	.44	.02	.12	.16	.24	1.15	1.30
—of which, medical care	.39	.12	.24	.30	.47	.49	.75

Source: Ministry of Health and Welfare, Minister's Secretariat, Policy Planning and Evaluation Division, *Income Redistribution Survey*, 1987.

the age of the head of the household, and shows large transfers of income from those under 60 to those over 60 and, more especially, to those over 70.

(4) Numerical data are not provided here, but the income redistribution rate is highest for assisted households, followed by female-headed households.

Now let us look briefly at the two mainstays of the social security system, health care and pensions.

3. HEALTH CARE

With the exception of the national hospitals, which grew out of the old army hospitals, and the national sanitariums, health care in Japan was supposed to be supplied by private clinics and hospitals. However, during the growth process, local communities built a number of public hospitals to meet the growing demand for medical care, and they continue to do so to this day. Since 1961, a national insurance system has covered the entire population, and the vast majority of treatment has been paid for by the insurance fund. The individual patient pays for only a small portion of the cost of diagnosis, treatment, and medications. The largest portion of the cost is billed to the central government, health insurance unions, and local governments that function as insurers. They pay the claims against them through special payment institutions. Figure 4-2 gives a schematic representation of the system.

There are two principal insurance systems at the present time: one for company employees (called Employees' Health Insurance) and one for the general public (National Health Insurance). Under the former, insurance for the employees at larger companies is administered by insurance unions; for those at smaller companies there is a government-administered insurance plan. There are large differences between the premiums paid to different insurance unions, but as of March 1989 the average insurance premium was equivalent to 8.2% of the employee's remuneration, and payment was split evenly between the employer and employee. To this are added subsidies from the central government. For the government-administered insurance plan, premiums work out to 8.4% of the employee's remuneration, again split evenly between the employee and the employer. Additionally, the government subsidizes 16.4% of all benefits paid.

Under the National Health Insurance program for the general public, the government pays for a full 50% of the benefits, but there are vast differences in the premiums paid from city to city. In the most extreme cases, those at the top of the scale will be paying seven times more than those at the bottom. National Health Insurance also suffers from the fact that a large percentage of policyholders are in low-income brackets, which places disproportionate burdens on middle-income policyholders. Further, the percentage of elderly people in the system is larger for the National Health Insurance program than for the insurance unions, which means more visits to doctors and consequently higher premiums. To counter the disparities between income and expenditures and to even out the burden of financing medical care for the aged, each insurance plan divides its burden proportionately. Those with fewer elderly policyholders than average pay higher contributions, thus evening out the burdens for geriatric medical expenses. This method, however, does not take into account policyholders' ability to pay, and, given the expected increase in the need for medical care for the aged, there are limits to what it can accomplish. One of the largest challenges facing the system is to find

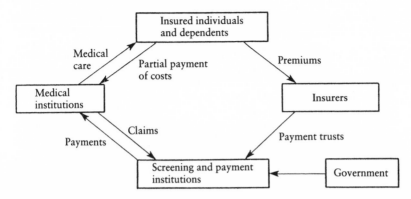

FIGURE 4-2   Medical Insurance System

ways to stabilize health care for the aged while taking into account the ability to pay of those of working age. As can be seen from Figure 4-2, medical institutions receive payments from insurers. These payments are made according to a point system determined by the Minister of Health and Welfare.

In 1988 there were 113.7 medical institutions in Japan per 100,000 population. Of these, 8.2 were hospitals; 65, private practices; and 40.5, dentists. Compared to 3.1 hospitals per 100,000 population in the United States (1980), 5.3 in West Germany (1980), and 6.7 in France (1977), Japan's percentage is high (even in 1980, it had 7.7 hospitals per 100,000 population). The only country with a greater density of hospitals was Sweden, with 8.6.

As shown in Table 4-5, Japan has 57 dentists and 160 general practioners per 100,000 population. Judging from the students enrolled in university medical courses, the number will reach 220 in 2000 and 300 in 2025, which indicates that a glut of doctors could be on the way. However, fewer and fewer newly accredited doctors want to go into private practice, opting instead for employment at larger institutions. Japan has fewer nurses than the United States or Sweden, but the gap is not that large. However, there are large regional differences, and the surge in the number of hospitals has created a serious shortage of nursing personnel. The supply of nurses has not been able to keep pace with the increase in hospital beds, and the large numbers of nurses quitting or retiring has only aggravated the problem.

TABLE 4-5   Number of Medical Personal per 100,000 Population

		Physicians	Dentists	Pharmacists	Nurses
Japan	(1988)	164	57	117	634
USA	(1984)	214	59	67	830
Britain	(1981)	164	31	31[1]	325
W. Germany	(1984)	256	57[2]	51[1]	504
France	(1985)	319[3]	72[3]	93[1]	
Sweden	(1985)	264	110[3]		846

Notes: (1) Includes chemists. (2) Includes oral surgeons. (3) Includes *ordres des medicins.*

On the demand side, the establishment of the medical insurance system and the aging of the population have produced marked rises in medical care needs, especially for geriatric medicine. Advances in medical technology and increased specialization within the medical profession have made hospitals, particularly general hospitals, the preferred choice of people seeking care.

Health care is notorious for its "asymmetry of information." Patients and doctors are not equal; patients have no means of judging their own condition except with such information as the doctor gives them. In addition, patients and their families seek the best medical care available, which makes it easy for the supply side (the medical profession) to create "induced demand." If patients are told they need an examination, they have one. If they are told they need an injection, they grit their teeth and suffer through it. It is therefore natural that medical costs rise, and the establishment of the medical insurance system has only accelerated that spiral.

The relationship between doctors and patients can also be expressed in terms of "principals" and "agents." The patient (the principal) lets the doctor (the specialist agent) make the decision about a particular problem (in this case, diagnosis and treatment). But the principal does not have the capacity to judge or monitor whether or not the agent is fulfilling his commission properly. All he can do if he is dissatisfied is move to another doctor or hospital. This asymmetry of information has combined with the rather irrational Japanese idea that it is better to "take shelter under the largest tree" to produce today's preference for larger hospitals.

All insurance carries with it moral hazards, and the special nature of health care makes it easy for doctors to perform unnecessary examinations and treatments. The "moral hazard" in insurance is that being insured may cause a person to act in such a way as to collect insurance benefits, which increases the probability that the situation insured against will occur. Medical insurance, for example, influences the way the insured manage their health: it may cause them to be ill and seek medical attention more often than if they were not insured. An even more serious problem than higher rates of illness, however, is greater frequency of hospital visits, or hospitals stays beyond the length that is necessary and care in excess of what is required. Medical expenses are dependent on hospital visitation rates and prices as well as on illness rates. Insurance encourages unnecessary visits, and also encourages practitioners to provide medical services beyond what the patient requires. The result of both is to drive medical expenses up.

Japan's national health bill is increasing by about ¥1 trillion a year. Obviously the biggest issue facing the country is how to supply "efficient, quality care." Particularly urgent are the costs of care for the aged. Japan's population is rapidly growing older, and without changes, it is doubtful that future generations will be able to bear up under the burdens.

Several proposals are on the table to remedy the situation, not the least of which is to strengthen monitoring functions with stiffer checks on doctors' billings to the health insurance system. Another proposal is to increase the burdens of the insured by, for example, enacting a "differential payment system" (in which the system pays only set benefits for the services provided, with anything over and above that to be paid by the insured), or by paying set benefit rates at a fixed percentage of costs, with the rest to be paid by the insured, or by adopting a system in which the patient pays the entire bill and then can file for reimbursement for all or a part of it from the insurer. In this case, benefits are paid in cash rather than in kind.

From the other side of the coin, there is a proposal for radically reforming the points system in favor of set benefits for specific diseases. This, however, would also create problems, since doctors might be less careful in their diagnoses and treatments. Recent trends have also emphasized preventive health care, given greater sway to the health care plans of local communities, and tried to define the problem of the aged in conjunction with welfare rather than as a medical issue alone. Other countries, we should note, face similar rises in medical costs and shortages of personnel.

Despite its problems, the Japanese health and medical care system performs very well by most measures. At present, medical costs are just a bit above 6.0% of the national income, which is low compared to the United States (10.9%), France (10.9%), Germany (9.8%), and even Britain (approximately 7%). The infant mortality rate, meanwhile, has gone from 60.1 per 1,000 live births in 1950 to 39.8 in 1965, 10 in 1975, and 5.5 in 1985. Average life spans have also increased. In 1955, Japanese men could expect to live 63.6 years; in 1975, men 71.7, women 76.9; in 1985, men 74.8, women 80.4; in 1988, men over 75, women over 81. The Japanese are now the longest-lived people in the world—and that despite the fact that in 1955 their life expectancy was far shorter than that for the British, Americans, West Germans, French, or Swedish.

The emphasis in the future must therefore not be merely on extending life, but on improving its quality and providing "things to live for." On the other hand, the problem of costs is looming larger. While it is ultimately up to the people what percentage of the national income is spent on health care, given the slower growth rates expected for national income and GNP and the rise in medical expenses brought on by an aging population, health care is virtually certain to command a bigger slice of the national pie, and it is urgent that Japan begin thinking about how those burdens are to be borne.

4. PENSIONS

Japan has three main categories of pensions: public, corporate, and individual. Corporate pensions are for employees of specific companies or groups of companies. Individual pensions are financial commodities that are sold by trust banks and insurance companies to individuals. Both of these are discretionary; employees and individuals are free to join pension plans or not, as they wish. All, however, are obligated to join the public pension system. Like medical insurance, the public pension program came out of the drive to have the entire nation insured and retirements provided for. Everyone in Japan is, in theory, a member of some public pension plan, and this membership entitles them to old-age annuities, disability annuities, and survivors' annuities.

The most important of these from the standpoint of social security are the old-age annuities for which an employed person becomes eligible upon retirement. We will therefore focus our comments on these annuities, though most of what we say also holds true for disability payments or survivors' annuities.

The first question to be dealt with is why a public pension system is needed at all. Neoclassical theory, with its emphasis on personal responsibility in all aspects of life, would hold that saving and providing for old age are up to the individual and not something the government should be involved in. Indeed, many economists have advanced just that argument. But public pensions have some benefits that do not accrue in private plans.

First, while recognizing that it would be best if each individual thought about his or her old age and formulated a rational plan for his or her life, proponents of public pensions point out that everyone may not act rationally. Many of those who were content to "live for the moment" may find themselves facing poverty in their old age. If it is socially unacceptable not to help these people just because it is their own fault they are in these circumstances, then it is desirable to avoid the situation entirely by making it mandatory to join a pension plan that will provide them with a minimum standard of living.

Second, pension benefits last a long and undetermined time. Thanks to medical advances, the average life span is increasing, and during that time prices can be expected to rise and economic conditions to change. Private pensions cannot by themselves deal fully with these changes. Unlike public pensions, it is impossible for them to have a built-in slide mechanism that would index them to prices, and there is nothing they can do about people living longer.

These considerations have convinced the majority of industrialized countries to set up public pension plans.

There are two broad categories of public pensions: funded schemes and pay-as-you-go schemes. Funded schemes work much like private pension plans. The insurer invests the premiums paid by people during their working years and uses the principal and interest it earns on them to pay annuities after the person retires or reaches a set age (say, 65). If funds are to maintain their balance, then the total of the insured's principal and interest at the time he starts to receive benefits must be equal to the (discounted) present value of the benefits that he will receive. Compare this to pay-as-you-go schemes, in which balance is maintained if premiums received during a fiscal year are equal to benefits paid out. Japan's public pension system is a hybrid of the two, which it calls a "corrected funded scheme." Funding for the pension system comes both from premiums and from contributions made by the central and local governments.

As long as an overall balance is maintained, there is no difference between funded public pensions and funded private pensions, and, as a rule, no transfer of income from younger generations to older takes place. But the basic objective of public pensions is to guarantee minimum living standards regardless of the recipients' income levels during their working years, so by their very nature they involve transfers of income within the same generation. To borrow a metaphor from Aesop, the diligent ants help pay for the retirement of the prodigal grasshoppers.

In pay-as-you-go schemes, the working generation supports the pension benefits paid to the aged. If the proportion of elderly people receiving pension benefits to workers rises, there is a transfer of income from the young to the old; if it declines, the result is savings for the pension fund.

Japan's "corrected funded scheme" involves both kinds of income transfers. Income is being transferred from the young to the old as the population ages and life spans grow longer; a considerable amount of income is also being transferred within the same generation.[3]

As was discussed briefly earlier, the public pension system has its critics, mainly from the classical liberal school of thought. First, they argue, with a large amount of pension income guaranteed upon retirement and that sum indexed to prices, more and more people will decide that they do not really need to work very hard and will opt instead for early retirement. Today's elderly subscribe to a work ethic that says "no work, no food"; but their numbers are rapidly declining. When the large majority of people learn to appreciate leisure and look forward to an enjoyable retirement, even those who may in their hearts want to continue working could be forced to choose retirement for appearances' sake. (Whether one considers that to be the mark of an affluent society or a decadent society is a value judgment best left up to individuals.)

Second, it is said that the pension system encourages people to

---

[3] Some of the same-generation income transfers stem from the fact that Japan was slow to enact its pension system and is therefore paying benefits to people who never contributed premiums.

raise fewer children. When there were no pensions, people had to depend on their children to look after them in their old age and so they had as many as possible. Now that there is a pension system, though, people can avoid the trials of child-rearing and rely on their pensions to see them through when they grow old. This is a variation on the free-rider phenomenon.

Third, Martin Feldstein and others criticize public pensions for being a form of mandatory savings, which has the negative effect of decreasing voluntary savings. As a matter of fact, that is exactly what happened in the United States. The establishment of the public pension system there caused national savings rates to fall, which then became a drag on capital accumulation and resulted in lower productivity gains and economic growth. Feldstein argues that the difference in growth rates between the United States and Japan can partly be explained by the fact that for a long time Japan had no public pension system. While no one denies that public pensions have an impact on personal savings, opinions are mixed on how much of an impact is indicated by the empirical evidence, and many doubt Feldstein's claims that the pension system cut America's capital accumulation by one-third. There is little support for the hypothesis that public pensions and private saving are completely substitutable.

The most fundamental criticism of public pensions is that they distort the spirit of self-reliance, but this is not a problem for old-age annuities alone. Insurance by its very nature is a system of mutual aid. Healthy people pay the medical costs of those who are sick; people who escape disaster bear the losses of those who do not. If we are to criticize public pensions for dampening self-reliance, then we must call into question the very existence of insurance itself.

The problems of pensions and early retirement or pensions and savings are the classical moral hazards inherent in insurance. When people are forced to participate in an old-age pension program, they lower their voluntary savings, or they decide to retire early because they can live quite well with the money promised to them. If, however, people consider their pension benefits insufficient, they will save on their own or work even after they have started to receive benefits. And the habit of savings enforced by mandatory pension contributions may actually heighten their desire to save. Thus, an effective way to avoid the moral hazards is to keep pension benefits low or to leave room in the system for voluntary choices. That is one of the reasons why pension benefits are limited to about half of one's average working income, and a major reason why the government provides encouragement and incentives for corporate pension plans.

Having developed rapidly in the sixties, Japan's pension system began to face serious problems in the eighties. As the system matured, there was an increase in the number of beneficiaries who had paid into the system for a long time before they collected. This obviously drove up the amounts of money being paid out. Added to this was the rapid aging of the population, which increased the number of retirees and elderly to be supported by the working generation. This imbalance between premium income and benefits paid out made a rise in premiums seem inevitable, while the diversity of pension plans that had been set up by necessity made the system too complex and argued for the adoption of something simpler and more uniform. Reforms in 1985 introduced a "basic pension system" into the National Health Insurance system. As a result, normal health insurance is composed of two parts: a basic pension component and a voluntary income-proportional component.

That still leaves the imbalance between income and outlays to be dealt with. The only way to keep premiums at levels that are bearable for future generations is to reduce benefit levels. One option is to extend the mandatory retirement age for those who find their work meaningful and fulfilling. Another is to raise the age of eligibility for benefits. Should insurance premiums reach 30–35% of income and the tax burden 30%, then Japan will face the same kinds of problems Scandinavia is confronting today: social security burdens that are too high prompt companies to move their manufacturing offshore, and individual citizens migrate to other countries where the tax load is not so onerous.

5
INTERNATIONAL BALANCES OF PAYMENTS

1. THE POSTWAR ERA

In 1949, the Dodge Line set the exchange rate at ¥360 to the dollar, which, as we saw in Chapter 1, was a bit high compared to prevailing market prices at the time or the rate that would have achieved trade equilibrium. Being poor in resources and dependent on foreign imports for its raw materials, Japan was forced by the overvalued exchange rate to promote exports and discourage imports. Had it not done so, it would have been unable to earn the hard currency it needed to buy its raw materials overseas.

Japan also had to adopt strict trade and foreign exchange controls to ensure that what hard currency it earned was used to the country's best advantage. It started by adopting a "foreign exchange budget" under which the government centrally controlled all the foreign exchange earned through exports and then reallotted it to priority industries. The two primary objectives of the "industrial policies" administered by the Ministry of International Trade and Industry were 1) to protect export industries and thereby encourage higher export volumes and 2) to encourage import substitution industries and thereby hold down imports. The most effective way to accomplish both of these goals would have been to devalue the currency (i.e., lower the foreign exchange rate), but that was not one of Japan's options. The rate was set by the Occupation forces, and the country had no choice but to work with it as a "given." Much time and effort were therefore spent to adjust the economy to the ¥360 rate. Aid from the United States (called "GARIOA" and "EROA" for "Government Appropriation for Relief in Occupied Areas" and "Economic Rehabilitation Account for Occupation Areas," respectively) helped Japan to maintain equilibrium in its balance of payments, although just barely.

Luckily for Japan, however, the Korean War broke out in 1950 and Japan became a base for supplying many of the U.S. military forces' needs. The surge in demand for Japan-made goods and parts helped keep the balance of payments above water and in the latter part of the decade provided the economy with a springboard from which to take off. Thanks to U.S. military demand (called *tokuju*, or "special procurements," in Japanese) Japan embarked on a path of steady economic reconstruction and development, and it grew as a trader.

One reason for Japan's development at this time was that the world economy as a whole was growing and there was an upsurge in trading around the globe. Amid these trends, Japan's industrial policy of protection and encouragement for infant industries succeeded in boosting the country's share of the whole. The other reason was that prices for oil and other raw materials remained low through much of this period, which was again advantageous to Japan as it switched from its traditional textiles and processing industries to such industries as steelmaking and petrochemicals.

The easiest way to track a country's balance of payments over the long term is to use what is known as the "absorption approach." Table 5-1 shows Japan's balance of payments in dollar figures for the three most recent years at the time of this writing. When discussing the balance of payments, it used to be common to urge countries to balance their current accounts, or the aggregate of their current account and capital account. This, however, was largely superseded by the "basic balance," which is the sum of the current account and the long-term capital account. Then, with the increasing proportion of securities investments in the long-term capital account, it became harder to classify which capital exports were "long-term" and which "short-term," which weakened the significance of distinguishing between overall balances and basic balances. Today, the emphases are placed on the current account and capital account, which make up the long-term capital account, and on the short-term capital account. In stock-flow analysis, the current account is on the "flow" side of the picture, representing the supply and demand for goods

TABLE 5-1   The Japanese Balance of Payments (in Dollars)

(Unit: $100 million)

	FY1988	FY1989	FY1990
(1) Trade balance	953	700	699
Exports	2,674	2,681	2,899
Imports	1,721	1,981	2,200
(2) Non-trade balance	−135	−126	−225
(3) Transfer balance	−45	−40	−136
(4) Current acct. balance	773	534	338
(1) + (2) + (3)			
(5) Long-term capital balance	−1,214	−997	−168
(6) Short-term capital balance	311	193	13
(7) Errors and omissions	−7	−303	−173
(8) Overall balance (4) + (5) + (6) + (7)	−137	−573	10
(9) Financial balance	−137	−573	10
Foreign exchange sector	−264	−164	−13
Public sector	127	−409	3
Foreign exchange reserves	994	735	699

Note: The balance of payments table is set up so that the addition of the capital account (including the financial account) to the current account balance equals zero. If it does not equal zero, the gap is considered "errors and omissions." Negative figures on the capital balance indicate an outflow of capital (increase in assets); negative figures on the financial account equal a worsening external position (decline in assets and/or increase in liabilities).

Source: Bank of Japan, International Statistical Comparisons.

and services. To the extent that it directly influences a country's production and employment, the current account is now the most closely watched indicator of economic health.

The absorption approach starts with the idea that the current account of a country is what is left over when "absorption" is subtracted from the country's national product (aggregate supply):

$$\text{Current account balance (CA)} = \text{National product (Y)} - \text{Absorption (A)}. [1] \qquad (1)$$

[1] The relationship shown in Equation (1) always holds after the fact. Thus, from the standpoint of absorption analysis, it does not matter what sort of changes are seen in a country's international competitiveness: if the increase in national product does not outpace the increase in absorption, the current account balance will not improve. This insight was one of the major contributions made by this school of analysis to general economics.

Domestic absorption is the country's total demand, including the demand for imports, so we can rewrite the equation as:

$$\text{Absorption} = \text{Private consumption (C)}$$
$$+ \text{Private investment (I)} \qquad (2)$$
$$+ \text{Government expenditure (G)}.$$

Likewise, national product is equivalent to the sum of national consumption (C), private savings (S), and government tax revenues (T), so substituting from Equation (2) gives

$$\text{Current account balance} = [\text{Private savings (S)}]$$
$$- [\text{Private investment (I)}]$$
$$+ [\text{Tax revenues (T)} \qquad (3)$$
$$- \text{Government expenditures (G)}].$$

Furthermore, government expenditures are equal to government purchases of goods and services, which we can further divide into consumption expenditures and investment expenditures:

Current account balance
$$= (\text{Private savings} - \text{Private investment}) + (\text{Tax revenues}$$
$$- \text{Government consumption} - \text{Government investment}) \qquad (4)$$
$$= (\text{Private savings} - \text{Private investment}) +$$
$$(\text{Government savings} - \text{Government investment}).$$

The conclusion, therefore, is that the current account surplus is equal to the sum of the excess savings (or overinvestment) of the private sector (S − I) and that of the government and public sector. When the country is running a domestic surplus, the right side of Equations (3)

TABLE 5-2   Current Account Balance   (Unit: ¥1 billion)

Calendar year	S − I	T − G	Statistical error	Net foreign investment	Current account balance
1971	1,495.8	410.1	639.7	2,135.6	1,992
1976	7,339.0	6,155.9	138.6	1,361.8	1,078
1981	10,160.4	9,666.4	879.0	1,372.9	1,147
1984	12,060.7	5,858.1	2,814.5	9,017.3	8,350
1985	12,594.4	2,485.9	1,974.8	12,083.4	11,518
1988	425.2	10,682.0	1,205.3	9,901.8	10,192

Source: Economic Planning Agency, *National Income Statistics Annual;* Bank of Japan, *Economic Statistics Annual.*

and (4) must be equal to the net foreign investment or the net increases in foreign assets. Table 5-2 traces this relationship for Japan for six fiscal years between 1971 and 1988. The figures do not add up exactly because of differences in the statistical principles employed in real life and those envisioned in theory. Nevertheless, we can see that the sum of the private-sector savings surplus and the government savings surplus is equal to net foreign investments or the net increase in credits held against other countries. The difference between this and the current account surplus stems from non-recurring (net) capital transfers such as war reparations and economic cooperation. If these outlays are excluded, we find:

Current account balance = Net foreign investment   (5)
                       = Net increase in private foreign assets
                         (credits).

This relationship can be seen clearly in Table 5-2. Note that this does not take into account changes in asset prices, which will obviously have an influence on the size of the country's foreign assets. We

TABLE 5-3   Stage of Economic Development as Defined by Investment and Savings Balance

Stage of development	Investment and savings balance	Capital & technology etc.
(1) Stagnation	I<S	No domestic investment opportunities; capital goes overseas; production stagnates.
(2) Commercial revolution	I>S	Mercantilistic period.
(3) Economic growth	I>S M>X	Economy takes off; capital and technology imported from overseas.
(4) Maturity	I<S M<X	As income levels rise, savings increase, but with fewer domestic investment opportunities capital is exported; independent technological development; greater inclination toward services.
(5) Decline	I>S M>X	Consumption increases; savings decline; another round of excess investment ensues, causing capital and technology to be imported.

Note: M stands for imports, X for exports.
Source: Charles Kindleberger, *International Economics.*

should also point out that one of the implications of Equation (5) is that a surplus in the current account leads to an increase in invisible trade income. The current account surplus produces an increase in net foreign investments, which naturally means an increase in foreign asset holdings and therefore a rise in the proportion of the current account coming from investment income and other invisible trades.

Charles Kindleberger uses the investment and savings balance to divide countries into five stages of development depending on their balance-of-payments standing (Table 5-3).

A contrasting approach is that taken by the Economic Planning Agency in the 1984 *Economic White Paper*. The EPA classified Japan's postwar economic development into six stages by looking at the impact of increases and declines in the balance of payments on foreign assets (stock) and the investment income derived from them (Table 5-4).[2]

With this foundation in place, let us now turn to Japan's postwar balance of payments. Disregarding the EPA's chronological categories, we can see that in the late sixties Japan began to run current

TABLE 5-4   Development of Balance of Payments

	Goods & services	Invest- ment income	Current account balance	Long- term capital
Immature debtor (postwar to early 1950s)	−	−	−	+
Mature debtor (late 1950s–early 1960s)	+	− −	−	+
Repayment of debts (late 1960s–early 1970s)	+ +	−	+	−
Immature creditor (after late 1970s)	+	+	+ +	− −
Mature creditor	−	+ +	+	−
Creditor drawing down credits	− −	+	−	+

Note: "−" indicates negatives (deficits), "− −" larger deficits than "−". Similarly, "+" equals positives (surpluses), "+ +" larger surpluses than "+."
Source: Economic Planning Agency, *Economic White Paper*, 1984.

[2] Karl Popper in *The Poverty of Historicism* delivers a scathing criticism of the "stage of development theories" espoused by Marxists and the German historical school. Rather than being unchanging laws, he says, they can never be more than mere trends. Still, it is hard to deny their heuristic value.

TABLE 5-5   Investment Income Balance   (Unit: $1 million)

	Investment income receivable	Investsment income payable	Overseas direct investments
1970	710	919	355
1975	3,616	3,889	1,763
1980	11,115	10,261	2,385
1985	22,107	15,267	6,452
1986	29,087	19,613	14,480
1987	49,245	32,575	19,519
1988	74,837	53,805	34,210
1989	101,785	78,343	44,130

Source: Shigetsugu Okumura et al., eds., *World Economic Data* (University of Tokyo Press, 1990).

account surpluses and reached the stage of a "mature debtor." However, as Table 5-5 clearly shows, in the late seventies, and particularly in the eighties after the second oil crisis, the country began to record an investment-income surplus that undoubtedly turned it into an "immature net creditor"—a capital exporter.

To explain what happened very briefly, during the growth period of the sixties, Japan was importing capital and technology from overseas. Domestic investments were higher than domestic savings (I_d [domestic investments] $> S$); imports were higher than exports ($M > X$). When the gap between domestic investments (I_d) and domestic savings (S) became too large, the economy would overheat, and a serious shortage of foreign exchange reserves would result, prompting the authorities to clamp down on finance as a way to adjust the country's adsorption ($C + I - G$). This pattern was repeated over and over and over throughout the period.

2. FROM BRETTON WOODS TO FLOATING RATES

Two major changes came in the late sixties. The Vietnam War brought on an "oversupply of dollars" that triggered simultaneous inflation around the world, and there began to be marked differences in the growth rates and productivity gains achieved by different countries, which led to chronic surpluses for West Germany and Japan. The two combined to weaken confidence in the dollar, and eventually led to the Smithsonian Accord in December 1971 that raised the yen's exchange value from ¥360 to ¥308 against the dollar.

Before we go any further, let us review how the adjustment mechanism worked under the Bretton Woods system. Like the gold standard or the gold exchange standard, Bretton Woods was a system of fixed exchange rates led by the International Monetary Fund (IMF). IMF members pegged their currencies either against gold or against the dollar, which was an acceptable substitute for gold, and were obligated to keep their currencies within 1% of the official rate of exchange. Unlike under the gold standard, however, there were provisions by which countries could, within certain limits, change their exchange rates when there were chronic surpluses or deficits in their balances of payments. It was also possible, when circumstances warranted, for countries to negotiate even larger adjustments in their exchange rates with the IMF. This was called the "adjustable peg" system.

The demand for foreign exchange is the result of imports of goods and exports of capital; the supply comes from exports of goods and imports of capital. When the point at which the demand for foreign exchange is equal to the supply of foreign exchange (point E) is within the upper and lower limits shown in Figure 5-1, E will be the determining factor in trading volumes and rates on the foreign ex-

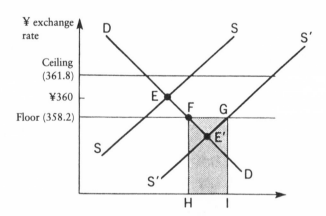

FIGURE 5-1   Determination of Foreign Exchange Rates

change markets. Let us now assume that Japanese exports increase because of an oversupply of dollars. When the exporters want to trade their dollars for yen, the supply of foreign exchange increases and the supply curve SS shifts far to the right, to S'S'. This changes the supply/demand equilibrium point to E', and the foreign exchange rate may, as a result, fall below the lower limit. To prevent this, the monetary authorities defend the dollar by buying it on the open market. But to keep it above the lower limit, they must buy dollars equivalent to FG. This causes Japan's foreign exchange reserves to grow larger, meaning there are more yen funds (FGIH) on the market and consequently there is more inflationary pressure on the Japanese economy. Were the same thing to occur at the same time in, for example, West Germany, then there would be a danger that the dollar would drop even further. This would create more pressure to exchange dollars for gold, which would undermine confidence in the dollar and further accelerate the outflow of gold from the United States, which, to stop the outflow, might then enact a moratorium on dollar/gold exchanges and slap a 10% surcharge on imports.

In fact, that is exactly what President Richard Nixon did on August 15, 1971. In response, European foreign exchange markets closed their doors; when they reopened, they adopted a market-based floating exchange-rate system. Surprisingly enough, Japan kept its foreign exchange markets open for business as usual right through August 31, which resulted in massive buying of yen by speculators wanting to profit from the rise in the value of the yen after exchange rates had been readjusted.

In December of that year, finance ministers and central bankers from ten countries gathered in Washington, where they signed the Smithsonian Accord on multilateral exchange-rate adjustments. Under the accord, the yen went from ¥360 to the dollar to ¥308, with an allowance of 2.25% on either side. This, however, did not restore confidence in the dollar, and in February 1973, Japan too floated its currency. The intervening time period was one of much wasted effort on the part of Japanese authorities. Pressured by business and financial leaders who feared the impact on both domestic and export industries of further appreciation of the yen, the government spent just over a year trying to stimulate the economy and boost imports under the ¥308 exchange rate.

One of the main advantages of floating exchange rates was that changes in rates would adjust balances of payments,[3] which would leave countries free to pursue independent economic policies.

As Note 3 explains in greater detail, changes in foreign exchange rates in theory always maintain equilibrium in the balance of payments, which means that the fiscal and monetary authorities are free to concentrate on price stability and full employment without having to worry about achieving an external equilibrium. At least, that was the way it was *supposed* to work. Unfortunately, in the real world, exchange-rate variations have failed to perform this function adequately. We have seen from experience that, whatever happens over the long term, over the short term, foreign exchange rates are not determined so as to keep an equilibrium in the balance of payments. Worse yet, they fluctuate far more wildly than most people ever imagined. Under the floating system, how exchange rates are determined has become a matter of vital theoretical and practical interest to many people.

3. DETERMINING FOREIGN EXCHANGE RATES
IN FLOATING SYSTEMS

The classical theory of how exchange rates are determined under floating systems is the "purchasing power parity" or "PPP" theorem, so that is where we will start.

Purchasing power parity says that if competition were perfect, there would be a single price for each item available in the market. For instance, if we assume transaction costs to be zero, the same pencil would go for the same price regardless of whether one bought it in the United States or Japan.[4] If prices are higher in the U.S., then one could buy pencils in Japan and export them to the U.S. at a profit. This would drive the price of pencils up in Japan and the American price down. If, therefore, a pencil costs ¥100 in Japan and 50¢ in the U.S., the exchange rate will be equal to purchasing power parity:

[3] The basic idea behind floating rates is that equilibrium will automatically be maintained for the overall balance. Under the floating rate system we have today, exchange rates are determined in correlation to point E_0 in Figure 5-2, which means that the equation "Exports + Capital imports = Imports + Capital exports" is valid. When Japanese exports rise and the foreign exchange supply curve shifts from SS to S'S', the floating rate system will switch to a new equilibrium point E', at which the equation Exports + Capital imports = Imports + Capital exports" is again valid.

[4] For this reason, it is common to limit evaluations of purchasing power to traded goods.

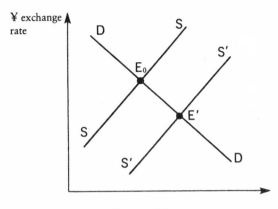

FIGURE 5-2

$$\text{Exchange rate} = \text{PPP} = \frac{¥100}{\$0.5} = \frac{¥200}{\$1} \tag{6}$$

This represents an "absolute" purchasing power parity. When there are many different goods on the market, purchasing power parity is expressed not in terms of a single item, but in terms of a basket of goods that are available in all countries.

If we assume that purchasing power parity is $\$1 = ¥200$ at the present time, and that over the next year Japanese prices will rise 10% while U.S. prices will rise 20%, then Japanese prices one year from now will be 110 (taking current prices as 100), and American prices will be 120. Therefore,

$$\text{PPP 1 year hence} = \text{PPP at base point } (¥200) \times \frac{110}{120} = ¥183.33. \tag{7}$$

Or, to put it in more general terms:

$$\frac{\text{Current PPP}}{\text{PPP at base point}} = \frac{\text{Japanese price index}}{\text{U.S. price index}}. \tag{8}$$

This is a relative purchasing power parity, rather than the absolute purchasing power parity we began with.

Relative purchasing power parity is the more widely used index today, but there are a number of problems with it. First, there is the question of what to take as the base point. The normal practice is to choose a year when current accounts were close to equilibrium, but if large differences in the economic structure subsequently emerge, there will be a wide gap between relative and absolute purchasing power parity.

Second, there is the question of what to use as a price index. There are many to choose from—the consumer price index, the wholesale price index, the GDP deflator—but they all include non-trade goods, and there are questions as to whether purchasing power parity derived from indexes that include non-trade goods is an appropriate standard for foreign exchange rates.

The results of empirical studies have been mixed, though the general conclusion is that in the absence of any structural changes, exchange rates will tend to converge with purchasing power parity over the long term.

During the interwar years of the twenties, the yen was floated and exchange rates matched purchasing power parity quite well. Similarly, purchasing power parity goes a long way toward explaining exchange rates between 1973, the year the yen was again floated, and about 1975–1976, because the government adopted stiff controls on the inflow and outflow of capital. When the yen appreciated, the authorities restrained capital inflows; when it depreciated, they

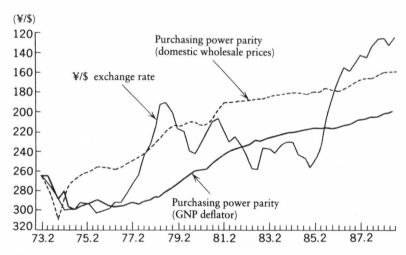

FIGURE 5-3   Purchasing Price Parity and Foreign Exchange Rates
Source: Fukao Mitsuhiro, Seminar on International Finance, Toyo Keizai Shimposha.

restrained outflows. After 1977, however, and particularly in the eighties, international movements of capital began to accelerate, which led to the wide gap between prevailing exchange rates and purchasing power parity shown in Figure 5-3. A new theory was needed to explain how exchange rates are determined.

Many have been proposed, and one of the things they all have in common is that they emphasize the impact of portfolio choices (including the supply of and demand for the foreign-currency assets that have begun to accumulate in the process of economic development) rather than such traditional factors as current accounts and balances of trade. This change in emphasis is a recognition of the new reality associated with increasing amounts of international capital. Financial assets move far faster than real assets, and exchange rates have become more responsive to them.

Of the many theories proposed, the one that is most widely accepted is the "portfolio balance approach," which says short-term foreign exchange rates are determined by the following equation:

$$
\begin{aligned}
\text{Actual exchange rate } (e_0) = {} & \text{Long-term equilibrium rate } (e^*) \\
& + k \times (\text{Real U.S. interest rates} - \\
& \quad \text{Real Japanese interest rates}) \\
& - \text{Risk premium}
\end{aligned} \tag{9}
$$

In plain English, actual exchange rates are equal to the long-term equilibrium rate, plus the part that depends on differences in real interest rates in the two countries, and a risk premium. In other words, the difference between the long-term equilibrium rate and the actual rate can be accounted for by differences in real interest rates and risk premiums.

Let us look at how this relationship is derived. Suppose a Japanese investor invests his wealth in domestic assets, for which he will receive a return of unit interest rate, i (i could be an annual rate, but note that if the investment period were only three months rather than a year, i would represent a three-month interest rate rather than an annualized interest rate, and so on throughout this discussion). We will further assume that the interest rate in the United States is i_f. In order to invest in the U.S., the Japanese investor must change his yen into dollars, and then after a certain period of time change them back into yen again. If we assume the current exchange rate to be e_0 and the future (three months from now) exchange rate to be e_1, then the

Japanese investor could expect profits per unit of $i + (e_1 - e_0)/e_0$ from his foreign investments. If, for simplicity's sake, we use "x" to express $(e_1 - e_0)/e_0$ (the expected rate of change in the foreign exchange rate), then the expected rate of return from foreign investments is $i_f + x$. If we further assume transaction costs to be zero and perfect substitutability between domestic and foreign assets, then interest-rate arbitrage will ensure that

$$i = i_f + x. \tag{10}$$

In other words, the return must be the same whether you invest your money in the U.S. or in Japan.

But when you hold foreign currency, you are subject to different risks from those for domestic investments, so unless $i < i_f + x$, no one will invest in foreign-currency-denominated assets. A risk premium is required, which we shall call β, so that

$$i = i_f + x - \beta. \tag{10'}$$

This risk premium increases as more foreign-currency-denominated assets are held. If there is an increase in dollar-denominated assets, for example, there will be a greater subjective risk that the value of the dollar might fall, so the risk premium will rise by the amount required to offset this.

Let us assume that the expected rate of change in the foreign exchange rate depends on the spread between the long-term equilibrium rate and the actual rate, so that

$$x = \alpha(e^* - e). \tag{11}$$

If the actual rate is lower than the long-term equilibrium rate (of which we will consider purchasing power parity a good indicator), the rate will be expected to rise. If it is higher (if the yen is undervalued), it will be expected to decline (the yen will appreciate). For our purposes, this seems to be a convincing argument.

We can now make substitutions back from Equation (11) to Equation (10') to find

$$i = i_f + \alpha(e^* - e) - \beta.$$

This we can rewrite as

$$e = e^* + \frac{1}{\alpha}[(i_f - i) - \beta]. \tag{12}$$

Now let us look at the impact of price fluctuations. The expected rate of change in the foreign exchange rate, x, depends on differences in the expected price growth rates for Japan and the United States. If Japanese prices are expected to grow more quickly than American prices, x will rise; if American prices are expected to rise faster than Japanese, x will fall. We can therefore rewrite Equation (11) to read

$$x = \alpha(e^* - e) + (\pi - \pi_f)$$

where π and π_f stand for the expected price growth rate for Japan and the United States, respectively. We can therefore conclude:

$$e = e^* + \frac{1}{\alpha}[(i_f - \pi_f) - (i - \pi) - \beta]^5. \tag{13}$$

Let us use these tools to look at Japanese foreign exchange rates since the yen was floated. (Figures 5-3 and 5-4 display the information graphically.)

Equation (9) explains foreign exchange in terms of purchasing power parity, real interest rate differentials, and the risk premium, so we will begin by looking at the relationship between purchasing power parity and actual exchange rates.

Figure 5-3 shows that for a while after the yen was floated, Japan was able to maintain a close correlation between actual rates and purchasing power parity (PPP). Beginning in 1977, however, actual rates began to fall below PPP, which drove the yen higher. This continued until about 1981 or 1982, after which the actual rate was higher than PPP and the yen began to depreciate. The next change came with the meeting of finance ministers from the Group of Five economic powers in September 1985. The yen shot upward and did not fall again until it was at almost ¥120 to the dollar.

Figure 5-4 explains why there was such a gap between purchasing power parity and actual exchange rates. Looking at real interest rates in the two countries, we can see that from 1976 to 1981 real Japanese long-term interest rates were higher than American, which increased the demand for yen, particularly among foreign investors in securities. The yen therefore appreciated (which translates to a decline in the rate when expressed in yen terms) more than purchasing power parity would have warranted. But in the eighties, American

[5] In Equation (9), $1/\alpha$ equals k and β/α equals risk premium.

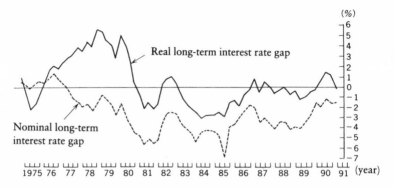

FIGURE 5-4   Japan–United States Interest Rate Gaps
Source: Economic Planning Agency, *Current Status of the Japanese Economy.*

policies[6] forced the country's interest rates higher, which caused funds to shift from Japanese securities to U.S. securities. This expanded the demand for the dollar, which caused the yen to be undervalued; the yen-based rate was higher than purchasing power parity would have warranted.

The undervalued yen encouraged Japanese exports, giving the country a large surplus on its current account, and more particularly, in its trade balance, which allowed it to accumulate growing amounts of dollars and other foreign-currency assets. The increase in the dollar-asset balance boosted the risk premium, which should have caused the yen to appreciate, but did not do so immediately. At most, there was a very slow correction of the overvalued dollar at the beginning of 1985. That set the stage for the Group of Five meetings in September of that year. The mood in the United States had shifted. Rather than wanting to maintain the strong dollar, Americans had become pessimistic about interventions on the foreign exchange markets. This shift, combined with lower U.S. interest rates (because inflation had been quelled), sent the dollar tumbling and the yen skyrocketing. (In May 1985, $1 was worth ¥250; six months later it

[6]To realize its objectives of a "strong America" and a "strong dollar," the Reagan administration cut taxes and boosted military spending, which brought on a sharp expansion in the fiscal deficit and a deterioration of the balance of payments. As a result the monetary authorities were forced to maintain high interest rates even after inflationary pressures had been quelled in order to improve the U.S. balance of payments.

was worth less than ¥200 and by 1988 it was worth just over ¥120.) Inasmuch as the strong dollar was supported by an illusion, its maintenance was a "bubble" and the events after 1985 resulted in its rupture.

Many hoped that changes in foreign exchange rates—the move from a weak yen to a strong yen—would help rectify the imbalances in the country's trade and current accounts. The appreciation of the yen would raise the dollar prices of Japanese exports, causing them to decline, while lowering the domestic prices for imports, causing them to grow. Ordinarily, this would lead to a decline in the (dollar-based) trade surplus, as long as the Marshal–Lerner criterion were met. It did not work out that way, however. Dollar-based export prices changed immediately after the yen began to appreciate, but export volumes did not generally decline, or at least not as much as the price rise would have indicated. Import prices, on the other hand, did not change very much, or at least not as much as the yen, so again there was little change in volume. In fact, what happened over the short term was that the dollar value of Japanese exports rose, so rather than contracting, the trade surplus actually expanded. It was only later that exchange rates began to make themselves felt and the trade surplus began to decline. This phenomenon is known as the "J curve." The sharp increase in Japan's trade surplus in 1986, the year after the yen began to appreciate, is a classic example.

Even after the effects of the J curve had passed, Japan's trade and current account surpluses did not decline as much as expected, which caused the United States to press for changes in the structure of the Japanese economy that would reduce the surpluses. To answer these demands, Japan formed a special committee under the direction of the Economic Council and headed by Haruo Maekawa, a former governor of the Bank of Japan, to examine ways in which the country could comply. Meanwhile, it enacted a "general economic policy package" (September 1989) of public-works spending and market-opening measures designed to switch from exports to domestic demand as the leading sector in economic growth. This was indeed a drastic change, the end of the era of trade-based prosperity that had begun in the Meiji Era.

These Japanese policies finally began to have some effect, but as we saw from Equation (4) above, the United States, to cut its current account deficits, needed to 1) hold down domestic absorption by reducing its giant fiscal deficit, and 2) increase its export competitiveness by devaluing the dollar. Unfortunately, the U.S. government had little enthusiasm for these kinds of fiscal and monetary policies and opted instead to take a more protectionist line by demanding "voluntary restraints" in Japanese exports of steel and automobiles. Naturally, the U.S. current account deficit and the Japanese surplus did not decline by as much as had been hoped, and friction between the two increased.

If, however, the reason that the trade balance did not improve as much as expected even after a dramatic appreciation of the yen was, as Americans say, because of the closed nature of Japanese market business practices, complex administrative guidance, *keiretsu*, and the like, as well as the downward rigidity of prices (domestic prices not declining as much as the higher yen would warrant), then it goes without saying that Japan needs to redesign its markets so that foreign exchange fluctuations have a more immediate effect and their workings are more transparent to outsiders.

4. EXTERNAL INVESTMENTS

We saw at the beginning of this chapter that during the late seventies and early eighties the Japanese economy matured and in all likelihood entered the "immature net creditor stage" in the six-stage schema. As this was happening, the relative position of the United States, which had in the past supplied the world with capital and provided its key currency, was in decline and running enormous deficits on its current account. Japan therefore took on an increasingly large role as a supplier of capital.

In Section 1, we noted that domestic savings are allocated to domestic investments and the net increase in external assets; the latter is the same thing as net foreign investments, or the country's deficit on its capital account (since it is disbursing more capital than it is taking in).[7] In short, the net increase in foreign assets (credits) is the net total of the long- and short-term capital transactions between Japan and other countries. This also reflects a surplus on Japan's current account because the country returns the money it has made on its current account to other countries in the form of long- and short-term capital exports. Japan and lately the NIEs are often criticized

---

[7] We can easily conclude from Equations (4) and (5) that
    Domestic savings = Domestic investment + Net increase in external assets.

for their current account surpluses, but we should point out that this money is always recycled abroad and that the funding it provides has financed economic growth in many countries.

The problem is not with surpluses themselves, but with the way the funds are accumulated and recycled. If they are held in the form of silver and gold or buried deep underground in Fort Knox (where the U.S. keeps its reserves) and not circulated back into the world's markets, they have a deflationary effect on the world economy and could bring on a global slump.

That is not the case with Japan, as shown in Table 5-6, a breakdown of the country's balance of external assets and liabilities. On its long-term accounts, Japan has a large asset surplus. This was brought on by a sharp increase in private-sector securities invest-

TABLE 5-6 Balance of Foreign Assets and Liabilities

(Units: $1 billion)

	1980	1985	1989 year-end
Total foreign assets	159.5	437.7	1,771.0
Long-term assets	87.8	301.2	1,019.2
(1) Private sector	66.5	264.4	901.7
—of which, direct investments	19.6	43.9	154.3
Export deferments	9.7	23.6	52.8
Credits	14.8	46.8	137.0
Securities investments	21.4	145.7	533.7
(2) Government	21.3	36.8	117.4
—of which, credits	15.5	23.2	60.4
Short-term assets	71.6	136.4	751.7
(1) Private-sector financial acct.	46.0	108.7	666.7
(2) Govt. financial acct.	25.6	27.6	85.0
Total foreign liabilities	148.0	307.8	1,477.7
Long-term liabilities	47.7	122.3	447.4
(1) Private sector	35.2	91.7	405.4
—of which, direct investments	3.2	4.7	9.1
Credits	1.6	1.2	18.8
Securities inv.	30.2	84.8	373.9
(2) Government	12.5	30.5	41.9
—of which, securities investments	12.3	30.4	41.9
Short-term liabilities	100.2	185.5	1,030.3
(1) Private-sector financial acct.	93.9	176.9	1,004.1
(2) Government financial acct.	6.2	8.5	26.2
Net assets	11.5	129.8	293.2

Source: Bank of Japan, *Economic Statistics Annual.*

ments. But the main influences on the short-term or "financial" accounts are foreign-exchange banks and the monetary authorities, and they are seeing larger and larger surplus liabilities. Overall, therefore, Japan is borrowing short and lending long. One of the things that characterizes its external investments is that indirect investments, particularly in securities, are far larger than direct investments. It is worth noting in this connection that the deficit on Japan's long-term capital account is far larger than the surplus on its current account. To make up the difference, the country is borrowing short-term. Or, to approach it from a different angle, rather than just investing domestic savings in other countries, Japan is raising short-term funds abroad and then also investing them abroad. It has gone from "domestic–foreign" transactions to "foreign–foreign" transactions. The ability to do so is one of the things that defines an international financial center, which is why Tokyo has grown to rival New York and London as a key center of international finance. There is, however, some question as to the permanence of this situation. Many say that it was a temporary aberration, that the increase in foreign securities investments was the result of the low interest rates that have been in effect since 1986 and that the trend will reverse when interest rates rise. If Japan is truly to develop into an international financial center, it will need to continue with its external investments, provide active support to prevent the blockage of funds that comes from incomplete information, and reform its financial system so that its markets are open and accessible to all who wish to use them no matter where they come from.

6
PRICES

1. POSTWAR TRENDS

In Chapter 1 we saw how the restrictive monetary policies of Joseph Dodge quelled inflation in the immediate postwar years. During the fifties, however, Japanese prices began to rise again because of the munitions boom during the Korean War. The extraordinary demand from the war ended once the armistice was signed (1953), and in 1955 prices began to fall. Once stabilized, both wholesale and consumer prices in Japan remained relatively flat until about 1960, though the business cycle did produce small fluctuations.

Price trends since 1960 can be divided into three basic periods, as Figure 6-1 illustrates. The first period takes us all the way through the sixties and up to about 1972, the year of the first oil crisis. Wholesale prices were generally stable or a bit slack during this time, while consumer prices rose at an average of 5–6% a year (the lowest rise was 4.2% in 1967). Thus, taking 1960 as 100, wholesale prices in 1965 were only 102.6, and in 1970 only 113.6; consumer prices, however, had risen to 134.3 and 175.1, respectively. The period therefore ends with a large gap between the indexes.

The second period takes us from 1972 to 1981. The dividing line is the December 1971 Smithsonian Accord for multilateral currency adjustment, which, as we saw in Chapter 5, brought the yen up from ¥360 to the dollar to ¥308. Even that, however, was not enough to restore confidence in the dollar, with the result that currencies continued to be volatile. Japan, trying to defend the new level of ¥308, lowered interest rates and enacted an economic stimulus program de-

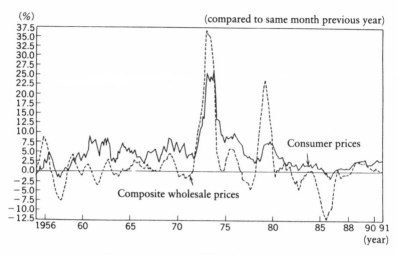

FIGURE 6-1   Consumer and Wholesale Prices
Source: Economic Planning Agency, Bank of Japan surveys.

signed to reduce some of its current account surplus. These moves, combined with the spending programs initiated under the Tanaka government's goal of "building a new Japan," caused land and equity prices to soar and, by the end of 1972, wholesale and consumer prices to turn sharply upward. With some reluctance, the authorities finally switched to tighter monetary policies in April 1973 with a hike in the official discount rate. But the move was "too little, too late." Before its effects could become fully manifest, war broke out in the Middle East and oil prices quadrupled almost overnight. Fears that supplies would be cut off caused speculators to hoard their supplies and keep them from the market. "Wild inflation" resulted. The public was outraged with oil companies, trading houses, and banks for their part in the process, and a militant consumer movement emerged. (One of the victories of this consumer movement was the 1977 strengthening of the antimonopoly laws, the first since the end of the war.) Inflation was only quelled by the ultra-tight monetary policies of 1975, and in 1976 there were signs that prices had recovered some semblance of stability. The Iranian revolution at the end of 1978 touched off another oil crisis, which boosted petroleum prices by 40%. Worldwide inflation was again the result. Japan recorded a 24% rise in wholesale prices during the fiscal year ending March 13, 1979, but it had learned its lesson from the bitter experiences of the first crisis. The authorities moved quickly this time, and by 1981 prices were again stabilized.

The third period takes us from 1980 to the present. Tight monetary policies enabled Japan to overcome the price volatility brought on by the oil crises, and stable prices were made the top objective of the country's financial policies. Thanks in part to private-sector confidence in the monetary authorities, the country has by and large been successful in achieving its aims. People from other countries are often astounded by this stability, and many rank it as one of the "mysteries of the Japanese economy," often putting it in the same league as the high-growth period of the sixties.

This discussion should have produced at least two questions in the reader's mind: Why, during the first period (which roughly corresponds to the 1960–1975 high-growth period), did consumer prices rise while wholesale prices remained stable? And why was it that Japanese prices stopped rising so quickly after the second oil crisis and remained so stable thereafter?

2. WHY PRICES CHANGE

One of the key questions that has continued to interest economists is why prices fluctuate, and many theories have been developed that try to explain the phenomenon. Before we look at Japanese prices in detail, we will briefly review the price theories proposed since Keynes.

KEYNES.   Keynes held that that price levels were determined by the aggregate supply of and demand for final goods, just as the price of any individual commodity is determined by the supply of and demand for that particular commodity. For simplicity's sake, let us assume money wages, available capital, and technology as givens. When prices rise, aggregate supply will increase because real wages—money wages divided by price levels—decline, so it is to companies' advantage to increase employment and production. Aggregate demand, on the other hand, will increase if the price level decreases, assuming the money supply, fiscal deficits, and exports as givens. When price levels decline, the real quantity of money increases, so demand increases as well. As can be seen in Figure 6-2, prices are determined by point E, the intersection between the aggregate supply curve AS and the aggregate demand curve AD. It should be obvious

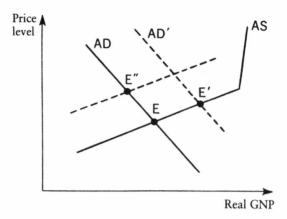

FIGURE 6-2   Determination of Price Levels

therefore that an increase in one of the givens—the money supply or exports, for example—will move AD to the left, resulting in higher prices. Similarly, an increase in wages will push AS upward, again resulting in higher prices. Conversely, if imports increase or technological progress brings productivity gains, prices will fall.

That is how Keynes explained it in his *General Theory*, but it is not yet complete. The *General Theory* has often been called "the economics of depression," because its analysis focuses on slumps in which large numbers of people are unemployed, and Keynes assumed that money wages would not rise until the economy had returned to close to full employment. But it was found that higher employment (or, a lower unemployment rate) will cause money wages to rise in spite of the fact that there is still unemployment in the economy, which will shift the AS curve higher, resulting in higher prices. The Phillips curve is used to express this relationship between the unemployment rate and the rate of change of money wages and prices. This insight has become one of the foundations of post-Keynesian economic thinking.

A simplified version of the Phillips curve holds that

Rate of change of money wages = F (Unemployment rate).   (1)

In this equation, F stands for a function that expresses the dependence of the rate of change of money wages on the unemployment rate. Figure 6-3 shows that the rate of change is a decreasing function

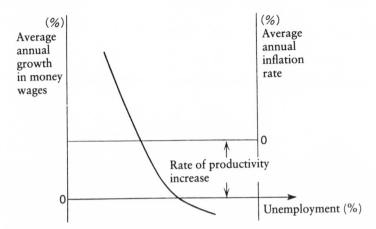

FIGURE 6-3   Unemployment Rate and Inflation (Phillips Curve)

of the unemployment rate—the lower the unemployment, the higher the rate of change of wages. There is also a relationship between the average rate of inflation and the rate of change in money wages:

Average inflation rate = Rate of change in money wages
  − Rate of change in labor productivity
  − Rate of change in labor share.   (2)

This relationship necessarily follows.[1]

We can now make substitutions from Equation (1) into the first factor in Equation (2) and, if we consider the labor share to be given (constant), arrive at:

Average rate of price inflation =
F (Unemployment rate) − Rate of productivity growth.   (3)

If we then assume the rate of change of productivity in Equation (3) to be given, Equation (3) shows the relationship between the unemployment rate and the rate of inflation. This relationship can be illustrated by shifting the base of the vertical axis of Figure 6-3 up-

---

[1] If the labor share is d, then $d = wL/py$, where w stands for the money wages per unit, L for the amount of employment, p for price levels, and y for real output. The denominator is therefore the nominal gross national product; the numerator, labor income. From this definition it is possible to express the price inflation rate ($\dot{P}/p$) as the right-hand side of Equation (2).

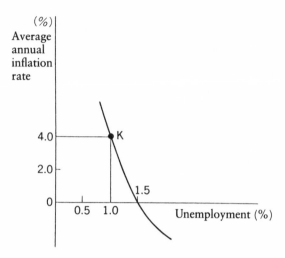

FIGURE 6-4   Relationship between Inflation Rate and Unemployment Rate

ward by an amount corresponding to the rate of change of productivity growth. Figure 6-4 illustrates the relationship between the rate of price inflation and the unemployment rate. It should be obvious that if the authorities try to stabilize prices, unemployment rises (for example, an unemployment rate of 1.5% may be required to produce price stability, or an inflation rate of 0%); conversely, if they try to hold unemployment down, prices rise. There are tradeoffs whichever route is chosen.

Because of these tradeoffs, Keynesians gave up looking for simultaneous achievement of full employment and stable prices. Instead, they see the goal of macroeconomic policy to be finding an optimal point along the Phillips curve (say, point K in Figure 6-4, where the unemployment rate is 1% and the price inflation rate 4%). Keynesians are also known to propose wage control policies (sometimes called income policies) that aim to keep the wage growth rate below the productivity growth rate. The United States in the Kennedy/Johnson era of the early sixties followed policies that were extremely close to this post-Keynesian thinking.

The chief critics of Keynesian and post-Keynesian ideas are Milton Friedman and Edmund Phelps, who began their analysis by wondering why the Phillips curve sloped down and to the right.

Their answer starts by pointing out the obvious—that the demand for labor is a decreasing function of real wages: if real wages decrease, the demand for labor increases, and conversely, if real wages increase, the demand for labor decreases. If prices are stable and the government adopts expansionary policies to try to increase jobs and decrease unemployment, what happens is that prices rise more than people expected, so real wages decrease, more jobs are created, and the unemployment rate goes down. Thus, Friedman and Phelps conclude, the unemployment rate is dependent on the difference between the real inflation rate and the expected inflation rate. In mathematical terms:

Unemployment rate =
f (Actual rate of inflation π – Expected rate of inflation π_e). (4)

We can rewrite this to read[2]

$$\pi = F(\text{Unemployment rate}) + \text{Expected rate of inflation } \pi_e. \quad (5)$$

What this equation means is that the actual rate of inflation depends on changes in the unemployment rate and the expected inflation rate (and the productivity growth rate).

The unemployment rate when $\pi = \pi_e$—when the actual rate of inflation equals the expected rate—is called the "natural rate of unemployment." There are therefore actually two Phillips curves: the long-term Phillips curve that shows the relationship between the inflation rate and the unemployment rate when the actual rate of inflation and the expected rate are equal, and the short-term Phillips curve that shows the relationship between unemployment and the inflation rate when the short-term inflation rate is given (see Figure 6-5).

Now let us consider what happens when the expected inflation rate is 0% and the government adopts expansionary policies in order to achieve point K on the short-term Phillips curve. First, the inflation rate rises from 0 to π_1. People begin to expect prices to rise at a rate of π_1, which raises the expected inflation rate π_e from 0 to π_1. The Phillips curve shifts upward as a result. Real wages are raised, and the unemployment rate increases as shown by the dotted line in Figure 6-5. But in order to maintain unemployment rate U_1, the government must accelerate inflation. Assume that prices rise as shown by line ABC in the figure. Even if the authorities try to stop inflation at this point, there are still strong inflationary expectations and the

---

[2] Strictly speaking, F in this case is the inverse function of f, f^{-1}.

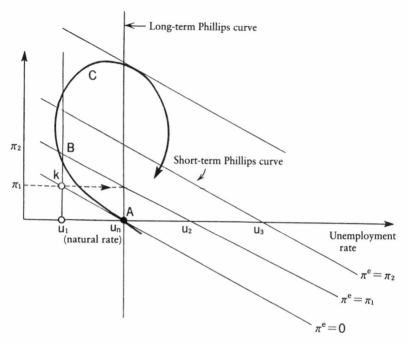

FIGURE 6-5   Natural Unemployment Rate

short-term Phillips curve has already shifted upward, so prices do not come down very rapidly. Thus, rising prices and high unemployment exist side by side in the same economy. That phenomenon is called "stagflation," and according to Phelps and Friedman it is the direct result of Keynesian policies.

THE MONETARISTS' VIEW.   The monetarists have a different way of explaining prices. According to this school of thought,

$$MV = Py. \qquad (6)$$

In this case, M is the money balance (stock of money), V the average velocity of circulation of money,[3] P price levels, and y real national income. We can rewrite Equation (6) to read

$$P = MV/y \qquad (7)$$

---

[3] This is often called the "income velocity of money."

And from this we can see that

Price inflation rate = Growth rate of M + Rate of change in income
velocity of money − Real growth rate.   (8)

If we assume V to be constant, then from Equation (8) we can conclude that if the money supply is expanding to keep pace with the
real growth rate, then price levels will not change (disregarding in-
stability on the supply side of the economy). However, V generally
tends to decline (the demand for money tends to increase), so for
prices to be stable, the growth rate for money M must be kept equal
to the real growth rate plus the rate of decline in the circulation
velocity.

THE GAP BETWEEN CONSUMER PRICES AND WHOLESALE
PRICES.   These tools can be used to analyze Japanese prices. First
let us look at why consumer prices rose between 1960 and 1972 even
though wholesale prices remained stable.

Before we begin, however, we should point out that consumer
price indexes and wholesale price indexes deal with different goods
and services. Wholesale prices are the prices at which goods are
traded between firms: they have no direct relation to consumer
sales. Still, many of the same goods are included on consumer and
wholesale price indexes; so while they are different, the two are
closely related. To be more specific, consumer prices emphasize
things like fresh food, general services, and utilities costs; wholesale
prices emphasize instead the intermediate and raw materials that go
into manufactured goods. A rise in oil prices, therefore, will affect
wholesale prices much more noticeably than consumer prices, while
crop damage will affect consumer prices much more than wholesale
prices. When economists want to eliminate these influences, they
often use an "index of consumer prices excluding fresh foods."

We should also note that while Japan made great strides in productivity during the high-growth period, the gains were vastly different for different types of goods and sizes of factories. Many of the
manufactured goods that make up the wholesale price index are produced in large factories; there were large gaps between the productivity gains made in such factories and those made by smaller-scale
manufacturers and service industries. More of the goods and services
that make up the consumer price index are supplied by smaller
firms, and in most cases their productivity gains were less than for
the goods and services that make up the wholesale price index.

Third, when there are gaps in productivity growth rates, theory predicts that prices will drop for products that are experiencing higher productivity gains, thereby adjusting relative prices. But in reality, demand was strong throughout the high-growth period, so the adjustment was effected instead by prices rising for low-productivity-growth areas. To look at the matter from a different angle, wages rose in high-productivity sectors, and these rises spilled over into sec-

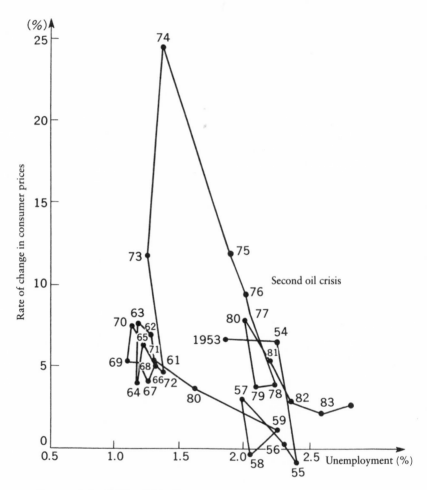

FIGURE 6-6   Phillips Price Curve
Source: Prime Minister's Office, Consumer Price Index, Report of Labor Survey.

tors with lower productivity growth, which caused consumer prices to rise. Figure 6-6 is a Phillips curve for Japan; the vertical axis shows the consumer price inflation rate; the horizontal, the unemployment rate. In 1955, consumer price inflation was negative, and the unemployment rate was 2.4%, but in the years that followed, unemployment declined. As Japan came close to achieving full employment, the rise in money wages began to accelerate until their growth rate surpassed the productivity growth rate for consumer goods. As it did so, the consumer price inflation rate began to steepen. Figure 6-6 also illustrates that it was not until the oil crisis of 1973 that the consumer price inflation rate began to rise more sharply than the gentle up-to-the-right slope of the normal Phillips curve. During this period, high productivity growth and low oil prices helped maintain stable wholesale prices.

Then, around 1972 and 1973, the government tried to defend the new rate of ¥308 to the dollar agreed upon in the Smithsonian Accord. The extremely easy credit policies it adopted resulted in a surge in the Marshallian k (the inverse of the income velocity of money) far above the trend line (see Figure 6-7 (a)), which combined with the boom created by the government's program to "build a new Japan" to spur a sharp increase in investments in land and equity. The results were higher prices and "inflationary expectations." The credit tightening did not come until April 1973, and before it could have any effect, war broke out in the Middle East, causing oil prices

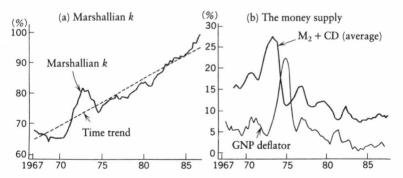

FIGURE 6-7   Marshallian k and Money Supply
Note: a–1) Marshallian k = {M2 + CD (average)/Nominal GNP} × 100. a–2) Time trend period: first quarter 1967 to fourth quarter 1986. b) Comparisons with same period previous year.
Source: Bank of Japan, *Economic Statistics Annual,* etc., for both.

to quadruple. Speculators aggravated this external shock to the economy by hoarding their oil supplies—either refusing to sell or buying anything they could find. The wild inflation that came in its wake increased the inflationary expectations, pushing the short-term Phillips curve far higher. The government responded with stringent financial controls that held back money supply growth and, as Figure 6-7 (b) and Figure 6-6 show, quelled inflation relatively quickly without producing massive unemployment. Then, in 1979, the Iranian revolution plunged the oil markets into crisis again.

In both cases it was oil that caused the inflation. Because of the differences in the makeup of the two indexes, the inflation was much more pronounced for wholesale prices than for consumer prices.

3. PRICE STABILITY IN THE EIGHTIES, AND FRICTION WITH THE UNITED STATES

By the time the second oil crisis rolled around, Japan had learned from its mistakes of the first. The authorities quickly cut the money supply in order to prevent the price rises caused by exogenous factors converting into endogenous inflation (see Figure 6-7 (b)). Prices settled, and by 1982 they regained full stability. Most economists see two factors at work in this:

(1) The Japanese authorities had credibility. The public had faith that they would cut the money supply growth rate, and that faith erased any inflationary expectations, quickly shifting the short-term Phillips curve downward and allowing Japan to stabilize prices in a short period of time without experiencing the slumps and massive unemployment that plagued other countries.

(2) The Japanese economy proved to be very elastic. Labor and management were able to work together to achieve the rationalization necessary to absorb higher raw materials costs. (By contrast, British labor unions were far more likely to oppose mechanization and other forms of rationalization, seeing them as stealing jobs from workers.) Part of this was because labor organization rates are almost as low in Japan as they are in the United States, part because both labor and management understood that rationalization was necessary to keep costs down after the oil price hike. Furthermore, most Japanese labor unions are organized on a company-by-company basis rather than on the skill-by-skill basis common in Europe. Wages in Japan are therefore

more sensitive to corporate profit rates and other indexes of corporate health, which makes it easier to resist wage hikes that are unwarranted by productivity growth. Instrumental in this is the keen competition among domestic companies, which makes it essential for firms that want to survive to invest in rationalization and cut their costs.

This is not to say that no problems were created by the tight money policies. One reason Japan was able to successfully stabilize its prices without generating large numbers of unemployed workers was that the policies of the United States at this time encouraged Japan to use exports as a way of preventing an economic stall. The end result, however, was economic friction. We have discussed in other chapters how the Reagan administration attempted to achieve its goal of a "strong America" and a "strong dollar" through large cuts in taxes and non-defense spending. Unfortunately, Congress, which was quite willing to go along with the tax cuts, resisted spending cuts. The budget deficit ballooned, and the authorities were forced to jack up interest rates.

As the gulf widened between the real interest rates being paid in the U.S. and those being paid in Japan and West Germany, capital flooded in, the dollar shot higher, and exports to the U.S. surged. Without falling into the trap of "what-if history," without this explosion in external demand, Japan's tight money policies and the corresponding decline in domestic demand could very well have sent the country zigzagging down the road to recession and unemployment. In short, the key to the second miracle of the Japanese economy, the post-oil-crisis price stabilization, seemed to be Amercian policy—or, more ironically still, its failure.

4. SKYROCKETING ASSETS, DISSONANCE WITH THE REST OF THE WORLD

We still have two price issues to left to deal with: skyrocketing land and equity prices and their influence on prices in the real economy, and the difference between prices in Japan and those in other countries.

SKYROCKETING ASSET PRICES. When the prices of assets—land, equity, and the like—rise, rent increases are not long to follow. Many therefore worry that rising asset prices pose the threat of inflation, and some have even advocated that asset prices be incorporated into price indexes.

Akiyoshi Horiuchi, in his *Theory of Finance* (*Kin'yūron*), calls this an "issue of presentation" and provides an extremely enlightening analysis. He begins by asking the reader to analyze the following statement from a critical perspective: "Land on the east side of Shinjuku Station, in central Tokyo, is extremely expensive. Therefore, in reflection of those land prices, meals at restaurants in the area will have to be higher than elsewhere."

The price of assets is generally thought to be determined by two factors: the stream of expected income derived from the asset over the long term (in the case of land, rent) and the stream of expected interest rates on alternative assets. If we consider expected interest rates to be a given, then the price of land is determined by the stream of expected income from it. In the case of a restaurant, expected income (or "rent") is the net profit derived when the total costs are subtracted from its sales. Let us assume that the restaurant raised its prices higher than those of nearby competitors because it was situated on more expensive land. All that would happen is that its customers would migrate to other establishments and its sales would go down, eventually forcing the restaurant to go out of business or relocate elsewhere. In other words, if land does not produce a rent in line with its price, its price drops. It is the expected rent that determines the price of land, not the other way around. Land prices rise because the land can be put to more valuable uses: the expected rent rises, the tax laws change, or the return on alternative assets declines. As we saw in Chapter 3, for investors who only want to hold a piece of land for one year, the deciding factors are the rent that can be obtained by owning the land *and* the capital gains that can be expected at the end of the year. This can easily lead to speculation. The rises in Japanese land and equity prices in the latter half of the eighties were the product of easy money policies enacted in the fall of 1985 and held over until 1989. Easier money caused the price of land and equity to rise, and these rises produced expectations of further rises, which pushed prices even higher. This spiral, however, has since been shown to have been a bubble. When the authorities switched to a tight-money stance at the end of 1989, the stock market crashed and land prices began to fall.

THE GAP BETWEEN DOMESTIC AND FOREIGN PRICES.   With both wholesale and consumer prices stable, the public has turned its attention instead to comparing the "level" of those prices with those in other countries—the gap between domestic and foreign prices. Japanese price levels are high by international standards, which gives the country a higher per-capita GDP and national income than Britain, Germany, and even the United States, but no corresponding sense of prosperity or affluence.

Let us assume that it costs ¥200,000 a month to live in Japan, and that the same bundle of goods and services would cost $1,000 if purchased in the United States. Purchasing power parity (PPP) between the yen and the dollar (as shown by living expenses) would be ¥200,000 ÷ $1,000 or $1 = ¥200. If, however, the prevailing exchange rate (in yen) is ¥150 to the dollar, you could maintain the same standard of living in the United States for only ¥150,000, and Japanese living expenses are therefore 30% higher than American. Expressed mathematically, Japanese price levels are:

$$\frac{\text{(Purchasing power parity as measured by living expenses)}}{\text{(Exchange rate)}}.$$

In the example above, this works out to be 1.3.

If, as in the example above, Japanese living expenses truly are higher than those in other countries, then people in Japan will have no sense of affluence or prosperity even if the country's per-capita national income and GDP, as calculated by the nominal exchange rate, are high. The price differential, however, is caused by a gap between purchasing power parity as measured by living expenses and prevailing exchange rates. If the two were equal, there would be no price differential. The 1990 *Economic White Paper* says that in 1985, purchasing power parity for consumption expenditures was $1 = ¥218, whereas the exchange rate was $1 = ¥239. Japanese prices were therefore lower than American prices on the average. The price differential only became an issue afterwards, when the yen's value began to appreciate. Therefore, if the yen turns and begins to decline, interest in the price differential will quickly fade.

But even if that explains the general differences in prices as measured by living expenses, there are still price differentials for individual products (even after transportation costs are taken into account) to be dealt with. It is almost unavoidable that different countries will have different prices for goods and services that are not traded—for example, land. The problem comes when there are differences between countries in the price for goods and services that *are* traded.

If imports and exports were entirely free, then price arbitrage would quickly remedy any long-term price differentials for traded goods in excess of transportation costs and taxes. It follows, therefore, that if there are price differentials, then it is either because domestic prices are slow to adjust under the floating exchange-rate system or because the structure of the market limits competition and keeps prices that should be falling from actually doing so. If the differentials are long-term, then market structure probably plays some role, and the solution is to enact policies that will promote competition and thereby make for more elastic domestic price changes. That means liberalizing imports, allowing grey-market importers to operate freely, and jettisoning restrictive business practices and unneeded government regulations.

7
STRUCTURAL CHANGES IN THE ECONOMY

1. IMPACT OF THE OIL CRISES

During the high-growth period, the leading industries in Japan were those that were able to rely on mass-production technology to pursue economies of scale: steelmaking, petrochemicals, shipbuilding, industrial machinery manufacture, and so on. But rapid growth brought with it changes in the Japanese industrial structure. The higher energy prices that came out of the oil embargoes of the seventies served to further accelerate these changes in some sectors, and brought new changes as well. Industries like petrochemicals, shipbuilding, and steelmaking contracted, and in their place arose electronics. The changes Japan is experiencing go by several names. Some call them an orientation toward services (or, in Japanese, toward "software" as opposed to "hardware"), others an orientation to higher value-added sectors, and still others, the realization of the "post-industrial society." This process can be seen most clearly in the changes in the income and employment structures between the three industrial divisions delineated by Colin Clark.

Table 7-1 shows how the importance of primary industries (agriculture, forestry, fishing, etc.) in both the income structure and the employment structure declined all the way through the high-growth period. In 1960, primary industries produced 14.9% of all Japanese income; in 1985, 2.8%. Similarly, employment in primary industries went from 30.2% of the population to 8.8% over the same period of time.

By contrast, the share of tertiary industries rose from 48.3% of income and 41.8% of employment to 62.7% and 56.9%, respectively.

TABLE 7-1   Changes in Income and Employment Structures (%)

	1960	1970	1980	1985	USA 1985	W. Germany 1985
Income structure						
Primary	14.9	6.1	3.6	2.8	2.4	1.7
Secondary	36.3	41.8	37.6	34.4	28.0	42.8
Tertiary	48.3	52.1	58.8	62.7	69.6	55.5
Employment structure						
Primary	30.2	17.4	10.4	8.8	3.0	5.3
Secondary	28.0	35.2	34.8	34.3	26.9	41.0
Tertiary	41.8	47.3	54.6	56.9	70.2	53.7

Source: Bank of Japan, International Statistical Comparisons.

The story is more complex for secondary industries (primarily mining and manufacturing). They experienced strong gains until 1970–1972, and have since been flat or seen slight declines. Most industrialized countries see the share of primary industries decline as their economies grow, and Japan has been no exception in this regard. But it does stand out for the sharp structural changes that it experienced in the eighties and early nineties, and the speed with which the economy has reoriented toward services and higher-value-added sectors.

This is so even for secondary industries. In automaking, for example, the amount of "non-material input" (input required for improvements in performance, design, and marketing) is growing faster than the amount of "material input" (required, say, to produce the body). For our purposes, we will call the percentage of aggregate input accounted for by non-material input the "service orientation rate," or "softonomization ratio." In formula, this rate is

$$\frac{\text{Non-material input}}{\text{Non-material input} + \text{Material input}}.$$

Two things are happening in Japan: first, the service orientation rate ("softonomization") is growing; and second, industries with higher service orientation rates are accounting for a higher proportion of total industry.

At the same time, the economy is reorienting toward the production of higher value-added products. This we will measure with a "real value-added ratio" that shows the proportion of real value-added to the real total value of output:

$$\frac{\text{Real value-added}}{\text{Real total value of output}}$$

This ratio has also been increasing. (Note, however, that defined in these terms the service orientation rate and the real value-added ratio are extremely similar concepts.)

2. GREATER ORIENTATION TOWARDS SERVICES AND VALUE-ADDED

Just as an increase in incomes brings about a decline in the Engel coefficient for households, when an economy becomes more affluent, the share of primary industries declines and the share of tertiary industries rises. This is called Petty's Law, after Sir William Petty who formulated it in the seventeenth century.

Here again, Japan has experienced the same phenomenon as other industrialized countries. What sets it apart are the speed with which the share of tertiary industries has risen and the existence of a parallel trend toward services, high value-added, and knowledge-intensive sectors in other industries as well.

Three factors are commonly pointed to:

(1) *Changes in the demand structure*, of which the most striking are the changes in the consumption structure. Having achieved a level of material consumption in which the daily necessities are no longer lacking, people are moving away from material goods toward greater comfort and well-being. Likewise, people's tastes in objects are changing. The Japanese now emphasize quality over quantity, and their tastes are becoming more diverse and individualized. Between 1960 and 1970, the share of consumption expenditures going for services rose from 42.4% to 49.1%, and within service expenditures itself, a greater proportion of the money was spent on "discretionary" cultural and recreational services rather than "required" services.

Similar changes have occurred in industry. With consumers demanding wider choices and better products, and the NIEs of Asia catching up, Japanese industry has been forced to become more sophisticated. To survive, companies are employing advanced manufacturing technology to turn out high value-added, knowledge-intensive products. In line with this, investments in research, development, and computerization are commanding a larger share of the pie.

(2) *Changes in the employment structure.* Directly following the war, Japan experienced shortages in the absolute quantities of food available. Boosting the output of rice and other agricultural products therefore ranked alongside boosting production of coal and steel as one of the country's primary policy objectives. The development of chemical fertilizers and hydrid plant species helped make the land more productive, and this combined with the high-growth process to create a surplus of labor in agriculture and other primary industries. The surplus labor streamed into secondary and tertiary industries, but employment in secondary industries, too, began to stagnate in about 1975. Several factors contributed. Partly because the newly industrialized economies of Asia were catching up with Japan, 1) production stagnated in industries like shipbuilding and steelmaking, 2) sectors like electrical equipment and automobiles invested in labor-saving equipment to increase their productivity, and 3) the appreciation of the yen during the eighties caused exports to stagnate and imports to increase. The end result was that secondary industries did not need as many people as during the high-growth period of the sixties, and the only place left for this labor force to turn was tertiary industries. We should note, however, that the economic boom of the late eighties produced a general shortage of labor in Japan. Job growth among secondary industries was particularly sharp for knowledge-intensive sectors.

(3) *Technological advances.* During this period, high technology areas—particularly microelectronics—achieved remarkable progress. The technology developed by the heavy and chemical industries of the sixties sought to push economies of scale to their limits. These industries used mass-production to cut their costs, but doing so required them to invest huge sums of money in their facilities. They were dependent on technological progress embodied in capital, because it was only by investing enormous sums in facilities and equipment that technological progress had any effect.

By contrast, the technology used in high value-added areas is of necessity more wide-ranging and better able to respond to changing needs. In this regard, great advances have been achieved in microelectronics and new materials. Automobile assembly lines provided a good example. Even twenty years ago, auto assembly was not much different from Charlie Chaplin's depiction of it in *Modern Times*.

Down the conveyor belt came exactly the same parts to be connected to exactly the same cars, in exactly the same order. At first, automation merely changed who was doing the work; machines took over for people. But in order to make a different model car, you had to either use a different production line or use the same line at a different time. Things are different in today's plants. Robots are able to choose and install the right parts for the car in front of them, so the same assembly line can produce cars built for many different people and preferences. Advances in electronics have enabled robots to respond to a wider range of needs and wants, and the availability of that technology has caused people's preferences to become still more diverse. It is not only in microelectronics where this has happened. Advances in biotechnology have brought improvements to crops and pharmaceuticals and will probably spur the development of new industrial sectors that will take over from the huge chemical fertilizer plants of the past.

Finally, products have become more compact and software more sophisticated. Computers and word processors are the classic examples. Without these advances, it would not have been possible for the economy to become as service-oriented as it is today.

If we are to define one characteristic that distinguishes the technological advances of today's service-oriented economy from those of heavy-chemical-industrial economy of the high-growth period, it is that the latter consisted of technological advances embodied in capital and required enormous facilities, whereas the former consist of knowledge-intensive technological advances for which physical size is generally not an issue.

3. IMPACT OF STRUCTURAL CHANGES ON SOCIETY AND LABOR

These structural changes have had profound socioeconomic effects. Let us look at a few.

First, there has been some regional diversification. Semiconductor production does not require large factories or huge facilities. During the heavy-industrial period, the key words for products were "heavy," "thick," "long," and "big;" now they are "light," "thin," "short," and "small." As long as there is a supply of quality labor and a convenient airport, factories can be located anywhere, and there is little to be gained by concentrating them all in the same place. As a result, companies have moved their production out of the big cities and into areas like Kitakyushu (known as "the Silicon Valley of Japan"), Kumamoto, Nagano, Yamanashi, and Tohoku. This has however not been that strong a trend, and there are signs that industry is once again moving back to the cities, especially Tokyo. Factory siting will be something to keep an eye on in the future.

Second, big factories are becoming a thing of the past. Massive investments in facilities are not required for new technologies, and there is a growing risk that changing consumer preferences or technological advances may render large facilities obsolete overnight. With some exceptions such as electric power production, companies are avoiding giant investments.

One autumn in the late seventies, I went with a group to visit Manchester, after traveling through the Lakes District of England. We were startled by the abandoned old spinning mills we saw just outside the city. Spinning was what had led the British Empire to greatness, after all, and we were unprepared for the sight of its ruin. This is not, however, a uniquely English phenomenon. It is happening in Japan as well, most notably with mining, especially of coal. Other industries like textiles, and even steel and non-ferrous metals, are having to diversify their business and introduce advanced microelectronics, new materials, and biotechnology in an effort to move into higher value-added areas. The clearest indicator of this is the percentage of sales in the textile or non-ferrous metals industries that comes from non-core businesses. Even in precision machinery, non-core businesses bring in more than 60% of firms' sales. During the nineties, core businesses are expected to decline even more in importance. In fact, it has become evident now that the boom of the late eighties was, for these companies caught in the competition for survival, nothing more than a welcome respite from the fray.

The new strength of the service sector has had an even greater impact on the employment market.

Tertiary industries have traditionally employed a higher proportion of women and part-time workers than have the other sectors. Demand in service sectors tends to be seasonal or cyclical (it might all concentrate at the end of the month, for example), so it is to companies' advantage to use part-timers rather than full-timers. Thus, the service-orientation of the economy has undoubtedly brought more women and part-timers into the work force and reduced the average duration of employment. This has also helped to lower organization rates for labor unions. Granted, workers in such tertiary sectors as transportation, telecommunications, electric power and gas, and government have some of the highest organization rates in the economy, while those in areas like wholesaling, retailing, and services in the narrow sense have some of the lowest. However, it is in these low-organization areas that new jobs are being created. If anything, the high-organization areas are losing jobs.

There is said to be a correlation between union organization rates and wage growth rates. Wages generally grow faster in countries with high rates of organization than in countries with low rates. Similarly, there is a higher correlation between wage growth rates and corporate profitability indexes when unions are organized on a company-by-company basis than when they are organized on a skills basis. In the case of Japan, its organization rates are as low as those of the United States, and 99% of its unions are company-based. This is considered to be one of the reasons why Japan's Phillips curve is so close to vertical. Its money-wage growth rate is flexible. When business is good, wages grow faster; when it is down, they grow more slowly. If this trend can be strengthened by increasing the service-orientation of the economy, then the shift to services has given Japan more economic flexibility.

There is more at work than just this, however. Japan's natural unemployment rate is lower than that of other countries. From the mid-fifties to the mid-seventies, it stood steady at 1%. Some expect it to rise a bit in the future, citing three factors: 1) an increase in "fluid" unemployment among younger workers; 2) a mismatch in the supply and demand for labor as the population ages; and 3) an increasing desire on the part of women to enter the work force.

"Fluid unemployment among younger workers" refers to the trend among today's young people, who, thanks to economic growth, have been liberated from the threat of starvation, to change jobs in search of greater fulfillment and enjoyment and to have no compunctions about hunting until they find a job they are satisfied with. For their parents, this would have been dishonorable, and also difficult in practical terms to do.

Meanwhile, Japan's population is becoming longer-lived, and more of its senior citizens want to work; companies still prefer to hire younger workers, however. There is thus a difference between what the demand side wants and what the supply side can deliver.

Finally, it used to be that the number of female part-timers in the work force would increase during boom times and decline when business turned sour. Women, in fact, bore the brunt of the unemployment during slumps, and when slumps were prolonged, they would abandon the search for work and return to the home. Because of this, Japan used to see a decline in the number of people seeking jobs during slumps. Now, however, women have a greater desire to work, so fewer of them are leaving the work force.

The common perception is that Japanese women have only recently achieved high employment rates, but this is mistaken. In 1955, 56.7% of Japan's women held jobs, which was a far greater percentage than for other industrialized countries (and than for Japan today). As Figure 7-1 illustrates, what happened was that the number of people working in family enterprises (generally farms) underwent a rapid decline, which brought the female employment rate down to 45.7% in 1975. But while the agricultural sector contracted during the growth period of the sixties, the number of women employed in industry increased steadily. In 1975, the increase in the number of women employed outside the home finally outpaced the decline in that of women working in family enterprises, causing the female work-force participation rate to bottom out that year and begin to turn upward. By 1988, it had reached 48.9%.

Still, many of the women in the work force are part-timers, and, as always, their numbers tend to increase when business is good, while when business is bad they leave the work force entirely. Tadashi Yamada and Tetsuji Yamada (1985) provide an interesting, if now somewhat dated, analysis of this trend (see Table 7-2). In looking for variables that could explain participation rates for married women, they found that the wages earned by the male head of the household were just as important as those earned by the woman wage-earner, especially in the full-time participation rate. Furthermore, business conditions (for which the unemployment rate was used as a proxy) had a clear impact on part-time employment. When business slumped and the unemployment rate rose, part-timers lost their desire to work and withdrew from the work force. Finally, the availability of day-care centers has had a positive impact on both part-time and full-time employment. However, the impact of greater employment opportunities is a bit more troublesome. It is obvious that it should have a positive impact on the part-time participation rate, but why a negative impact on the full-time rate? The authors postulated

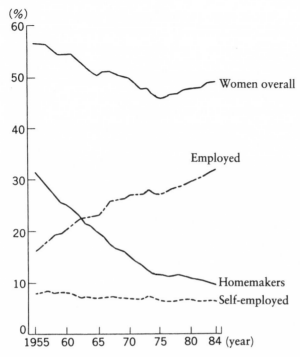

FIGURE 7-1 Percentage of Women in the Japanese Work Force
Source: Management and Coordination Agency, *Labor Survey.*

TABLE 7-2 Impact (Elasticity) of Different Variables on the Participation Rate of Women: Prefectural Cross-Section

Explanatory variable	Explained variable	Part-time participation rate	Full-time participation rate
Women's wages		0.65**	0.15***
Men's wages		−0.13*	−0.18***
Unemployment rate		−0.25***	−0.11
Employment opportunities		1.28*	−3.49***
Women's education		−0.40***	0.10
Day-care facilities		0.32**	0.80***

Note: *Significant at 10% level; **significant at 5% level; ***significant at 1% level.
Source: Tadashi Yamada and Tetsuji Yamada, NBER Working Paper No. 1608, April 1985.

that it may have been an anomaly that had something to do with the timing of the survey (1980).

Finally, let us look briefly at the impact of structural changes on macroeconomic performance.

At the top of the list is the decline in inventory fluctuations. The development of computer networks has combined with better transportation methods to reduce the need for end-users to carry inventory. This has helped rationalize inventory management throughout the economy. Service industries, by their very nature, do not require inventories at all. If you are providing a specific service on a specific date—say, transportation from Osaka to Tokyo on September 11 —you cannot hold that over until the next day (because transportation on September 12 is a different service from transportation on September 11). Inventories therefore play less of a role in service-oriented economies, and the impact of inventory fluctuation on economic activity is consequently smaller. Japan experienced many inventory cycles even after the first oil crisis, but since 1975 there has been a dramatic drop in inventory investments, and inventory accounts for a smaller proportion of final demand. (This does not mean that business inventory cycles never occur.)

Second, there is the impact of service-orientation on capital investments, though this impact is not necessarily clear. Personal consumption tends to fluctuate less than other areas of demand, so if investments induced by consumption account for a large share of total investments, this is generally thought to help stabilize the economy. But spending for discretionary services and durable consumer goods is more fluid, so if service-orientation brings about an increase in spending for this kind of consumption, investment levels will be more volatile. Another factor destabilizing capital investment rates is the accelerating pace of technological progress.

Third, it is common to say that service-orientation causes the economic growth rate to decline. During the high-growth phase, resources shifted from low-productivity primary industries to high-productivity secondary industries, which helped boost overall growth. Tertiary industries, however, tend to be low on productivity, so a shift of resources in that direction is thought to undermine the overall growth rate. Another drag on growth is thought to be the fact that recent technological progress does not require the enormous investments that progress in heavy and chemical industries did, which consequently lowers the capital investment rate and therefore the economic growth rate. In Japan's case, there has indeed been a sharp drop in the growth rate compared to the sixties, but the growth rate is still higher than that for other industrialized countries. The competition to bring new technologies to market is still fierce in the electronics and computer industries; there is still room for investments that bring greater productivity; better integration between industrial sectors is helping to improve productivity; and smaller companies, which have been slower to computerize than their larger competitors, still need to make technology-intensive, capital-intensive investments. The labor crunch that hit Japan in the late eighties forced firms to install more labor-saving equipment, and the prolonged period of easy credit made it possible for the country to sustain high investment rates, and consequently high growth rates. Whether or not growth rates will be able to stay this high, however, is entirely dependent on the pace of technological progress.

4. TRADE FRICTION: THE CHALLENGE ON THE HORIZON

American economists and officials often say that Japan's industrial structure is responsible for the trade imbalance, which in turn is responsible for economic friction. According to the American analysis, new macroeconomic policies and changes in the industrial structure will be required to alleviate this friction. We saw in Chapter 5 how, following the war, Japan encouraged exports and suppressed non-essential imports as a way to earn the hard currency needed for raw-material imports. This necessarily led to policies that protected exporters and import-substitution industries. At the time, Japanese trade consisted of exports of processed goods (principally textiles produced by the country's abundant labor supply) and imports of raw materials and capital-intensive machinery. In this, the Japan–U.S. trade structure was quite similar to the "Heckscher–Ohlin principle" which states that countries tend to export goods produced through intensive use of their relatively well endowed factors. During the rapid growth period, however, Japan actively introduced and improved new technologies, and in the process its exports changed from simple processed goods to heavy industrial products. Then, about the time of the oil crises, economic orientation switched in the direction of high value-added, and high-tech products became the leading exports. In U.S. and European markets, these Japanese products competed directly with domestic products and eventually replaced them. Trade friction was the result. The Heckscher–Ohlin principle does not do a very good job explaining these horizontal divisions and trading patterns between industrialized countries, which makes this issue one of intense interest for economists. Most today concede that as economies grow, the comparative advantages of different countries change.

Working from the idea of changing comparative advantages, we can conclude that Japan first specialized in industries requiring economies of scale (for example, steel, shipbuilding, and automobiles), where it attained comparative advantage, and then turned to knowledge-intensive industries where it again attained comparative advantage. But in uncertain markets, competition (which is prerequisite for the Heckscher–Ohlin principle) is, according to Stiglitz, not just a matter of simple price competition but one of price and quality competition. Thus, one explanation is that the U.S. concentrated on price competitiveness, whereas Japan was more interested in achieving a reputation for quality. This point certainly should not be ignored in looking at recent competitiveness in areas like semiconductors (Japanese chips are known for their consistent high quality and few defects). American criticisms, however, are that Japan's competitiveness is the product of a protectionist industrial policy.

The U.S. marshals three arguments to its cause: 1) Japanese policy emphasizes the interests of producers over those of consumers and tends to protect export industries. (2) Even though an antimonopoly law was passed after the war, many cartels have been declared legal; business practices and government directives tend to limit competition just as cartels would, and for all practical purposes there is little scope for free entrance to Japanese markets, which suppress competition between Japanese and foreign companies. (3) Corporate cross-shareholding arrangements have resulted in the development of industrial groups (*keiretsu*) that have much the same effect as cartels. To remedy the situation, American critics say that Japan should enforce its anti-monopoly provisions more thoroughly and exact more stringent punishments from offenders. Doing so, they claim, would create transparent markets.

In Chapter 1 we saw how Japan adopted many protectionist measures during the process of economic growth. Almost all of these measures, however, have been jettisoned today. Much of the American argument is therefore based on misunderstandings and miscon-

ceptions. But much is also right on target. The solution to the problem is to change from an export-driven, producer-oriented industrial
structure to a domestic-demand-driven, consumer-oriented one, and
to try to make markets as transparent as possible. But inasmuch as
the Japanese economy espouses free market principles rather than a
centrally planned economy, that transformation will have to come
through changes in *relative* prices such as are brought about by
changes in the exchange rate. Japanese political leaders often rather
naively state that they intend to "do all we can to improve the situation." This merely exacerbates trade friction and creates unnecessary
misunderstandings, since it gives people overseas the impression that
the transformation can be accomplished by government fiat.

8
PROBLEMS AND CHALLENGES FOR THE FUTURE

Japan was late to industrialize—the process only began in the 1870s—and in the process of catching up with the West, it built for itself a "development-oriented" economic system. Surrounded by industrialized and generally unfriendly powers, the country had no choice but to modernize quickly. It was therefore natural that what emerged was a government-driven market economy, even more so when it is remembered that the Meiji Restoration was led by lower-class samurai who by that time were the equivalent of lower-ranking bureaucrats. The government-driven system showed some signs of change during the brief period of "Taisho Democracy," but after the depression of the early Showa years, Japan switched to a war footing, and its economy remained under strict control until its defeat in 1945.

The Occupation forces tried to democratize the country, and succeeded in effecting great changes in Japan's socioeconomic makeup (see Chapter 1 for a fuller discussion). But with the onset of the Cold War and U.S.–Soviet hostilities, the emphasis of Occupation policies changed from democratizing Japan to transforming it into a key member of the Western alliance. As this happened, the Japanese people began pulling together to rebuild their country from the ashes of defeat. The development-orientation of the past was thus carried over into this century, and what emerged was a market economy that, unlike those of the United States or Britain, was led by bureaucrats in the broad sense of the term—elite corporate and economic leaders as well as government officials.

The American model would have the government authorities set up rules to be followed by individual economic units and step in with fines, criminal punishments, or orders to cease business should the rules be violated. Everything else, however, is up to the free will of the individual, and each takes responsibility for the consequences. The antimonopoly laws and Fair Trade Commission introduced by the Occupation are classic examples of the Anglo-American version of markets.

The Occupation ordered Japan to set up a committee to oversee its securities markets, too. This committee was originally modeled on the U.S. Securities and Exchange Commission (SEC) and, like the Fair Trade Commission, was independent of the administrative authorities. The body no longer exists today. It was absorbed by the Ministry of Finance as part of the revisions to the Securities and Exchange Law that were passed in 1952, after the peace treaty formally ending the war had been signed. Undoubtedly, the development-oriented thinking of the time held that it would be easier to assist in the sound development of the securities markets if administration and supervision were carried out by the same organization. Similar things happened with many of the other administrative committees set up by the Occupation. Only a few, like the Fair Trade Commission, are still functioning today. And until very recently, even the Fair Trade Commission was routinely criticized by business leaders and the Ministry of International Trade and Industry as being "unsuited to Japan."

This development-oriented (or "goal-oriented") economic system emerged out of a process of trial and error that began in the Meiji era, but it saw fundamental changes during the rapid growth of the sixties and early seventies. These changes in the economic base caused corresponding changes in how people in Japan thought and acted. Growth freed people from the threat of starvation, and as the Japanese began to enjoy their new-found prosperity, their values and tastes broadened. Mass production was no longer enough. Rather than cheap, standardized goods, people began to demand more individualized products and to place a higher premium on comfort and enjoyment (see Chapter 6). With a greater range of values to take into account, it became harder and harder to forge the broad consensus on goals that had allowed the traditional development-oriented system to be so effective. That undermined efficiency and set the stage for something new.

The answer has been to move to a more American-style system that gives priority to market efficiency above all else. Recent waves of deregulation represent the first steps toward this transformation. Japan is trying to abandon the bureaucrat-led system of "administrative guidance" that has underpinned its economy, but it will not happen overnight. The old system, after all, took decades to build and will take time to dismantle.

The development of the Japanese economy may have been aided by the qualities and efforts of the Japanese people, but it owes much to the favorable environment of the postwar world, and more than a little to luck. Japan's high-growth period corresponded to a worldwide boom, a time of unprecedented growth in the global economy and expansion in world trade. That is why Japan was able to invest in new technologies from overseas, import cheap raw materials, and export *quality* products at reasonable prices—and that ability was what powered the country's economic development. We should remember that, as we saw in Chapter 2, the source of much of this competitiveness—the reason Japanese products were able to beat out those from the U.S. or Britain—was the relatively young vintage of Japan's capital.

The seventies saw the United States's absolute position in the world economy undermined by growth in Japan and West Germany and by war in Vietnam. This in turn posed a threat to the foundations of the Bretton Woods system and prompted most countries to float their currencies (1973). Right around the same time, the world was hit with two sharp hikes in the price of oil that threatened the economies of non-oil-producing countries. This was a direct blow to Japan, which was dependent on imports for virtually all of its oil, and it took the country almost a decade to recover.

Floating rates are, by nature, a nationalistic economic system, and as such in conflict with the idea of economic internationalism. The "adjustable peg" of the Bretton Woods system came out of the world's experiences with floating rates during the interwar period. It was an attempt to hold on to the advantages of fixed rates while eliminating their faults. Together with the General Agreement on Tariffs and Trade (GATT), Bretton Woods provided an international economic order that was founded on the idea of free trade between nations. Together, they helped eliminate nationalism and trading blocs. The reason Bretton Woods failed was that it was, in the end, a system based on the U.S. dollar, and the U.S. (to finance its war in Vietnam) was printing too many dollars. The markets lost confidence in the currency and began to speculate against it.

There is much good to be said about the floating rate system. For instance, it is very adept at sealing itself off from external shocks. But it has at least three major faults: 1) it magnifies uncertainty, and therefore is a hindrance to economic development; 2) it makes prices more volatile; and 3) it caters to destructive speculation. Efforts to counter these problems and provide for more stable economic growth lead to a fourth problem: the emergence of blocs. For example, the EC made what it called a *"joint float"* in 1973. European currencies joined the floating-rate system *en masse* with the exchange rates between them more or less set. This pushed Europe closer to becoming a "common-currency bloc" designed to give it the economic strength necessary to compete with Japan and the United States. Granted, the EC is not the same as the prewar trading blocs in that it has not used tariffs to close itself off to the outside world, but the danger that it will do so is always there. One way to remove these dangers would be to create a new system to take over for the failed dollar-based Bretton Woods system—say, a system based on special drawing rights (SDRs). But that will not happen overnight. The next best would be to try to minimize the inconsistencies of the floating-rate system by supporting GATT and encouraging greater international policy coordination. Countries all over the world have a duty to do at least that much, especially Japan, which is one of the chief beneficiaries of free, multilateral trade.

While the West was searching for stability through international coordination, the East (principally the Soviet bloc), which had grown so robustly after the war, saw its economies stagnate in the late seventies. Once a real threat to the West, Eastern Europe faced the need for reforms if it wanted to break out of the slump.[1] The two main problems with the economies of Eastern Europe were that they had sacrificed consumption in order to make wasteful investments and that the weaknesses of bureaucrat-run command economies (bloating, inefficiency, corruption) could no longer be ignored. Reform was the only answer. Governments tried, to a limited extent, to give producers some incentives by making them responsible for their own profits and losses, and reducing the amount of government interference they were subject to. But, owing in part to resistance

---

[1] Table 8-1 illustrates two points: first, that Japanese growth corresponds to the postwar economic boom; and second, that until about 1975, the Soviet Union and Eastern Europe were growing at rates high enough that they were indeed a threat to the West.

TABLE 8-1   Real GDP Growth Rates Worldwide

	1965/ 1960	1970/ 1965	1975/ 1970	1980/ 1975	1985/ 1980
Soviet Union	3.6	6.5	3.6	2.3	2.1
Poland	4.5	4.1	6.5	0.7	0.7
Hungary	3.9	3.1	3.3	2.0	1.0
Yugoslavia	6.8	5.7	4.5	5.7	1.2
E. Germany	2.9	3.3	3.5	2.3	1.8
U.S.A.	4.6	3.0	2.1	3.3	2.7
Japan	10.5	11.0	4.3	5.0	3.9
World Total	4.9	4.5	2.8	3.4	2.5
OECD	5.2	4.5	2.8	3.4	2.5

Note: Dollar-based 1985 prices used.
Source: Japan Economic Research Center, *World Economy at a Turning Point*, 1991.

from the entrenched governing class (as represented by the Communist Party), these reforms were less than fully successful. When Mikhail Gorbachev came to power in the Soviet Union, he embarked on the strategy of *perestroika* to try to overcome the crisis; but by providing for freedom of speech and information, he provided Eastern Europe with the opportunity to jettison communism altogether, and sparked democratic movements and criticism of the party within the Soviet Union. In virtually every socialist country except China, socialism died, and for the most part there was no system waiting to take its place.

This marked the failure of the "grand experiment" in Soviet-style socialism that Lenin had begun; it demonstrated the superiority of market economies over command economies. Whatever its faults, the market system, with its incentive mechanisms, has proven itself a better way to organize economies than systems of centralized planning.

The world was unprepared either politically or economically for the rapid disintegration of Cold War structures. Conflict between the United States and the Soviet Union was the basis on which the world had been running, and it ended more quickly than anyone had expected. Into this turmoil came the Gulf War, a test case that illustrated the limits of Soviet power, accelerated the final demise of Cold War institutions, and made it clear that the United States was the new hegemon—albeit one with limited economic power.

The world is now choosing the direction it will take in the next century. The choice it makes will be as important for Japan as for anyone else.

In his book *Economic History* (*Keizai-roku*), Shundai Dazai, a follower of Sorai Ogyu,[2] says: "There are four things that those who wish to discuss economics should know: first, know times; second, know reason; third, know forces; and fourth, know human nature." (The commentator Eiichi Tanizawa notes that by "times" Dazai is referring to the turning points between periods and epochs; by "forces" he is talking about the unexpected—it is not enough just to know facts and reason, you must have an instinctive ability to understand the currents of the times as well; and by "human nature" he is referring to what actually happens, what people actually do.[3]) Those who discuss the Japanese economy should take Dazai's advice to heart. Whatever benefits hindsight may give, it is no easy task to spot the turning points when you are caught up in the process.

I have long been impressed by an editorial written by Tanzan Ishibashi[4] in in the August 25, 1945, issue of *Toyo Keizai*, right after Japan's defeat. Most of the population was stunned and distraught. But Ishibashi promised that if the country were to concentrate on peace and science, "there is a future of boundless plenty ahead for a renewed Japan." He followed up on this theme in the September 1 issue, writing, "As I wrote in the [last] issue, there is boundless hope for the renewed Japan. Of this there can be no doubt. When I try to envision the way in which we will proceed, it is not full of obstacles. Rather, before my eyes I see a broad and level path. All that we need is for the people of Japan to be prepared not to close their minds, not to be willfully led astray by obstacles because they fail to see the broad path before them."

The order that had been supported by the Cold War has now come crashing down, giving rise to an outpouring of racialism from the Soviet Union, Eastern Europe, the Balkans, and on to the Middle East. We had assumed racialism to be a thing of the past, but in

[2] Ogyu (1666–1728) was an influential exponent of Japanese Confucianism and founder of the Sorai school.
[3] *One Hundred Sayings, One Hundred Tales* (*Hyakugon Hyakuwa*) (Chuko Shincho, 1985).
[4] Ishibashi (1884–1973) was an influential journalist, economist, and politician who served as finance minister and minister of international trade and industry in the early postwar years before becoming prime minister in 1956.

reality it had only been held in check by superpower hostilities. Meanwhile, neither the United Nations nor the United States has been able to function as in the past. In this kind of environment, it is almost impossible to draw a picture of what awaits the world. It will be particularly hard for the leaders of Japan to understand their situation and make the correct choices. Up until now, the only interest of the Japanese government and the intelligentsia has been in maintaining good relations with the United States. Not only do they lack a proper understanding of the reality of the Cold War structures, they do not even realize that those structures are something they need to understand. But Japan was not mistaken when after the war it chose to seek a position of respect for itself as a pacifist nation. Now that it has the world's respect, it must make commensurate contributions. In economic terms, that means providing more global public goods. Only by doing so will Japan be able to keep the honor that it has worked so hard to achieve.

AFTERWORD: THE "BUBBLE" AND ITS AFTERMATH

To understand the Japanese economy as it now stands, it will be necessary to go back and review the formation of the "bubble" that began to form in 1985 and its subsequent collapse, even at the risk of a bit of repetition. In Chapter 6 we saw how the yen's exchange value rose sharply after the Plaza Accord of 1985. This was a shock to the Japanese economy, which up until then had experienced steady, export-driven expansion. The result was the "high-yen slump." The government reacted with a series of cuts in the official discount rate beginning in 1986, bringing it down to a postwar low of 2.5% by February 1987. Combining with this were economic measures—mostly public works projects—that had been enacted in October 1985 and were designed to expand the country's domestic demand.

Japan overcame the high-yen slump in short order and went on to post solid growth. The real growth rate for capital investments between 1987 and 1989 was reminiscent of the high-growth sixties (Table 1-13). Price levels, however, were stable at both the wholesale and consumer levels thanks to the rising exchange rate and falling prices for oil and other raw materials. As the economy geared up, the full unemployment rate went from 2.6% in 1986 to 2.1% in 1990; the ratio of job offers to applicants from 0.65 in 1985 to 1.4 in 1990. As the labor crunch grew more serious, wages began to rise more quickly.

Figure A-1 illustrates how the easy money policies adopted in 1986 pushed share prices higher. By 1987, Japanese stocks were already trading at prices well above their theoretical value. Likewise, land

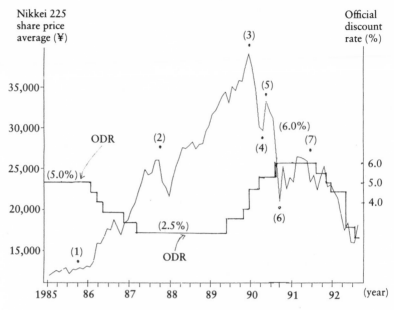

FIGURE A-1   The Nikkei 225 and the ODR
Notes: (1) Plaza Accord (closing price September 24: ¥12,755)
         (2) Black Monday (closing price October 19: ¥15,746)
                    (closing price October 29: ¥21,710)
         (3) 1989 closing price: ¥38,915
         (4) April 2, 1990: ¥28,002
         (5) June 7, 1990: ¥33,192
         (6) October 1, 1990: ¥22,211
         (7) June 1991 (end of May closing price): ¥25,789

prices, especially in the Tokyo area, surged sharply upward. In February 1987, the joint communiqué known as the Louvre Accord called on the Group of Seven countries (with the exception of Italy) to maintain their exchange rates "around current levels." If this was not enough to stay the hand of Japanese monetary authorities, the "Black Monday" stock market crash of October 20 was. The crash began on the New York market, but it was feared that any tightening of Japanese monetary policies might trigger a global recession. Japanese authorities were forced to leave matters alone, despite the fact that asset (share and land) prices were soaring and the money supply was posting double-digit growth. Though Japanese share prices crashed on Black Monday just like share prices everywhere, it only took six moths for them to regain their pre-crash levels. By the end of 1989, the Nikkei share price index stood at 38,900, compared to 12,750 in September 1985, immediately before the Plaza Accord.

The course of land prices is slightly different from shares because of regional gaps. Commercial land prices in the Tokyo area began to rise around 1985 or 1986; those rises eventually spread to residential land in the city as well, but did not reach Osaka or Nagoya until 1988 or 1989. Moreover, the 1985–1986 rises in Tokyo commercial districts were somewhat justified by the rising demand for office space as more and more of Japan's economic activity concentrated in the capital. By 1988 or 1989, land price growth had begun to slow. And as the Tokyo market peaked, Osaka and Nagoya emerged as replacements.

We have examined how asset prices are set; they tend to be equal to the discounted present value of the flow of revenues that can be expected from ownership. For shares, this means that they are equal to the discounted present value of expected dividends, or, over the short term:

Share price = Expected dividend + (Expected) Share price at end of
term / 1 + Interest rate + Risk premium.

In other words, asset prices depend on the income streams from expected interest rates and expected dividends (or rents or other expected revenues) or on this term's dividends, expected prices at the end of the term, current interest rates, and the risk premium. The hardest part is how to set the risk premium. Generally, the premium charged when economic conditions are stable and market participants expect relatively calm share price fluctuations is considered the "normal premium" and from this is extrapolated a "theoretical" or "fundamental" price.

From this point of view, the bull market that took off in early 1988 was indeed spectacular, but the gap between prevailing prices and theoretical or fundamental prices was still within acceptable limits. Afterwards, however, prices rose so far as to alarm market participants. A "bubble" had formed.

A similar trend was seen in land prices. The rise in commercial Tokyo land prices that peaked in early 1988 may have been justified by an increase in demand, but that was not the case for residential Tokyo, nor for Osaka or Nagoya. There, the rises were part of a speculative bubble in which actual demand played very little part.

In 1989, the Bank of Japan raised the official discount rate for the first time in two years and three months, and the authorities put a cap on the amount of money banks could lend against real estate. The bubble soon burst. Prices plummeted for virtually all assets—shares, land, even golf club memberships.

HOW THE BUBBLE FORMED

There were four direct causes of the bubble.

First is the fact that the easy-money policies adopted to combat the high-yen slump were kept in place for well over two years in the name of "international coordination." When prices remained stable in spite of the low interest rates, people grew overly optimistic about the economy. Low interest rates meant that both interest costs and risk premiums were lower, so share prices rose.

Second, there were changes in the economic behavior of industrial corporations and financial institutions. Optimism about the future convinced firms in both sectors to invest. For industrial concerns, this meant higher capital investment; for institutional investors and financial institutions, it meant a reduction in what Keynes called "lender's risk," which became a spur to further loans and equity shares. Larger companies began to raise funds directly from the capital markets, which forced banks to turn to nonbank lenders, who dealt mostly with smaller businesses and real estate ventures, as the principal borrowers of their funds. The non-banks, in fact, served as the chief conduit by which cash-rich banks became active real estate lenders.

Third, the experts, who should have been encouraging investors to take long-term positions and promote sound price formation, began to engage in short-term trading, which sent prices soaring far beyond what the fundamentals justified. Japanese securities markets have always had a strong short-term streak to them, but that became even more pronounced during the late eighties.

Finally, there was the fast-paced deregulation of the Japanese finance industry designed to bring it into line with worldwide trends toward the internationalization, globalization, and securitization of financial products, and the diversification of financial services (see Chapter 2 for details). But while regulations governing interest rates, fees, and areas of business were all in the process of being changed or scrapped, financial institutions (including securities companies) were still closely protected thanks to permit requirements that all but barred new entries. They became lax in their screening and examination of lending and underwriting proposals. In fact, they became overly aggressive in their efforts to place loans, and rather cavalier in their underwriting. A vicious circle ensued: easy lending caused the prices for land and shares to rise, which increased their collateral value, which convinced institutions to loan even more money against the "new" collateral. After the bubble ruptured, several banks became embroiled in scandal and it was learned that securities houses routinely made up losses to their larger investors. These, however, were just the extreme manifestation of the lax screening processes that had taken hold in financial institutions grown used to fixed fees and government protection.

THE CURRENT SLUMP

In early 1990, share prices crashed, bursting the speculative bubble in their wake. At first, most thought that the impact would be fairly light. But following the preventive hike in the discount rate to 6% at the time of the Gulf War, another crash occurred in October 1990, and share prices were still sliding downward in July 1991 after repeated rate cuts. Meanwhile, land prices were dropping in the Kansai (Osaka) area, and for all practical purposes there were no buyers in the markets. The effects were beginning to be seen in the real economy as well. Private-sector capital investment, which rose 12.1% during fiscal 1990, declined 3.0% in 1991 and another 2.2% in 1992. The real GNP growth rate also slowed, and as of this writing no one expected the 1993 government target of 3.0% to be met.

One school of thought maintains that this is just a normal downward phase in the business cycle. But while the underlying causes for the inventory and capital stock adjustments are the same, they will require more time than usual because of the extreme length (over two years) of the boom.

Another theory is that this is a "compound recession." Unlike normal downturns, this one is fueled by a combination of several factors: the bubble caused by the financial deregulation that began in the mid-eighties; the correction of that bubble; and the effects of the bubble's rupture on the real economy. The main proponent of this idea is Professor Yoshikazu Miyazaki, though the term "compound recession" is commonly used in Japanese economic circles in spite of the fact that it has never been clearly defined. It is worth noting, however, that the compound recession school maintains only that finance became far removed from the real economy and took on a self-propogating life of its own, not that the slump was caused by the compounding of real and financial factors.

There are yet others who say that this slump is different from those of the past because it occurred while the economy was in a period of structural transition.

Indeed, this downturn is structurally different from the normal cyclical downturn. After the authorities switched from tight to easy money policies, one would have expected consumer demand to rise, which would have prevented further declines and sparked a recovery in business conditions. But it has not happened. Consumer demand has been weak. Industries like automobiles and electrical machinery, which in the past had been the driving forces behind recovery, find demand for their products sluggish and are being forced to restructure. Meanwhile, no other industry has emerged to replace them. These factors alone set the current downturn apart. Added to this are the mistakes made by corporate managers who, lured by rosy pictures of ever-rising profits, failed to make the rationalizations they should have in order to prepare for the structural shifts that were coming. Instead, they opted for ill-advised investments in higher capacity. The people who lent them the money for this are also to be blamed, since they underestimated the risk of default and engaged in overly aggressive lending practices. But behind all of this lies the unique nature of competition between Japan's regulated and well-protected companies and institutions. The problem is one of "hothouse competition."

As is well known, the rupture of the bubble brought about a "negative asset effect." In the "asset effect," higher asset values spur greater consumer spending. Now, however, declines in the real value of assets are dampening consumer spending. More importantly, the collapse of the bubble has increased the "lender's risk" Keynes talks about in his *General Theory*. According to Keynes, when investments are made with borrowed money, lenders are exposed to risks above and beyond those that inevitably come with investment. Keynes called the latter "borrower's risk" and the former "lender's risk." Lender's risk is the lender's subjective evaluation of the chances that the borrower will default. When the economy is good, lender's risk declines, so there is little point in making the distinction between the two, but when the economy slumps, lenders perceive a greater chance that borrowers will default. Thus, even if borrower's risk remains unchanged, the increase in lender's risk impedes the smooth flow of finance.

Two important cushions protecting financial institutions from bad debts are collateral and owned capital. The slump has wiped away much of both. Not only has the crash brought prices down for the shares and land used to collateralize loans, it has also erased many of the unrealized gains on their stock portfolios that make up a large part of the capital claimed by Japanese institutions and corporations. As lender's risk increases, therefore, institutions are more cautious about making loans, and securities companies are more wary about underwriting new issues, even assuming the capacity to do so. These "prudential policies" are natural and desirable for individual institutions, but not for the economy as a whole, since the "fallacy of composition" could very well spur a contraction in economic activity. This is what is known as a "credit crunch," and it is generally considered to have been one of the principal factors aggravating the American depression of the thirties.

When it lowered the official discount rate to 2.5% at the beginning of 1993, the Bank of Japan was probably hoping to stave off a contraction in financial and economic activity. But if one considers structural changes responsible for at least part of the current slump, it will probably still take longer than normal to recover. At the same time, the policies adopted now will have a marked influence on the shape of the Japanese economy in the future.

Some of the policies the fiscal and monetary authorities have turned to in their quest to avoid a crisis of confidence in the credit system are troubling in their own right, since they seem to foretell a return to Japan's traditional bureaucrat-led economics. Examples include the attempts to forestall a stock market crash by telling investors not to sell and excessive interference in the scope of business allocated to the subsidiaries that financial institutions will now be allowed to establish under the Financial Reform Act. While measures of this sort may ostensibly preserve stability, let there be no mistake—the resulting search for loopholes and decline in attractiveness mean reduced international standing for Japanese markets in the future.

BIBLIOGRAPHY

Note: This bibliography is a selective list concentrating on book-length publications, not a comprehensive list of information sources.

A. Works about the Japanese economy in general

Kanamori Hisao. *New Dimensions in the Japanese Economy (Nihon Keizai no Shinjigen).* Nihon Keizai Shimbunsha, 1972. (in Japanese)

Komiya Ryutaro. *Modern Japanese Economic Studies (Gendai Nihon Keizai Kenkyu).* University of Tokyo Press, 1975. (in Japanese)

———. *The Modern Japanese Economy (Gendai Nihon Keizai).* University of Tokyo Press, 1988. (in Japanese)

Kosai Yutaka. *The Era of High-Speed Growth (Kodoseicho no Jidai).* University of Tokyo Press, 1986. (English translation of original Japanese published by Nihon Hyoronsha, 1983)

——— and Ogino Yoshitaro. *The Contemporary Japanese Economy (Nihon Keizai Tenbo).* Macmillan, 1984. (English translation of original Japanese published by Nihon Hyoronsha, 1980)

Kurosaka Yoshihisa and Hamada Koichi. *Macroeconomics and the Japanese Economy (Makuro Keizaigaku to Nihon Keizai).* Nihon Hyoronsha, 1984. (in Japanese)

Minami Ryoshin. *Turning Points in the Japanese Economy (Nihon Keizai no Tenkanten).* Sobunsha, 1970. (in Japanese)

Moriguchi Chikashi. *Theory of the Japanese Economy (Nihon Keizairon).* Sobunsha, 1988. (in Japanese)

Nakamura Takafusa. *The Postwar Japanese Economy: Its Development and Structure (Nihon Keizai: Sono Seicho to Kozo).* University of Tokyo Press, 1981. (English translation of original Japanese published by University of Tokyo Press, 2nd ed., 1980)

———. *Showa Economic History (Showa Keizaishi).* Iwanami Seminar Books, 1986. (in Japanese)

Patrick, Hugh, and Henry Rosovsky (eds.). *Asia's New Giant: How the Japanese Economy Works.* Brookings Institution, 1976.

Shinohara Miyohei. *Growth and Cycles in the Japanese Economy* (*Nihon Keizai no Seicho to Junkan*). Sobunsha, 1961. (in Japanese; portions of this volume were published in English in *Industrial Growth, Trade, and Dynamic Patterns in the Japanese Economy*, University of Tokyo Press, 1982)

Ueno Hiroya. *Competition and Regulation: Modern Industrial Organizations* (*Kyoso to Kisei: Gendai no Sangyo Soshiki*). Toyo Keizai Shimposha, 1987. (in Japanese)

Yoshitomi Masaru. *The Japanese Economy and New Crises in the World Economy* (*Nihon Keizai: Sekai Keizai no Aratana Kiki to Nihon*). Toyo Keizai Shimposha, 1981. (in Japanese)

Additional sources include the annual Economic White Paper published by the Economic Planning Agency, the EPA's *Current Status of the Japanese Economy* (*Nihon Keizai no Genkyo*), and the Bank of Japan's Comparative International Statistics.

B. Works on specific aspects of the Japanese economy
Modern economics and historical analysis

Blaug, Mark. *Economic Theory in Retrospect*. Cambridge University Press, 1978. Especially the Introduction and Chapter 16, "A Methodological Postscript."

Caldwell, Bruce J. "Clarifying." *Journal of Economic Literature*, 1991: 1–33.

Machlup, Fritz. *Methodology of Economics and Other Social Sciences*. Academic Press, 1978.

Popper, Karl. *The Poverty of Historicism*. Allen & Unwin, 1957.

———. *The Logic of Scientific Discovery*. Harper & Row, 1959.

Growth theory

Bruno, Michael, and Jeffrey Sachs. *Economics of World Stagflation*. Harvard University Press, 1985.

Corden, W. Max. *Inflation, Exchange Rates and the World Economy* (3rd ed.). University of Chicago Press, 1986.

Domar, Evsey D. *Essays in the Theory of Economic Growth*. Greenwood Press, 1982 (reprint of 1957 edition).

Dornbush, Rudiger, and Stanley Fischer. *Macroeconomics* (3rd ed.) McGraw-Hill, 1984.

Harrod, Roy F. *Towards a Dynamic Economics*. Greenwood Press, 1980 (reprint of 1948 edition).

Hicks, John R. *The Crisis in Keynesian Economics*. Basil Blackwell, 1974.

Sato Ryuzo. *Theory of Economic Growth*. (*Keizai Seicho no Riron*). Keiso Shobo, 1968. (in Japanese)

Solow, Robert M. "A Contribution to the Theory of Economic Growth." *Quarterly Journal of Economics*, Vol. 56, 1970.

———. Investment and Technical Progress." In Kenneth J. Arrow et al., eds., *Mathematical Methods in the Social Sciences*, 1960.

Economic growth and economic policy

Friedman, Milton. *The Optimum Quantity of Money and Other Essays.* Aldine, 1969.

Ito Motoshige, Kiyono Masaharu, Okuno Masahiro, and Suzumura Kotaro. *Economic Analysis of Industrial Policy (Sangyo Seisaku no Keizai Bunseki).* University of Tokyo Press, 1988. (in Japanese)

Johnson, Chalmers. *MITI and the Japanese Miracle: The Growth of Industrial Policy 1925–75.* Stanford University Press, 1982.

Komiya Ryutaro, Okuno Masahiro, and Suzumura Kotaro, eds. *Industrial Policy of Japan (Nihon no Sangyo Seisaku).* Academic Press, 1988. (English translation of book published by University of Tokyo Press in Japanese in 1982)

Lucas, Robert. "Econometric Policy Evaluation: A Critique," in Brunner and Meltzer, *The Phillips Curve and the Labor Market.* Carnegie-Rochester Conference Series, 1976.

Nambu Tsuruhiko. "The Utility of Industrial Policy" (*Sangyo Seisaku no Yukosei*), in H. Uzawa, ed., *The Japanese Economy: The Process of Accumulation and Growth (Nihon Keizai: Chikuseki to Seicho no Kiseki).* University Tokyo Press, 1989. (in Japanese)

Samuelson, Paul A. *Economics,* 11th ed. McGraw-Hill, 1980.

Tachi Ryuichiro. "Fiscal and Monetary Policy," (*Zaisei Kin'yu Seisaku*). In R. Komiya, ed., *Economic Growth in Postwar Japan (Sengo Nihon no Keizai Seicho).* Iwanami Shoten, 1963.

Tachi Ryuichiro and Komiya Ryutaro. *The Theory of Economic Policy (Keizai Seisaku no Riron).* Iwanami Shoten, 1963. (in Japanese)

Tobin, James. *Asset Accumulation and Economic Activity.* Basil Blackwell, 1980. (in Japanese)

U.S. Department of Commerce. *Japan: The Government-Business Relationship,* 1972.

Finance

Bank of Japan. *The Bank of Japan: Centennial History (Nikon Ginko Hyakunenshi).* 1982–86. (in Japanese)

Gurley, John G., and E. S. Shaw. *Money in a Theory of Finance.* Brookings Institution, 1960.

Horie Yasuhiro. "Asset Values and the Japanese Economy" (*Shisan Kakaku to Nihon Keizai*), *Kin'yu Kenkyu* (Journal of Finance), Vol. 9, No. 1, 1990.

Horiuchi Akiyoshi. *Japanese Financial Policy (Nihon no Kin'yu Seisaku).* Toyo Keizai Shimposha, 1980. (in Japanese)

———. *The Theory of Finance (Kin'yuron).* University of Tokyo Press, 1990. (in Japanese)

——— and Sakurai Kojiro. "The Opening of Financial and Capital Markets" (*Kin'yu Shihon Shijo no Tenkai*), in H. Uzawa, ed., *The Japanese Economy: The Process of Accumulation and Growth (Nihon Keizai: Chikuseki to Seicho no Kiseki).* University of Tokyo Press, 1989. (in Japanese)

Ikeo Kazuhito. *Japanese Financial Markets and Organizations: The Mi-*

croeconomics of Finance (Nihon no Kin'yu Shijo to Soshiki: Kin'yu no Mikuro Keizaigaku). Toyo Keizai Shimposha, 1985. (in Japanese)
Kin'yu Seido Chosakai (Committee on Financial System Research). Recommendations for a System of Specialized Financial Institutions (Senmon Kin'yu Kikan Seido no Arikata ni Tsuite), 1987. (in Japanese)
——. Recommendations for a New Financial System (Atarashii Kin'yu Seido no Arikata), 1991. (in Japanese)
Kure Bunji. Finance Reader (Kin'yu Tokuhon), 17th ed. Toyo Keizai Shimposha, 1988. (in Japanese)
Monetary Policy Research Institute, Bank of Japan. The Japanese Financial System (Wagakuni no Kin'yu Seido) (rev. ed.), 1986. (in Japanese)
Royama Shoichi. The Financial System of Japan (Nihon no Kin'yu Shisutemu). Toyo Keizai Shimposha, 1982. (in Japanese)
Shimura Kaichi. History of Japanese Bond Markets (Nihon Koshasai Shijoshi). University of Tokyo Press, 1980. (in Japanese)
Sudo Megumi. The Japanese Securities Industry: Organization and Competition (Nihon no Shokengyo: Soshiki to Kyoso). Toyo Keizai Shimposha, 1987. (in Japanese)
Suzuki Yoshio. Japanese Economics and Finance: Transformations and Adaptations (Nihon Keizai to Kin'yu: Sono Tenkan to Tekio). Toyo Keizai Shimposha, 1981. (in Japanese)
Tachi Ryuichiro. Theory of Financial Policy (Kin'yu Seisaku no Riron). University of Tokyo Press, 1982. (in Japanese)
——. Perspectives on Financial Realignment (Kin'yu Saihensei no Shiten). Toyo Keizai Shimposha, 1985. (in Japanese)
—— and Komiya Ryutaro. "What To Do about Japanese Financial Policy." Keizai Hyoron, supplement to April 1990 issue. (in Japanese)
—— and Royama Masaichi. Japanese Finance (Nihon no Kin'yu). Vols. I and II. University of Tokyo Press, 1987. (in Japanese)
Tsutsui Yoshihiro. Financial Markets and the Banking Industry: Economic Analysis of Industrial Organizations (Kin'yu Shijo to Ginkogyo: Sangyo Soshiki no Keizai Bunseki). Toyo Keizai Shimposha, 1988. (in Japanese)

Public finance
Ihori.Toshihiro. Japan's Fiscal Deficit Structure: Mid- and Long-term Empirical Analysis (Nihon no Zaisei Akaji Kozo: Chuchoki no Jissho Kihan Bunseki). Toyo Keizai Shimposha, 1986. (in Japanese)
Kaizuka Keimei. Public Finance (Zaiseigaku). University of Tokyo Press, 1988. (in Japanese)
——. Japanese Public Finance (Nihon no Zaisei Kin'yu). Yuhikaku, 1991. (in Japanese)
Musgrave, R. A. The Theory of Public Finance. McGraw-Hill, 1959.
Shibata Tokue, ed. Japan's Public Sector: How the Government Is Financed. University of Tokyo Press, 1993.
Stiglitz, J. E. Economics of the Public Sector, 2nd ed. Norton, 1986.
Takeda Takao, Hayashi Takehisa, and Imai Katsuhito. Overview of Japanese Public Finance (Nihon Zaisei Yoran), 3rd ed. University of Tokyo Press, 1987. (in Japanese)

Yabushita Shiro and Asako Kazumi. *Japanese Economics and Fiscal Policy: Analysis of Macroeconomics and Fiscal Deficits (Nihon Keizai to Zaisei Seisaku: Makuro Keizai to Zaisei Akaji no Bunseki).* Toyo Keizai Shimposha, 1991.

Social security
Arrow, Kenneth J. "Uncertainty and the Welfare Economics of Medicare," *American Economic Review,* 1963:941–73.
──────. *Essays in the Theory of Risk-Bearing.* 1971.
Friedman, Milton, and Rose Friedman. *Free to Choose: A Personal Statement.* Harcourt Brace Jovanovich, 1980.
Niki Ryu. *Medical Care in the Nineties (Kyuju Nendai no Iryo).* Keiso Shobo, 1990. (in Japanese)
Nishimura Shuzo. *Economic Analysis of Medical Care (Iryo no Keizai Bunseki).* Toyo Keizai Shimposha, 1987. (in Japanese)
Stiglitz, J. E. *Economics of the Public Sector,* 2nd ed. Norton, 1986.

International balances of payments
Dornbusch, Rudiger. *Open Economy Macroeconomics.* Basic Books, 1980.
Frenkel, Jacob, and H. G. Johnson, eds. *The Economics of Exchange Rates: Selected Studies.* 1978.
Fujino Shosaburo. *Trends in the International Currency System and Their Effect on the Japanese Economy (Kokusai Tsuka Taisei no Dotai to Nihon Keizai).* Keiso Shobo, 1990. (in Japanese)
Fukao Mitsuhiro. *International Finance (Kokusai Kin'yu).* Toyo Keizai Shimposha, 1990. (in Japanese)
Kindleberger, Charles P., and P. H. Lindert. *International Economics,* 7th ed. R. H. Irwin.
Onizuka Yusuke. *The Economics of Capital Exports: Issues in Japan's Balance of Payments and Capital Transfers (Shihon Yushutsu no Keizaigaku: Wagakuni no Kokusai Shushi to Shihon Ido no Shomondai).* Tsusho Sangyo Chosakai, 1985.
Shinohara Miyohei. *Industrial Growth, Trade, and Dynamic Patterns in the Japanese Economy.* University of Tokyo Press, 1982.
Tachi Ryuichiro et al., eds. *Seminar on International Finance (Kokusai Kin'yu Koza),* Vols. I–IV. Yuhikaku, 1974–75. (in Japanese)
────── and Royama Masaichi, eds. *Japanese Finance (Nihon no Kin'yu),* Vol. II. University of Tokyo Press, 1987. (in Japanese)
Ueda Kazuo. *International Macroeconomics and the Japanese Economy: Theory and Verification of Economic Systems (Kokusai Makuro Keizaigaku to Nihon Keizai: Kaiho Keizai Taisei no Riron to Jissho).* Toyo Keizai Shimposha, 1983.
Watanabe Taro. *International Economics (Kokusai Keizai),* 4th ed. Shunjusha, 1989. (in Japanese)

Prices
Horiuchi Akiyoshi. *Theory of Finance (Kin'yuron).* University of Tokyo Press, 1990. (in Japanese)

Kumagai Hisao. *Theory and Policies of Modern Capitalism* (*Gendai Shihon-shugi no Riron to Seisaka*). Sobunsha, 1986. Especially Chapters 6 and 9. (in Japanese)

Okina Kunio. *Economic Analysis of Expectations and Speculation: "Bubbles" and Exchange Rates* (*Kitai to Toki no Keizai Bunseki: "Baburu" Gensho to Kawase Reto*). Toyo Keizai Shimposha, 1985. (in Japanese)

Tachi Ryuichiro. *The Theory of Monetary Policy* (*Kin'yu Seisaku*). University of Tokyo Press, 1982. (in Japanese)

————. "Theory of Excess Liquidity" (*Kajo Ryudosei no Rironteki Kento*). *Keizai Hyoron*, August 1976. (in Japanese)

————, Komiya Ryutaro, and Niida Hiroshi. *Issues in Japanese Prices* (*Nihon no Bukka Mondai*). Toyo Keizai Shimposha, 1964. (in Japanese)

Changing industrial structure

Clark, C. *The Conditions of Economic Progress*. Macmillan, 1940.

Fuchs, Victor R. *The Service Economy*. National Bureau of Economic Research, 1968.

Gomulk, S. *The Theory of Technical Change and Economic Growth*. Routledge, 1990.

Lucas, R. "On the Mechanics of Economic Development." *Journal of Monetary Economics*, Vol. 22 (1988).

Maddison, A. "Growth and Slowdown in Advanced Capitalist Economies." *Journal of Economic Literature*, Vol. 25 (1987).

Miyazawa Ken'ichi. *Systemic Mechanisms in Modern Economies* (*Gendai Keizai no Seidoteki Kiko*). Iwanami Shoten, 1978. Especially Chapter IV. (in Japanese)

Nelson, R. R. "Research on Productivity Growth and Productivity Differences: Dead End and New Departure." *Journal of Economic Literature*, Vol. 19 (1981).

Romer, P. M. "Increasing Returns and Long-run Growth." *Journal of Political Economy*, 1986.

Tachi Ryutaro, ed. *Soft-nomics*. (*Sohutonomikkusu*) Nihon Keizai Shimbunsha, 1983. (in Japanese)

INDEX